Nationalism and Independence

BY THE SAME AUTHOR:

The Irish Free State: Its Government and Politics (1934)

The Government of Northern Ireland: A Study in Devolution (1936)

The Irish Question 1840–1921 (1940, 1965, 1975)

The Commonwealth Experience (1969, 1982)

Constitutional Relations between Britain and India: The Transfer of Power 1942–7 (Editor-in-chief, 12 Vols., 1967–82)

The Unresolved Question: The Anglo-Irish Settlement and its Undoing 1912–72 (1991)

NATIONALISM
AND
INDEPENDENCE

Selected Irish Papers

by

NICHOLAS MANSERGH

edited by Diana Mansergh

Foreword by J. J. LEE

CORK UNIVERSITY PRESS

First published in 1997 by
Cork University Press
Crawford Business Park
Crosses Green
Cork
Ireland

British Library Cataloguing in Publication Data
A CIP catalogue record for this book is available from
the British Library.

ISBN 1 85918 105 8 hardback
1 85918 106 6 paperback

Typeset by Tower Books of Ballincollig, Co. Cork
Printed by ColourBooks, Baldoyle, Co. Dublin

CONTENTS

Part II   THE INTER-WAR YEARS
           Liberalising influence of Ireland on the Statute of Westminster
           Commonwealth; de Valera in office, 1932–48; removal of the
           oath, the Governor-General, appeals to the Judicial Commit-
           tee of the Privy Council; the External Relations Act author-
           ising diplomatic appointments; 1937, the new Constitution,
           republican in all but name; 1938, the Anglo-Irish Agreement,
           which ended the economic war and ceded British rights in the
           Treaty ports to Ireland; future policy of neutrality.

Part III   POST-WAR IRELAND
           Ending partition the aim of all parties; 1948, the end of de
           Valera's sixteen continuous years in power; February, Mr
           Costello leads an inter-party government; November, the
           Republic of Ireland Act and repeal of the External Relations
           Act; 1949, Easter Day, the Republic proclaimed and Éire leaves
           the British Commonwealth; questions arising such as citizen-
           ship and trade; August, India becomes the first republican
           member of the Commonwealth.

EDITOR'S PREFACE

Nicholas Mansergh lived till he was eighty, luckily just long enough for him to sign the contract with Yale University Press for publication of his last full-scale book, *The Unresolved Question: The Anglo-Irish Settlement and its Undoing 1912–72*. To collect into one volume some of his many scattered essays and papers was the next thing he intended to do and the present volume is my attempt to make such a collection of his Irish papers.

Nicholas lived through the Irish revolution and there are glimpses of his childhood in parts of this book – the diary entry for Sunday, 13 February 1938 (p. 129), and the reference to the abrupt closure of the Abbey School, Tipperary (p. 235).

Endowed with these early experiences and later inspired by the creative atmosphere of Oxford in the 1930s, he had three books on Ireland published by the time he was thirty. He worked as a wartime civil servant in the British Ministry of Information and the Dominions Office, becoming increasingly absorbed by the transition from Empire to Commonwealth, particularly in relation to India, which he loved. After the war he became a Commonwealth Professor, first in London and then in Cambridge. This combination of experiences underlay his particular historical insights. Many of them retain freshness and immediacy and help to convey the climate of opinion in those days.

On the most recently published piece (Chapter 17), in 1985, the editor of the County History and Society series 'found it a most stimulating piece of work which gave local history a significant boost when it was developing. [He] was an ideal contributor'.

Diana Mansergh
Cambridge
October 1996

ACKNOWLEDGEMENTS

Far my greatest debt is to Professor Lee for so generously lending his name to this volume and writing the Foreword. I also thank most warmly, for their assistance in various different ways, my sons Philip, Martin and Nicholas and my son-in-law Paul Gilbert.

The essays are reprinted by the kind permission of the original publishers whose names appear in the table of contents. Previously unpublished chapters are 9, 13 and 18.

There has been no alteration to the text of these writings and where necessary they should be read in relation to the date of their publication.

Mrs S. French of Fulbourn has typed the whole book and I cannot thank her enough for all her help and friendship since times past.

FOREWORD

Nicholas Mansergh enjoyed a glittering career by the conventional criteria of English academe, culminating in the mastership of St John's College, Cambridge. But Mansergh was an Irishman, and an Irishman, moreover, who remained loyal to his roots.

It says something of Mansergh's scholarly stature that had he never written a word on Ireland his standing as a leading authority on Commonwealth history would be secure. But had he never written a word on the Commonwealth, his record as an historian of Ireland would equally ensure him an outstanding scholarly reputation. That record is quite extraordinary. By the age of thirty he had already three substantial pioneering books to his credit, *The Government of the Irish Free State* (1934), *The Government of Northern Ireland* (1936), and *Ireland in the Age of Reform and Revolution* (1940). And he would continue to build on the foundations so firmly laid. *Ireland in the Age of Reform and Revolution* would be extensively revised and expanded to appear as *The Irish Question* in 1965, and in a further edition in 1975. His later years were devoted to the posthumously published *The Unresolved Question: The Anglo-Irish Settlement and its Undoing 1912–1972* (1991), in which he meditated yet again on those issues of national identity, of Anglo-Irish relations, and of the making of partition, which he had explored not only in books, but in a long series of papers for a half century and more. The collection of these papers into a single volume now allows one to appreciate fully the range, depth and development of his thinking on Ireland, and enables us to place his contribution to Irish historiography in proper perspective.

Perspective is the key to the unique quality of Mansergh's scholarship: a perspective on the Commonwealth enriched by an Irish angle of vision; a perspective on Ireland enriched by a Commonwealth angle of vision, and not only a Commonwealth one, but a European one also. *Ireland in the Age of Reform and Revolution*, which remains, both in its original and in its revised editions, a seminal text for any serious student of modern Ireland, is an explicit pioneering attempt to place the Irish experience in European perspective. As such it remains a rare example of a historical study that not merely preaches, but practises, the comparative approach.

The comparative perspective reflects Mansergh's determination to stand back from the ebb and flow of events. In preface after preface to book after book, he insists that his purpose is not to produce straight narrative, but 'politico-historical analysis', or 'historical commentary on the events', as he puts it in the foreword to *The Coming of the First World War*.[1]

He actually does himself rather less than justice in this respect. Firstly, he makes light of the weight of his scholarship. His 'commentary' was based on a mastery of archival material, on the one hand, and of the great learning of a mind that was widely, deeply and discerningly read, not only in history, from classical to contemporary, but in prose and poetry, enabling him draw on a remarkable range of literary reference. Secondly, master though he was of political analysis in the narrow sense, he interpreted analysis to include analysis of political culture in the broad sense. He always remained conscious of the emotional and ideological impulses that underlay policy, displaying a profound understanding of the collective psychology of rulers and ruled alike, whether Irish or English, Hindu or Muslim, black African or Afrikaner.

Nowhere are these gifts more in evidence than in his study of partition. Mansergh is the pre-eminent authority on partition in the modern world. Nobody has pondered more profoundly the issue of Irish partition, or Indian partition, above all in his magisterial lecture, 'The Prelude to Partition: Concepts and Aims in Ireland and India'. The comparisons and contrasts that both his instincts and his scholarship enabled him to detect between these two classic cases of partition deepened his, and our, understanding of both, and of the issue of partition in general.

From his perspective, the Government of Ireland Act of December 1920 was the defining moment in the partition of Ireland, not least because it imposed not merely the principle of partition, but because it also decided the line of partition, and established the importance of territory.

The centrality of the Government of Ireland Act to Irish history, and to Anglo-Irish relations, most of all in the past twenty-five years, cannot be sufficiently emphasised. Even now, there is a reluctance on all sides to confront its centrality. It is natural that this should be the case. All the parties involved have a vested interest in focusing on the Treaty of December 1921, rather than on the Government of Ireland Act, a year earlier, as the origin of partition.

Irish nationalists, whether pro-Treaty or anti-Treaty, were loath to concede

---

[1] *The Coming of the First World War* (London, 1949), p. viii.

that partition existed before the Treaty. They could not continue to cherish the myth that they had 'won' the War of Independence in purely military terms if they conceded that partition had been successfully imposed on them by superior British military power. The anti-Treaty side, who at the time opposed the Treaty mainly on the question of the oath of allegiance, and only secondarily on the question of partition – which they chose to assume would be terminated by the Boundary Commission established under the Treaty – found it more congenial in retrospect to justify fighting the Civil War mainly on the issue of partition rather than on what appeared to most people to be the rather abstract issue of the oath, particularly when that oath was soon abolished. It suited both sides in the Civil War to present themselves as having been cheated by the Boundary Commission, when that failed to make the sweeping changes in the existing line of partition they had all chosen to assume would inevitably occur, thus preserving the sense of grievance that was for so long an essential component, naturally enough, of the Irish nationalist mentality. Public opinion in the south continues to delude itself to the present day that the Treaty negotiators, Arthur Griffith, Michael Collins, and their colleagues, somehow connived at bringing partition into being. They didn't. They could not concede what they had not got. The British did not negotiate partition with the representatives of Sinn Féin. Partition was not for negotiation as far as they were concerned. The consequence of a superior command of violence, it was already a *fait accompli*, imposed through the Government of Ireland Act, before the Treaty negotiations began.

It suited Ulster Unionists to assume that the Civil War was mainly about partition. They could then accuse the anti-Treaty side of being so anxious to rule the North that they were prepared to fight a civil war to clear the way for them to trample over Ulster Unionists. And of course it suited the British to attribute partition to the Treaty, as if this had been agreed in some sort of 'democratic' way by representatives of the majority of the Irish people, rather than having been imposed unilaterally by themselves without any consultation with, much less the consent of, a substantial majority of people on the island. This conveniently diverts attention from the fact that it was a condition on the British side for even entering preliminary discussions on a Treaty that Northern Ireland should be safely in existence before a settlement with Sinn Féin could be even contemplated. In an age when the idea of 'consent' has become much more fashionable than it then was, it is useful to be able to blur that particular issue by concentration on the Treaty rather than on the Government of Ireland Act.

Mansergh is the supreme authority on that Act. In the classic paper reprinted here, he unravels the tangled skein of plot and subplot with a clarity, a subtlety, and a precision that leaves no excuse for further delusion on anybody's part.

It was not, of course, that Mansergh underrated the importance of the Treaty in the wider sphere of Anglo-Irish relations. Indeed, few have done as much to illuminate the Treaty negotiations. It may even have been his mastery of the material on the Treaty that alerted him to the central relevance of the Government of Ireland Act. The Treaty, at the end of the day, and despite the substantial concessions made by British negotiators, compared with the Government of Ireland Act, remained a diktat, imposed under threat of renewed resort to violence by the militarily superior party. It was not a negotiation between equals. Mansergh never concealed his view that the British, from their own point of view, blundered in imposing Dominion status on the Irish Free State. Nowhere in the entire literature on the Treaty are the consequences of that blunder for Britain itself analysed more clearly than in his lecture, 'The Implications of the Irish Experience for the Indian Settlement', for which the British government was desperately groping in 1947. Mansergh insisted that Mr de Valera's concept of external association was far in advance of what even the cleverest British statesmen were capable of conceiving about the nature of the Commonwealth in 1921. By 1947 they had begun to catch up with de Valera's thinking, thanks in part to Mansergh's tutelage.

The shadow of de Valera hovers over much of Mansergh's work. Having personally observed virtually all Commonwealth statesmen over half a century, he ranked de Valera among the greatest. This might seem an unlikely verdict, given the animosity he must frequently have heard expressed against de Valera. It would have been understandable had he chosen to turn his back, emotionally and intellectually, on the new state, and make his life independently of it. His talents would have allowed him do so. He didn't need Ireland in any career sense. But for all his devotion to Britain, his loyalty to Ireland was formed early and remained steadfast.

And he would always remain loyal to Tipperary as well as to Ireland. It is entirely appropriate that this collection should contain his evocative essay on Tipperary local history. There is a certain irony in a scholar whose gaze girdled the globe, the most widely written and widely travelled of all Irish historians, who visited every country in the Commonwealth in preparing his *Surveys* and his *Documents* on Commonwealth affairs, noting in the introduction to the 1975 edition of *The Irish Question* that 'local history remains neglected in Ireland generally. Dublin perspectives continue to prevail'[2] – and then himself proceeding to show how the most cosmopolitan of scholars could write illuminatingly about local history.

Mansergh seems to have been almost prematurely mature, both as scholar and as man. He was singularly free of the various neuroses that afflict Anglo-Irish relations, even when those relations are at their friendliest. The

---

[2] *The Irish Question 1840–1921* (London, 1975), n. 1, p. 19.

fascinating extracts from the diaries he kept while still in his twenties, published here for the first time, reveal not only his gift for incisive summary, but the same extraordinary maturity of judgement that characterises even his earliest writings.

Mansergh, as Professor Harkness observes,[3] held firmly to certain basic values, especially tolerance, a sense of justice, and a sense of fairness, which many would regard as the essence of civilised society. But he never deluded himself that he was above the fray. It is tempting to think of him as the quintessential Olympian, and there was indeed a mandarin quality to his mind. But for all his remarkable ability to penetrate the dense complexity of human affairs, he had the humility of the true scholar in realising that the historian, whatever his stature, cannot look down, but only look around, or, as he put it himself in the preface to the second volume of his *Survey of Commonwealth Affairs*, cannot stand above events, but only stand aside from them. Mansergh comes as close as is humanly possible to showing how the historian can be emotionally engaged, yet intellectually detached. Recent trends in Irish historiography make it only too apparent that the lesson has to be learned anew in every generation.

The central theme of all Mansergh's writing, the relationship between imperial, or once imperial, powers and colonial and post-colonial states, between the strong and the weak, between rulers and ruled, constitutes a central theme of world history in general, and of Irish history in particular. Noting that 'the Anglo-Irish Treaty of 1921 marked the ending of an age' he observed that this simply meant that a new Irish question, or rather a new Anglo-Irish one, had emerged, for 'there would seem to be no ultimate, final or predestined solution of Anglo-Irish relations; there is only a continuous conflict of forces, whose direction and strength are always changing'. The past remains, he concluded 'to encourage, to influence, and most of all, to warn'.[4]

It is sad that the warning should still be necessary. Unfortunately, the quotation from Eliot which he cites at the end of *The Unresolved Question*,[5] 'we had the experience but missed the meaning', remains only too valid for too many of the actors on the Anglo-Irish stage. Diana Mansergh has put in her debt all of us, on both sides of the Irish border, on both sides of the Irish Sea, and on both sides of the Atlantic, who wish to foster lasting friendship between all the peoples of Britain and Ireland, by collecting here the essays of an historian who has done so much to give meaning to the tortured and tortuous experience of Anglo-Irish relations in the twentieth century.

J. J. Lee

---

[3] *Proceedings of the British Academy*, 82, 1993, p. 422.

[4] *The Irish Question* (London, 1965), pp. 287-8.

[5] *The Unresolved Question* (Yale University Press, New Haven and London, 1991), p. 352.

Part I

The Northern Situation

1

THE UNIONIST PARTY AND
THE UNION 1886–1916:
An Unresolved Dilemma*

Since 1886 the Unionist, or Conservative, party has been the major force in English politics. In the eighty years that have since elapsed the party has been in office either on its own, or in coalitions in which it has been the dominant partner, for close on sixty. The fact needs restatement only because English historians for the most part are apt to find their interest disproportionately drawn to Liberal or Labour administrations. This is not surprising. It is more exciting to write about change and reform than about conservation. Yet it can be, as it has been in the historiography of Anglo–Irish relations, misleading.

It is commonly accepted, for example, that it was more important that Gladstone should have proposed a Home Rule Bill in 1886 than that Joseph Chamberlain should have killed it. Yet was it really so? Could it not be argued that the rejection of Home Rule by the Radicals in association with Tories and dissident Whigs was the event that was decisive in its consequences for the next half-century? It had meant in the first place that the establishment, in terms of the traditional landed interest and propertied classes, was reinforced by radical lower middle-class and working-class votes, which were important, and at times possibly decisive electorally. But it had also a further long-term significance. The cause that united left with

* First published in the spring of 1966 in *The Irish Times* supplement, commemorating the fiftieth anniversary of the Easter Rising and subsequently included in the book, *1916 the Easter Rising*, edited by O. D. Edwards and F. Pyle.

3

right, deriving from common opposition to Home Rule, was maintenance of the Union. Their association accordingly brought into existence a party generally pragmatic in its outlook but, of political necessity, rigid and ideological on the issue which had brought it into being.

'Jack Cade vanished', as Professor Thornton has remarked of the archetypal Radical-Unionist Joseph Chamberlain, 'behind orchid and eyeglass, taking his radicalism with him'.[1] But his Unionism always retained its pristine importance. The Conservative party became the Unionist party and the change of name symbolized a modification, at the least, in character. Adaptable as the party might be in its response to changing interests in other fields, implicit in its very being was one unchanging element – support for the Union. In this respect it was a party depriving itself, from 1886 to 1921, of its customary freedom of political manoeuvre. Its attitude to Ireland did not, and could not, change in response to changing circumstances, as for example it did later with dramatic consequences in respect of Africa, because of the manner in which Home Rule was defeated in 1886. Unionism was a party dogma and was in effect written into its constitution. And it was this party, tied to dogma in this one particular, that dominated British politics for twenty-one of the thirty-six years between 1886 and 1921; and which in the remainder was generally able to call up sufficient reserves of establishment influence or electoral strength to block all but the most resolute of Liberal reformers in a period in which Liberal reformers were not generally remarkable for their resolution on Irish issues.

Was Unionist policy towards Ireland in these years then a study in political negation? The answer is qualified. Its unchanging premise was a negation – no Home Rule – from which there derived certainly a broad but by no means necessarily a detailed conclusion. Herein lay the area of debate and discussion within the party. Home Rule rejected, what was to replace it? Coercion? Or conversion? In essence those were the alternatives. Four-fifths of the Irish electorate supported Home Rule. Home Rule was not to be conceded. Were the Irish then to be coerced in perpetuity into acceptance of or, at the least, acquiescence in Union? Or was there some other way by which they might be persuaded to abandon, with secret satisfaction – open was too much to hope for – the Home Rule dead end? The second, it is not to be doubted, was the hope of all except a diehard (but possibly realistic) minority. Arthur James Balfour supplied the necessary conceptual foundation. 'He is', noted Sir Henry Lucy when Balfour first made some mark in the House of Commons in 1880, 'a pleasing specimen of the highest form of the culture and good breeding which stand to the credit of Cambridge University.'[2] But he was also something

---

[1] A. P. Thornton, *The Habit of Authority* (London, 1966), p. 291.

[2] Sir Henry Lucy, *A Diary of Two Parliaments, 1880–1885* (London, 1886), pp. 84–5.

more – 'a pretty speaker, with a neat turn for saying nasty things',[3] and, as Sir Henry had occasion to note in 1890, in him was to be 'recognized the most perfect living example of the mailed hand under the velvet glove'.[4]

Parnellism, in Balfour's view, was a superficial, dangerously misconceived political expression of ills which were real. Those ills were social and economic. They were endemic in the Irish social system, especially the land system. They were deep-seated, hard to alleviate, but given persistence, time and, above all, a sense of common British purpose, not beyond remedy. Such interparty agreement, in the Balfourian exegesis, should have been forthcoming if only by reason of British self-interest. For while the outward manifestations of Parnellism were political, its inward dangers were in equal measure social. The exploitation of agrarian distress for political purposes had resulted in an assault upon the rights of property in Ireland, where they were most vulnerable, and Balfour, like Salisbury and many others besides and before him, argued that the undermining of property rights in one part of the United Kingdom would by necessary consequence open the way to their impairment in others. Therefore, on this reasoning, the right course was to remedy Irish grievances, relieve Irish social distress, foster industries and the welfare of the Irish people and so not merely maintain but strengthen, through new contentment, the Union and incidentally, but significantly, reinsure the rights of property throughout the United Kingdom. The phrase was 'killing Home Rule by kindness'. The kindness, however, on the Unionist premise, was a precondition of the killing. But therein lay, as Balfour was to find, a familiar and inexorable dilemma. The moment of reform is always difficult, sometimes dangerous, for an autocratic regime. Hitherto, Balfour had said at the outset of his Chief Secretaryship in 1887, English governments had 'either been all for repression or all for reform. I am for both: repression as stern as Cromwell, reforms as thorough as Mr Parnell or anyone else can desire'.[5] He sought, in other words, to avert the risks associated with reform by 'resolution' in government. The price, however, was that the resolution counterbalanced, or outbalanced, the psychological effects of reforms. 'Bloody Balfour', 'the man of Mitchelstown', was not associated in the Irish mind with 'kindness'. That was a handicap for the Chief Secretary and more important, for the policy he propounded, which was never overcome.

Balfour, however, did not stand alone. There were twenty years of Unionist rule between 1886 and 1905, broken only by a three-year interlude

---

[3] Quoted in Kenneth Young, *Arthur James Balfour* (London, 1963), p. 100.

[4] Sir Henry Lucy, *Memories of Eight Parliaments* (London, 1908), p. 157.

[5] Quoted in L.P. Curtis, *Coercion and Conciliation in Ireland 1880–1892: A Study in Conservative Unionism* (Princeton, 1963), p. 179. This book provides the authoritative account of A.J. Balfour's Irish administration and the ideas behind it.

of uncertain, Liberal administration. In the Chief Secretary's office A. J. Balfour was followed by his brother, Gerald, and then by George Wyndham – an attractive, gifted personality and a romantic Tory, of whom it was said that Sir Walter Scott was 'his only outpost in the modern world'.[6] Yet, for all his gifts, Wyndham lacked one thing as important to politicians as Napoleon deemed it to be for generals – luck. Balfour's most recent biographer, Kenneth Young, has told a strange story of how in August 1892 Balfour wrote to Lady Elcho about a visit by her brother, George Wyndham, to a fortune-teller. 'She appears to have told him "everything which he ever did", to have prophesied many good things, but to have incidentally announced that he was to die at fifty.'[7] He died in 1913 just before his fiftieth birthday. But long before then his political hopes and with them something of the more attractive side of the new Unionism, by ill-luck, which may be another name for ill-judgement, had perished.

George Wyndham, whose mother was a granddaughter of Lord Edward Fitzgerald, was sympathetic and well-disposed to Ireland and its problems. He came to office resolved to settle the land question. It is hardly an exaggeration to say he settled it. The foundation laid by Lord Dunraven's land conference was used to frame an Act that encouraged landlords to sell and tenants to buy. The inducement to both was provided by a substantial Exchequer grant. The figure is said to have been worked out in the first instance by George Wyndham himself, who, having been good at sums at school, prided himself on his skill with figures. He produced compensation so generous for landlords as to provoke witticisms about 'brandy and soda' finance. But even scaled down, sufficient inducement remained. Wyndham, however, was not content to think of the Land Act as an end. It was a means, a means as his biographer, John Biggs-Davidson, has written 'of euthanasia for Home Rule'.[8] There was an element, or possibly a double element, according to the point of view, of illusion here. Even Liberals, by no means convinced of the reality of Irish nationalism, argued that if nationalism derived from social oppression, where was the assurance that it would end with it? If Irish nationalism was in itself not a derivative but an absolute, then there was no possible foundation for the notions Wyndham entertained.

Wyndham, himself, soon had reason for doubt. He had appointed Sir Antony MacDonnell, Lieutenant-Governor of the United Provinces, an Irishman and a Catholic with Home Rule sympathies, Under-Secretary at the Irish Office. Balfour's keen political nostrils scented the whiff of danger. But Wyndham, less perspicacious and relaxing abroad after the passage of the Land Act, inadvertently overlooked the extent (of which

---

[6] John Biggs-Davidson, *George Wyndham: A Study in Toryism* (London, 1951), p. 236.

[7] Young, *op. cit.*, p. 139.

[8] Biggs-Davidson, *op. cit.*, p. 132.

he was, albeit a little casually, informed[9]) of the Under-Secretary's commitment to a programme of devolution. There were first indignant rumblings and then angry protests from within the Unionist party at this supposed official commitment to a loosening of the bonds of Union. MacDonnell survived the storm but Wyndham resigned. In effect the Unionist experiment in killing Home Rule by kindness was ended. It had had its successes, notably the 1903 Land Act, on the road to final failure. Far from being killed, Home Rule was showing every sign of reinvigoration. Nor was it a question of Home Rule alone; it was self-evidently the larger question of Irish nationalism. Salisbury, Balfour, George Wyndham, all alike had denied the reality of its existence. That was an article of their Unionist faith. How much longer could the party subscribe to it?

Out of office from December 1905 until the formation of the first wartime coalition in 1915, the Unionist party moved, but not so rapidly as is retrospectively apt to be supposed, towards an extreme position, or perhaps more accurately, towards an extreme attitude, for it could be argued that Unionist insistence upon the Union and nothing but the Union was in itself the extreme, fundamentalist position. But at the least, so long as Balfour was leader of the party, it spoke the language not of violence but of reason. There could be no compromise about the Union, but were there not ways in which concessions might be made to Irish sentiment consistent with that fundamental purpose? There were not lacking indications that that was a possibility, a last chance, now more seriously weighed. No one can read English Unionist discussion about future Irish policy at this time without sensing, behind the policies, a mood of deepening perplexity.

In 1906 there appeared F. S. Oliver's *Life of Alexander Hamilton*. It enjoyed great success – except with historians; it had far-reaching influence. Its theme, in biographical form, was the making of the American federation. Oliver believed with George Washington that 'influence is not government' and the moral he drew from the early experience of the United States was the need for authority to ensure the triumph of centripetal over centrifugal forces. He sought to apply the lessons to the British Isles. In 1910 he published a series of letters under the title *Federalism and Home Rule*, the argument of which was that while 'the Union of the United Kingdom is a great thing, and to impair that would be to lose all', that Union was not necessarily inconsistent with federalism or even conceivably, and certain conditions being fulfilled, with Home Rule. In further pamphlets, *The Alternatives to Civil War* (1913) and *What Federalism is Not* (1914) Oliver elaborated his views. In so far as federalism or Home Rule were consistent with devolution of authority as distinct from division, he was prepared to favour them. He believed that a delegation of powers from

---

[9] *Ibid.*, pp. 152–3.

Westminster to the four national units in the British Isles on a permanent basis would at once preserve the Union and might be made a part of a larger plan for the federation of the whole of the British Empire, the 'grand federal idea' on which Oliver and his colleagues in *The Round Table* had set their sights. It was all a dream. Canadians and South Africans were as much opposed to the federation of Empire as Irishmen were to the federation of the British Isles. And in each case the reason was the same. They were aware that such a federation would not lead, and was not intended to lead, to recognition of their several and separate political identities, but to their merging with, and ultimate submergence in, a larger whole. At root, therefore, behind the forms, the phrases, and the idealism of the Round Tablers, lay unbridged the gulf between imperialism and nationalism. Oliver's conception of Home Rule was a delegation of power to all four national units in the British Isles, preserving 'The Union of these Islands', which as he wrote and as Stephen Gwynn who later edited his letters noted, was, to men of his views, 'by its nature; sacramental'.[10] In that context federalism implied not, as Oliver suggested, 'a new departure' for Unionism, but superficial rearrangement of the forms of Union to make it more palatable to Irish Nationalists.

In 1913, in the same year in which Oliver wrote of federalism, A. J. Balfour, now dispossessed of the leadership of the party by Andrew Bonar Law, reflected, also in pamphlet form, upon *Nationality and Home Rule*. His approach was closer to political realities. He conceded that there was an Irish problem. He argued that it lay neither in the existing parliamentary system, nor in the existing financial system, both of which indeed he claimed were more favourable to Ireland than to Britain. The land system was reformed, the administrative system was being reformed. Where then was the justification for Home Rule? 'It lies in the fact', noted Balfour, 'that the Irish Nationalist Party claim that Ireland, *on the ground of a separate nationality*, possesses inherent rights which cannot be satisfied by the fairest and fullest share of the parliamentary institutions of the United Kingdom. What satisfies Scotland cannot satisfy them, and ought not to satisfy them. It would be treason to Ireland.'

Balfour then proceeded to probe the foundations of Irish nationality and concluded that in respect of neither Irish institutions, nor Irish culture, nor Irish descent or civilization was there sufficient ground for the separate nationalism implicit in Home Rule. The explanation for that was to be found 'in the tragic coincidences of Irish history'. In them Irish nationalism originated and from them it derived its anti-British tradition. How should British statesmen respond? To Balfour there were only two alternatives.

---

[10] Stephen Gwynn (ed.) *The Anvil of War: Letters Between F. S. Oliver and his Brother* (London, 1936), p. 23.

The first was maintenance of the Union and the keeping of Ireland in full political communion with England and Scotland. The second was to give her complete autonomy. That was 'a counsel of despair'. Yet, Balfour noted, it was apparently suited to the disease. It gave Nationalist Ireland what it professed to desire. In that respect it was, at least, a solution to the Irish Nationalist problem. But what of Home Rule? It offered the middle course, but it solved no problem whatsoever. Financially, administratively, and constitutionally, he argued, it was at once indefensible and unworkable. His own answer was time, time in which to give the measures enacted by the Unionist administration a chance to have their remedial and beneficial effects. And to those who argued that 'Irish patriotism, in its exclusive and more or less hostile form, is destined to be eternal', he replied that they should think in logic not of Home Rule but of separation.

By 1913 Balfour possessed influence but no longer enjoyed power within the party. That rested in the improbable hands of Bonar Law, a pugnacious pessimist elected to the leadership because he was known to be politically a first-class fighting man. On the ground that the curbing of the powers of the House of Lords by the Parliament Act of 1911 had upset the balance of the constitution, Bonar Law felt warranted in urging the party of 'law and order' to take all steps to resist Home Rule. The Liberal government was, he declaimed at Blenheim on 27 July 1912, 'a Revolutionary Committee' which had seized by fraud upon despotic power. The Unionists accordingly would no longer be restrained by the bonds which would influence their action in any ordinary political struggle. They would use whatever means seemed most likely to be effective. Under Bonar Law's leadership, the English Unionist party committed themselves, even to the point of threatened violence, to the support of the Ulster Unionist cause. Yet Ulster was not to the majority of English Unionists, even if Bonar Law's own position on this point possibly by reason of his Ulster descent remained personal and distinctive,[11] an end in itself. It was a means to an end and that end was the preservation of the Union, and thereby of the integrity of the Empire. The imperial interest thus reinforced, in a way that has been insufficiently recognized, domestic opposition to Home Rule. It moved imperial administrators, soldiers, and even statesmen not otherwise interested in Irish affairs to action. Many of them had at most qualified faith in democratic processes.

Lord Milner provided the outstanding example. By temperament and by reason of his proconsular experiences in South Africa, he had nothing but contempt for the British parliamentary system. He felt 'only loathing for the way things were done in England in the political sphere' and despised

---

[11] Robert Blake, *The Unknown Prime Minister* (London, 1955), p. 531; Blake believed Ulster was one of the two things Bonar Law really cared about.

English politics.[12] He hated the pressure of parliamentary necessities, he disdained the whims of a 'rotten public opinion', and if in South Africa he had made sacrifices, they were not 'for this effete and dislocated Body Politic'.[13] In the supposed interests of Empire and without regard for British parliamentary tradition, Milner, as A. M. Gollin in his *Proconsul in Politics* first made plain, used his remarkable administrative gifts for the organization of opposition in Great Britain, chiefly through the Union Defence League, to Home Rule, securing by 1914 close on two million signatures for the British Covenant. He also sought, and apparently succeeded, in securing substantial financial backing for measures which he was only too ready to contemplate but from which even Craig and Carson shrank. Compared with all the other leaders, writes Mr Gollin, Milner 'was the least anxious to seek a solution to the Ulster problem'.[14] As for the English Unionist leaders, Milner himself noted that they preferred to talk rather than to enter into any definite plan for ridding themselves, by other than constitutional means, of the 'horrible nightmare' of Home Rule. If, therefore, these leaders are remembered for the great lengths to which they went, there were even greater being urged upon them.

In the last phase of Unionist opposition to Home Rule, posed as it was on the brink of violence, there were at least three identifiable elements in the Unionism. There were first the Irish Unionists (whose attitudes and assumptions were sufficiently distinct from the English allies as to require separate analysis), themselves subdivided between the Ulster and Southern Unionists; secondly there was the main body of English Unionists thinking of Home Rule chiefly as an issue in domestic politics; and finally there were the imperialists, accustomed to autocratic rule, some though not all of them – with Milner on the extreme right – little interested in Anglo-Irish politics for their own sake, but thinking of the unity of the British Isles as an essential condition of the unity and therefore of the greatness of the British Empire. Bound together by one supreme and testing issue, this was the formidable combination before which Liberals weakened and the cause of Irish constitutional nationalism succumbed.

For Unionism the Easter Rising was the moment of truth. Unionists had declined to credit the authenticity of Irish nationalism. That was not for them a matter of political opinion but something that had become in effect close to an article of political faith. The Rising, immediately for some but in the longer run for almost all, destroyed the conviction. Irish nationalism came to be recognized for what it was. In time this introduced a new

---

[12] A. M. Gollin, *Proconsul in Politics: A Study of Lord Milner in Opposition and in Power* (London, 1964), p. 45.

[13] *Ibid.*, pp. 45–6.

[14] *Ibid.*, p. 193. See generally pp. 184–94.

element of realism. Arthur Balfour had already argued, as we have seen, that there was no halfway house between Union and separation. In that important respect, at least, he was at one with Sinn Féin. The two extremes were agreed, if in nothing else, in discounting the possibility of a *via media*. After 1916, Home Rule discarded and discredited, they were left face to face. The outcome, almost inevitably, was violent. Not till 1921 was the Unionist dilemma resolved – with the abandonment of Union. Henceforward, British Conservative, and no longer Unionist, statesmen, freed from their ideological burden, returned to pragmatic paths and showed a steady resolve, as Baldwin remarked in the thirties, that there should not be another Ireland in India, or indeed elsewhere. If it be true that Unionist fundamentalism, lending countenance to threats and preparations for armed resistance in Ulster to Home Rule in the years before the First World War, bore a heavy, possibly a decisive, responsibility for creating a situation in which a violent resolution of the Irish question became probable, it has also to be remarked that with the qualified exception of Cyprus, the party, still dominant in English political life till the early sixties, was not again immobilized by credal conviction on a national issue on 'the wrong side of history'.

2

NORTHERN IRELAND:
THE PAST*

May I begin by saying how honoured I am to take part in this Memorial Lecture with Dr Conor Cruise O'Brien this evening. My pleasure in accepting the Institute's invitation was the greater because of the very high regard I had for Sir Alexander Carr-Saunders with whom I was associated on various committees when I was working in Chatham House. I formed then the greatest respect for the penetration of his mind and the integrity and balance of his judgement on all matters that came before him. It is an additional pleasure to me, having worked in Chatham House for six years, that this lecture is to be delivered here this evening.

I have conceived my responsibility as that of analysing the past of Northern Ireland with the focus sharply on those still most critical of questions: how and why in 1919–21, the years of the great revolution in Anglo-Irish relations, Northern Ireland came into being in the form in which it did. My purpose is to explain and explore, not to pass judgement, and to refrain from protest: 'it serves no purpose to expostulate with history', wrote Lewis Namier;[1] and however tempted on occasion, I propose not to do so.

---

* This Memorial Lecture on Northern Ireland was one of two lectures given in Chatham House (headquarters of the Royal Institute of International Affairs) the same evening at the meeting of the Institute of Race Relations – Nicholas Mansergh on 'The Past' and Dr Conor Cruise O'Brien on 'The Future'.

[1] L. B. Namier, *Avenues of History* (London, 1952), p. 44.

The existence of Northern Ireland as a distinct political entity stems immediately from Ulster Unionist opposition to Home Rule and, more especially, to the Third Home Rule Bill, which was introduced by Asquith in the House of Commons on 11 April 1912 and conceded a qualified measure of self-government to all Ireland. On the first day of the committee stage, 11 June 1912, two young Liberals, Agar-Robartes and Neil Primrose, moved an amendment making acceptance of the proposed Home Rule Parliament conditional upon the exclusion from its jurisdiction of the four north-eastern counties, Antrim, Armagh, Down, and Derry.[2] The amendment enlisted support neither from Unionists nor, still less, from Liberals, but it retains historical interest as a first specific proposal in this period for the division of Ireland. It was followed by a variety of other proposals for the 'veiled' or 'open', the temporary or permanent, exclusion of Ulster or some part of it, from Home Rule, many of them advanced with the avowed intent of buying off Ulster and English Unionist opposition to Home Rule. A presumption of partition in some form was thereby created, with the result that when the Home Rule Act[3] was placed upon the statute book, in October 1914, it was not only associated with an Act[4] suspending its operation till after the conclusion of hostilities, but there was also the understanding that Parliament would then have an opportunity of passing an amending bill making special provision for Ulster, or some part of it. The Liberal and Nationalist principle of unity, resting upon the declared will of the majority of the elected representatives of the Irish people with safeguards for the minority consistent with it, had, therefore, by 1914 been seriously eroded, by contemplated concessions extracted by Ulster Unionist readiness to use force and qualified English Unionist readiness to support them in so doing.

The remarkable thing about the Easter Rising 1916, in this particular context, is not how much but how little difference it made. If you doubt this, compare Lloyd George's negotiations with the Irish leaders in the early summer of 1916 with Redmond's record of the deliberations at the Buckingham Palace Conference, July 1914. Certainly there is a change in style – not, it may be thought, for the better – but little in content. The negotiations were about the same problems and the same solutions – about the exclusion of six counties on a short-term or a long-term basis. Common to both was what had in effect been determined by 1914 – though Redmond to his cost had failed to understand this – namely that Ireland should be divided. The outstanding question, accordingly, was no longer whether Ireland was to be partitioned but rather what was to be the basis of partition? Asquith posed it succinctly in a letter to Redmond dated

---

[2] H. of C. Deb., 1912, Vol. XXXIX, Col. 771.
[3] Government of Ireland Act 1914, 4 & 5 Geo. V c. 90.
[4] Suspensory Act 1914, 4 & 5 Geo. V c. 90.

28 July 1916, on the breakdown of the negotiations. 'The real point', he wrote 'is the future of the Excluded area. Carson (naturally) wants safeguards against "automatic inclusion". You (with equal reason) desire to keep open, and effectively open, the possibility of revision and review at an early date.'[5] That was the point – the future of the Excluded area – that was to be settled in 1919–20.

As this phase of the Irish question neared its climax, there were involved three principal parties: the Coalition Cabinet in London representing British interests, Sinn Féin, with its self-constituted political and military manifestations in Dáil Éireann and the Irish Republican Army, and finally the Ulster Unionists, also equipped with embryonic political and paramilitary organization. It was, if not easy, at least not unduly difficult, even taking into account past actions and future pledges, for the British government to reach agreement with either Ulster Unionists or Irish Nationalists separately, and in fact in 1920–2 Lloyd George negotiated a settlement with each in turn, that with the Ulster Unionists being embodied in the Government of Ireland Act 1920, and that with Sinn Féin in the Anglo-Irish Treaty 1921. Both were effected in the absence of a third party, Sinn Féin having boycotted Westminster in 1920 and the Ulster Unionists not being represented at the Treaty negotiations in October–December 1921. In neither case, neither at the time nor later, did the third party subscribe to the spirit[6] of a settlement reached in the absence of its representatives, although it was perforce compelled in greater or lesser degree to acquiesce in the letter of it. Historically the most surprising feature is the fact that the second settlement, contrary to expectation when it was negotiated, in no significant respect modified the first.

The Government of Ireland Act 1920,[7] was in all respects, save one, derivative, but that solitary departure from Home Rule precedent sufficed to ensure its place in history – and in politics. There was no mistaking the significance with which that deviation was regarded for it was embodied in Section 1 of the Act. It read:

> (1) On and after the appointed day there shall be established for Southern Ireland a Parliament to be called the Parliament of Southern Ireland consisting of His Majesty, the Senate of Southern Ireland, and the House of Commons of Southern Ireland, and there shall be established for Northern Ireland a Parliament to be called the Parliament of Northern Ireland consisting of His Majesty, the Senate of Northern Ireland, and the House of Commons of Northern Ireland.
>
> (2) For the purposes of this Act, Northern Ireland shall consist of the

---

[5] Redmond Papers, National Library of Ireland, Dublin.

[6] The 1925 Agreement [tripartite] probably represented the nearest approach to this.

[7] Government of Ireland Act 1920, 10 & 11 Geo. V c. 87.

Parliamentary counties of Antrim, Armagh, Down, Fermanagh, Londonderry and Tyrone and the Parliamentary boroughs of Belfast and
Londonderry and Southern Ireland shall consist of so much of Ireland
as is not comprised in the said parliamentary counties and boroughs.

The concept underlying these provisions of the Act of 1920 may in one
sense be readily defined. It was that a demand for self-government on the
part of the large majority of the Irish people, demonstrated first in electoral returns over more than a generation, and, later, in growing support
for those prepared to use force to obtain it, ought, consistent with British
interests, to be conceded on grounds of principle, irrespective of whether
it was at root a 'national' or a something less than 'national' demand.
On the same line of reasoning, subject to the same criteria of evidence
in respect of authenticity, i.e. electoral returns over a generation or more
and a readiness in extremity to use force, the demand of a minority in
Ireland should also, subject again to British national interest, be respected.
The minority had no right to stand in the way of the legitimate aspirations of the majority; the majority had no entitlement to refuse to the
minority the same degree of self-determination conceded to, or obtained
by, them. If for the majority this meant the abandonment of the idea of
national unity, and if for the minority it meant the abandonment of their
objection to self-government, or Home Rule, these were sacrifices consistent with the application to majority and minority alike of the fashionable
Wilsonian principle of self-determination. On this line of thinking the 1920
Act realistically reflected the wishes of the majority and minority sections
of Irish opinion about their future government and lent justification to
Austen Chamberlain's disclaimer, in the debate on the Government of
Ireland Bill, that it was not 'We who are dividing Ireland, not we who made
party coincide with religious differences',[8] but Ireland that was, so to
speak, self-determining its own division.

In the retrospect of half a century such a conceptual analysis, even on
its own terms, seems insufficiently probing. The provisions of the Act which
partitioned Ireland might be construed in terms of self-determination, if
each self-determining population had constituted a long-established
political community. But this was not so. In the preceding five centuries
of British rule Ireland had been regarded as an entity, in earlier centuries
with a parliament of its own and since 1800 as one of the kingdoms merging in the United Kingdom of Great Britain and Ireland. If that Union
were to be undone then, even having regard to British precedent alone,
should not the exercise of self-determination by Ireland be as a unit,
since it was as a unit that the Irish Parliament had approved of Union?
If not, why not?

---

[8] H. of C. Deb., Vol. 127, Col. 981.

In logic, the answer ought to have been the emergence in Ireland of something more than a minority community, namely, a separate nation. It was indeed asserted that this had happened. Redmond, in condemning the two-nation theory as 'an abomination and a blasphemy', displayed realistic sensitivity to the fundamental nature of the implicit challenge. Yet usually the claim was advanced in a qualified form, namely, not that a minority as such constituted a nation, which would imply the emergence of a separate state, but that they were part of another nation. That theoretical position was in 1920–1 – and Lloyd George explored it in the latter year – and remains to this day, inconsistent with dominion status or, still more, with a unilateral declaration of independence, but altogether consistent at all times with what is now called integration. But acceptance of this view, although it alters the conceptual basis, does not diminish the conflict in principle between the two fundamental concepts – that of self-determination on the basis of a historic nation by its people as a whole on the one hand and that of equal regard for minority and for majority views on the other. Both concepts have claims upon the allegiance of the liberal and enlightened and both have attracted the allegiance of those who are neither.

Both also have important implications. Of the first view, that of Ireland as a nation, there was not, or, alternatively, there ought not to have been, any third party. This was a matter of principle, though even on the Irish view, one which also had its practical implications. 'Nothing', de Valera and his colleagues told General Smuts on his visit to Dublin on 6 July 1921, 'could come from a conference of the three parties.'[9] The two antagonized parties, de Valera reiterated a week later, should first meet and discuss their differences including the Ulster difficulty, not least because, principle apart, a tripartite conference would only encourage Ulster to be unreasonable and enable Lloyd George to take shelter behind the Ulster difficulties.[10] For Lloyd George it was the practical implications that came first. When Arthur Griffith in the course of the Treaty negotiations asserted once again that Ireland was a nation and its destiny should be determined on that assumption, Lloyd George was asked to explain how successive Liberal governments had been compelled to abandon the principle of unity to which they were pledged. This is how he did it:

> Attempts have been made to settle the Irish problem since 1886 on the basis of autonomy. Gladstone, who was the outstanding figure of his time with 40 years of political experience, tried to do it but he came up against

---

[9] Thomas Jones, *Whitehall Diary*, Vol. III, *Ireland 1918–1925*, edited by Keith Middlemas (London, 1971), p. 82.

[10] *Ibid.*, p. 88.

Ulster . . . We tried from 1911 to 1913. Ulster defeated Gladstone. Ulster would have defeated us. Mr Churchill and I were for the Bill, Mr Chamberlain and the Lord Chancellor were opposed. They with the instinct of trained politicians saw that Ulster was the stumbling block. They got the whole force of the opposition concentrated on Ulster. Ulster was arming and would fight. We were powerless. It is no use ignoring facts however unpleasant they may be. The politician who thinks he can deal out abstract justice without reference to forces around him cannot govern. You had to ask the British to use force to put Ulster out of one combination in which she had been for generations into another combination which she professed to abhor and did abhor, whether for political or religious reasons. We could not do it. If we tried the instrument would have broken in our hands. Their case was 'Let us remain with you'. Our case was 'Out you go or we fight you'. We could not have done it. Mr Churchill and I warned our colleagues. Mr Gladstone and Mr Asquith discovered it. I cannot say I discovered it because I was always of that opinion. You have got to accept facts. The first axiom is whatever happened we could not coerce Ulster.[11]

It would be an oversimplification to say that it was an argument between principle and pragmatism, but it would be correct to say that in 1920–1 the pragmatists prevailed. In particular they, in the persons of Lloyd George and his colleagues in the postwar Coalition Cabinet, determined the nature of the partition of Ireland, that is to say the area to be excluded and the form of its government, and something of the pragmatic nature of their decision-making process may be gathered from the Cabinet records of the time.

On 7 October 1919, the Cabinet appointed a committee under the chairmanship of Walter Long to advise upon a new measure of self-government for Ireland. The committee presented its first report to the Cabinet on 4 November 1919.[12] The extension of Home Rule, not to all Ireland as a unit but to both parts of Ireland, was felt by the committee to possess many advantages. It would provide for the complete withdrawal of British rule from the whole of Ireland in the sphere of domestic government; it would be consistent, both with the fact that there was a majority in Ulster as opposed to Dublin rule as there was a Nationalist majority opposed to British rule in the rest of Ireland, and with pledges already given; and finally it would 'enormously minimise the partition issue', since there would then be no Nationalists under direct British rule and both North and South

---

[11] *Ibid.*, pp. 129-30.

[12] The author read a paper to the Tenth Irish Conference of Historians at University College, Cork, in May 1971, entitled 'The Government of Ireland Act 1920: Its Origins and Purposes – The Working of the "Official" Mind', which analysed these developments in longer perspective and greater detail. [Reproduced in this volume as chapter 5.]

would enjoy 'immediately *state rights* together with a link between them'.[13] With regard to area, the Cabinet accepted the committee's view that exclusion on a basis of county option was unworkable and that a plebiscite would 'do more to partition Ireland in spirit and in temper . . . than any separation from outside could do'. It was also noted that if ultimate reunification were the aim, the whole province of Ulster should be excluded.

On 3 December discussion advanced a stage further with consideration by the Cabinet of three propositions each made on the assumption that there should be a Parliament for the south and west of Ireland.[14] The first was that the six north-eastern counties of Ulster should be allowed to vote in favour of remaining part of the United Kingdom for all purposes; the second that there should be a Parliament for the whole of Ulster; and the third that there should be a Parliament for the six counties. The argument advanced in support of the first proposition, i.e. that the six counties remain an undifferentiated part of the United Kingdom, was that it conformed to the wishes of the majority of the inhabitants and, therefore, rested on a clear basis of principle – that of self-determination to be applied, if necessary, by plebiscite. The objections were that the 'Covenanters' would be opposed because they had bound themselves to treat Ulster as a unit, that the Nationalists would likewise be opposed and also all moderate elements in the south and west, with the result that prospects of the eventual unity of Ireland would be greatly diminished by the exclusion of the six counties on this basis.

In the light of these objections and practical difficulties the possibility of the continued *inclusion* of the six counties for all purposes in the United Kingdom was excluded, one further reason being that such direct rule would at once diminish prospects of Irish unity and suggest to the outside world – a point on which ministers were clearly sensitive – that partition was the aim of British policy. In fact, and *per contra*, unity in the long run was the professed purpose of the Cabinet, the conclusion reached after discussion being that 'a united Ireland with a single Parliament of its own bound by the closest ties with Great Britain' was 'the ultimate aim'. At a subsequent Cabinet meeting this was questioned on the ground that lifelong Unionists would prefer that there should not be a single Parliament in Ireland, but the general trend of Cabinet opinion, so the minutes read, remained in favour of adhering to the earlier conclusions.[15]

---

[13] Cab. 27/68.

[14] Cab. 23/28.

[15] Cab. 23/18, 10 December 1919. The diverging views of Ulster and English Unionists, which were of very considerable significance at this juncture, are analysed in depth by D. G. Boyce in 'British Conservative Opinion, The Ulster Question and the Partition of Ireland, 1912–1921', *Irish Historical Studies* (Vol. XVII, No. 65, March 1970), pp. 89–112.

With the idea of continuing direct Westminster rule for the six counties discarded, a local Parliament became a necessity and the Cabinet considered the alternatives in respect of area laid before it. Here the debate turned on the arguments for and against a separate Parliament for Ulster or for the six counties. One argument for the six-county area was the advantage of having people under a Northern Ireland Parliament as homogeneous as possible. But the critics of this view were hard to convince, and on 19 December it was once more urged in Cabinet that if the ultimate aim of the government's policy were a united Ireland, it would be better that the jurisdiction of the Northern Parliament should extend over the whole of Ulster which included Roman Catholics and Protestants, both urban and rural districts and by its size was more suited to possessing a separate Parliament. But on the other side were the views of the Ulster leaders, especially as reported to the Cabinet on 15 and 19 December. They had expressed doubts about the ability of a Northern Parliament to govern the three additional Ulster counties where there were large Nationalist majorities and had 'greatly preferred' that the scheme should be applied to the six 'Protestant counties'. As Captain Craig put it later in the House, the best way to safeguard Ulster was to 'save as much of Ulster as we knew we could hold. To try to hold more . . . would seem an act of gross folly on our part'.[16] In general, the initiative in respect of a separate Parliament was taken by the Cabinet, but the reported conversations with the Ulster leaders would seem to dispose of the widely publicized notion that the Ulster leaders were reluctant to accept it. On the contrary they were not unwelcoming to the idea of a separate Parliament on grounds of security – as Carson later observed in the House of Commons, 'you cannot knock Parliaments up and down as you do a ball, and, once you have planted them there you cannot get rid of them'[17] – and, once it was to be adopted it was they who pressed the Cabinet in favour of the limited area because, as the Cabinet had already surmised, 'the idea of governing three Ulster counties which had a Nationalist majority was not relished'.

There was no very obvious warrant for a six-county area. The Ulster Unionist leaders were seemingly aware of this, for Sir James Craig in a personal conversation with Sir Laming Worthington-Evans proposed the establishment of a Boundary Commission to examine the distribution of population along the borders of the whole of the six counties and to take a vote on districts on either side where there was a doubt about allegiance. This proposal was commended to the Cabinet on 15 December 1919 as being in accord with the practice and principles adopted in the peace treaties and is reported to have met with considerable favour. It was discarded

---

[16] H. of C. Deb., Vol. 127, Col. 992.
[17] H. of C., Deb., Vol. 127, Col. 1202.

however, on the argument, presumably advanced by Lloyd George himself, that any such enquiries would produce unrest. One consequence was that the partition of Ireland, unlike the partition of India, was carried through with no prior enquiry into delimitation of frontiers. A more important consequence was that a large minority was included within the six-county area. Michael Collins put the point to Lloyd George in the Treaty negotiations on 14 October 1921. 'You and Northern Ireland', he said, 'are faced with the coercion of one-third of its area.' The allegiance, he proceeded, of the majority in Tyrone and Fermanagh, more than half Armagh, a great deal of Derry and a strip of Antrim would be with the authority they preferred, namely a Dublin Parliament. Lloyd George did not contest the statement. He responded instead by saying:

> The real unit was Ulster. It was an old province and a recognised unit . . . That would have been a unit but it was felt to be handing over a large Catholic population to the control of the Protestants. There was almost an agreement for the partition of Ulster. Therefore we had to get a new unit . . . On the whole, the 6 county area had been acceptable to the Nationalists as preferable to a new delimitation of Ulster. True, if you took a plebiscite of Tyrone and Fermanagh, there would be a Catholic majority.[18]

The exclusion of the six counties as a *bloc* without consultation on a county or other regional basis and without a prior Boundary Commission would appear to have derived from an assumption of temporary as distinct from lasting partition on the part of a majority of the Cabinet. Had the latter been contemplated, a closer coincidence of frontier and allegiance would, if only as a matter of expediency, have been sought by the British government, if need be against Ulster Unionist wishes.

There was, and there remains, a closer correlation between area and form of government in Northern Ireland than is apt to be recognized. That correlation was implicit but never, so far as I can trace, made explicit in Cabinet discussions when these matters were being determined. It was possible to conceive of Ulster, as a whole, remaining part of a United Kingdom and administered from London but unrealistic, as the Ulster Unionist leaders themselves indicated, to think of the whole province sustaining a separate Parliament on so precarious a balance of political allegiance. Equally once the notion of subordinate parliamentary institutions was conceived of as the most appropriate device to protect the interests of the Protestant minority in north-eastern Ireland, it was unrealistic to think of a four-county area (as suggested in 1912) having the population and resources to sustain them. Once, therefore, political institutions of a subordinate character were

---

[18] Jones, *op. cit.*, Vol. III, pp. 129-31.

to be established, the only option remaining open which would at once give political security and sufficient sustenance was a six-county area with, or without, frontier modifications.

The most important conclusion deriving from a perusal of the Cabinet records is that the partition of Ireland was effected within, or from, a concept of continuing unity. This was reflected both in the records and in the provisions of the 1920 Act. In the Act the establishment of separate Parliaments in Section 1 was, on paper, in part counterbalanced by the constitution of the Council of Ireland in Section 2. 'A fleshless and bloodless skeleton', Asquith termed it, and he appreciated more clearly than any other critic the implications of parity as between North and South, as between minority and majority, in the composition of that Council. 'It is left', he said, 'to an Ulster minority for all time to veto, if it pleases, the coming into existence of an Irish Parliament.'[19] This was evidently true. None the less the bias towards unity was there, and it found expression once more in December 1921, when the Articles of Agreement were for a Treaty between Great Britain and Ireland, the terms of which applied to the whole of Ireland, unless and until Northern Ireland exercised its freedom to opt out.

In retrospect, however, it would seem reasonable to infer that Carson and Craig had a clearer notion of the consequences of the creation of a Parliament for Northern Ireland than had members of the Cabinet. The Act of 1920 states explicitly (Section 75): 'Notwithstanding the establishment of the Parliaments of Southern and Northern Ireland, the supreme authority of the Parliament of the United Kingdom shall remain unaffected and undiminished over all persons, matters, and things in Ireland and every part thereof'. That section remains on the statute book, and, that being so, it is otiose to talk of a federal or even a quasi-federal system within the United Kingdom. But at the same time the existence of a subordinate machinery of government has given administrative reality and opportunity for the institutionalized formulation of the views of the majority in Northern Ireland. At the very least this has proved, as the Ulster Unionists realistically anticipated, a continuing restraint upon the actual political freedom of action of successive British governments. In that context the enactment of the Ireland Act 1949, in reaction to the repeal of the External Relations Act by the interparty administration in Dublin, registered less a new departure than recognition of a situation that had been coming into existence over the years, by providing that 'in no event will Northern Ireland or any part thereof cease to be part of His Majesty's dominions and the United Kingdom without the consent of the Parliament of Northern Ireland', But even so, there has been no subtraction from

---

[19] H. of C. Deb., Vol. 127, Cols. 1112-13.

the overriding authority vested in Parliament at Westminster by Section 75 of the Government of Ireland Act 1920.

The constitution of Northern Ireland as embodied in the Govermnent of Ireland Act 1920 not only reflected the recent history of Ulster but went some considerable way to determining the future, not only of Ulster but of Ireland. This, and one must return to the point, was because the Irish question at the end of the First World War was a triangular question, which did not receive triangular or multilateral settlement. Had it done so, the obvious possibilities of a federal solution within Ireland could hardly have been so completely disregarded. It was, however, resolved in two bilateral arrangements, namely the Government of Ireland Act 1920, in respect of Ulster, and the Anglo-Irish Treaty 1921, in respect of the Irish Free State, which were concluded, moreover, not in a natural order, as in India, but with the settlement with the minority party preceding the settlement with the majority party and concluded without its concurrence. The bilateralism of the two settlements little modified, however, the multilateralism of the problem. It was not, therefore, if, but when, that multilateral character would re-emerge and seek to reimpose itself upon arrangements which were made in at least partial disregard of it.

The existence of Northern Ireland as a political entity dates from the opening of the Northern Ireland Parliament by King George V on 22 June 1921. That was the day on which 'direct' rule ended in the six counties; the day on which Ireland was in fact partitioned. In an Irish context the opening of a Northern Ireland Parliament was thus the symbolic moment of a division sanctioned by the legislative enactment of a Parliament at Westminster from which the large majority of Irish members were absent on the ground that it was an alien parliament or in the earlier phrase of Arthur Griffith 'the parliament of the conqueror'. Yet in retrospect, as indeed at the time, the moment so loaded with potentialities of provocation was softened with overtones of reconciliation. When General Smuts had lunched with the King on 13 June, he had found the King anxiously preoccupied with the speech he was about to deliver in Belfast, his preoccupation heightened by rumours that the Home Office were drafting 'a bloodthirsty document'. Smuts suggested an alternative draft, which he communicated to Lloyd George. It proved unacceptable, as it stood, to the Cabinet, neither Balfour nor Austen Chamberlain liking what they termed its 'gush', nor 'the innuendo of oppression' which lay behind it.[20] But enough remained for the speech to be accepted as a gesture of reconciliation. Among other things the King said: 'This is a great and critical occasion in the history of the Six Counties, but not for the Six Counties alone, for everything which interests them touches Ireland'. That at least is unaffected by the passage of half a century.

---

[20] Jones, *op. cit.*, Vol. III, pp. 75–9.

3

JOHN REDMOND*

John Redmond, born at Ballytrent, County Wexford in 1856, was educated at Clongowes and at Trinity College, Dublin. In 1876, cutting short his university career, he went to live in London with his father, William Archer Redmond, member of Parliament for Wexford city. The father was a supporter of Isaac Butt – the son, of Parnell. His first meeting with Parnell was dramatic. It was at Enniscorthy during the general election, 1880. There was, as Redmond later recalled, 'an awful scene'. Parnell was greeted by a hostile crowd, his speech was inaudible, his trousers torn, and the remains of a rotten egg lodged in his beard. But he remained unperturbed as ever and as they went home he noticed his young companion bleeding from an injury and remarked 'Well – you have shed your blood for me at all events'. It was symbolic. Redmond never wavered in his loyalty to his chief in life or death.

That same year 1880, Redmond's father died but John's expectation of succeeding him was disappointed because Parnell wished to have Tim Healy, that master of sardonic repartee, to support him in the House.

---

* Several series of lectures in honour of the Irish patriot Thomas Davis were broadcast by Radio Éireann over a number of winters and these were later published in book form. Chapters 3, 6 and 8 in this book were all Thomas Davis lectures in different series.

A letter dated 4 March 1956 from de Valera's private secretary reads: 'Mr de Valera was listening to your recent lecture in the Thomas Davis series on Radio Éireann. He liked the lecture very much and would be obliged if you could let him have a copy'.

Within a few months John Redmond was rewarded for his self-sacrifice by being returned unopposed at a by-election for New Ross.

The three influences that were to determine the outlook and career of John Redmond played upon him in his early, impressionable years. The first was Parliament. 'Redmond's entire life was centred in the House of Commons.' That is the opening sentence in Professor Denis Gwynn's biography; that is, that must be, the essential consideration in any assessment of his place in Irish history. Redmond was, and always remained, by temperament and heredity, a House of Commons man. At Westminster under the leadership of Parnell, the second great influence in his life, John Redmond found himself one of a well-drilled, pledge-bound phalanx of Irish Nationalist members whose speeches and votes were used at the discretion of their leader to enforce attention to Irish demands. In Parnell's hand the party was a weapon to be used in warfare – a warfare none the less deserving of the name because it was in theory constitutional. That was something deeply implanted in Redmond's mind.

As one of Parnell's followers in the House of Commons in the heyday of the party's power, Redmond participated in great events but had no voice in their direction. It was when he was away on an extended tour to raise funds for the party in Australia and in North America that his personality matured and his opinions crystallized. He married an Australian girl as did his brother Willie who accompanied him; he made many friends and he was influenced by those he met and by what he saw. This, the third enduring influence on his political outlook, is the most often overlooked. On his travels Redmond acquired both knowledge of that great body of Irishmen living overseas and something of the predominant outlook of the Irish in the Empire. This coloured his thoughts on Ireland's future. Not only did he think it undesirable that two countries so closely associated as Britain and Ireland should be wholly separated but, further, he had no wish to see any dismemberment of an Empire which Irishmen had had their share in creating. 'Let us', he said, 'have national freedom and imperial unity and strength.' From this ultimate aim Redmond never, I think, departed. It was the aim of Australian, Canadian and later of South African leaders. In so far as it helped to influence Redmond's later actions it served, psychologically at least, to widen the gulf between him and succeeding generations.

The rent in the party caused by the O'Shea divorce case first brought John Redmond into prominence at home: he was one of the small band who remained unquestioningly loyal to Parnell. He saw the issue in simpler terms than the majority of his colleagues and stated it forcibly in the bitter debates in Committee Room 15. It was the issue, as Parnell himself had chosen to present it, of whether the party was, or was not, to accept Liberal dictation in its choice of leader. To Redmond, Parnell could not, and should not, be replaced. The majority accepted neither the argument nor the conclusion and seceded. There followed ten barren years in a wilderness of division, recrimination and distraction from the national cause. In those years Redmond, within the House of Commons and without, displayed both growing qualities of leadership and oratorical gifts which earned praise from those well qualified to judge. But for the future these things could have availed him little had not the circumstances that led to the reunion of the party played into his hands.

It was William O'Brien and the United Irish League practising, not preaching, unity, at a time when the Boer War had drawn the two sections of the party closer together, that in fact gave the final impetus to negotiations for reunion; and it was John Dillon who generously suggested as a basis for reunion that the chairman of the reunited party should be chosen from the weaker, the Parnellite, section. It was this suggestion that opened the way for Redmond's election and in 1900 a national convention in Dublin confirmed him in that position. The most faithful of the Parnellites was thus invested with the mantle of Parnell. But by force of circumstance he had to wear it with a difference. The years of division had left their legacy; there were personal antagonisms not easily to be eradicated and there were, too, differences of principle about the organization and policy of the party. On the surface much was restored but something of the old spirit had gone. The Irish party was not destined to enjoy 'glad confident morning again'!

This was not the fault of John Redmond. He was not thought of as the inspired and chosen leader of the party but more prosaically and correctly as its chairman. This in itself placed him at some disadvantage by comparison with Parnell. But he suffered from a more serious disadvantage by the mere efflux of time. Parnell had conceived of the Irish party as a wholly independent party whose votes thrown now on one side and now on the other would make, and even more important threaten to unmake, governments. The effectiveness of the weapon at all times depended less upon the numerical strength of the Irish party than upon the relative strength of the two great English parties. As Redmond quite correctly argued in 1910, what mattered was not whether the party won eighty-six or seventy-six or sixty-six seats in the House of Commons but whether it held the balance. But over and above this there was the fact that the psychological impact of the organized Irish vote had weakened. In the eighties it was so great partly because it was novel. In the period of Redmond's leadership it was familiar and with familiarity had come, not contempt, but an appreciation of its limitations. In 1910 Redmond had nominal freedom of action but could he throw out a Home Rule Liberal government, however much they compromised, if the alternative were to be a violently anti-Home Rule Unionist administration?

It is in the light of such considerations that Redmond's leadership in the decisive years which began with the landslide Liberal victory of 1906 must be judged. At the outset there were Irish anxieties lest independence should make the Liberals neglectful of Home Rule. An Irish Councils Bill, which they introduced in 1907 and to which Redmond responded conditionally and as it proved imprudently, was indignantly rejected by Irish opinion as inadequate. But the new Prime Minister, Sir Henry Campbell-Bannerman, a wealthy, shrewd, Scottish radical who had never feared to champion unpopular causes and who in the words of T. P. O'Connor was honoured and loved by the Irish party, was in fact, and despite reservations in respect of timing, a convinced Home Ruler. In that same year, 1907, he gave striking evidence of his faith in national self-government by restoring the independence of the two South African republics, the Transvaal and the Orange Free State, within five years of their defeat in the Boer War. This 'magnanimous gesture', bitterly condemned by the Tories, converted two of the famous leaders of the Boer guerilla forces, Generals Botha and Smuts, into staunch upholders of the idea of a Commonwealth of free and equal nations. It also made a profound and lasting impression upon John Redmond. Time and again I have noticed how in his letters and in his speeches at critical moments he recalled Campbell-Bannerman's generosity and its reward. Do to Ireland, he was urging Asquith even as late as 1916, as your predecessor did to the Dutch republics and you will reap that same reward.

Why did the Liberals not do so? The answer in 1907 was that the House of Lords would have thrown out a Home Rule Bill as they had thrown out Gladstone's in 1893 by 419 votes to 41, and as they would have thrown out proposals for self-government in the Boer republics had not Campbell-Bannerman restored it by Order in Council. Such a device, however, could not be employed to repeal or amend the Act of Union. Home Rule was, therefore, conditional upon neutralizing the opposition of the House of Lords. This was no easy undertaking. In the early years of the Liberal administration almost every Liberal measure was mutilated or rejected by the Lords. The Tories spoke of ploughing the sands, the Liberals of 'filling up the cup', for it was Liberal strategy to allow the account between peers and people to mount up till an appeal could be made to the people themselves. In 1909 the cup was filled when the Lords, disregarding the opinion of the more statesmanlike Unionist leaders, decided to follow Lord Milner's advice, to reject Lloyd George's budget – the so-called people's budget – and 'to damn the consequences'. The Liberals dissolved, and in the ensuing election Lloyd George, who had earlier described the House of Lords as being no longer the watchdog of the constitution but Mr Balfour's poodle, with bitter invective in Limehouse denounced the 'gilded popinjays' who flouted the people's will. The outcome fulfilled Redmond's, but not Asquith's, highest hopes. The Liberals returned in 1910 with a majority over the Conservatives but dependent on Irish support. They were pledged to end or mend the House of Lords. There was a second election later in the year before the issue was settled. But settled it was in the Parliament Act of 1911. The Lords could henceforward delay, but they could not veto Home Rule. The Unionists complained bitterly that Asquith was the prisoner of the Irish party, his followers 'mere helots' of Redmond. This was wilful exaggeration but it suggests that while Redmond's influence was certainly great he might have been better advised to exercise it more discreetly. However in 1911 there seemed little need for discretion. Not only was the way clear for Home Rule but the Liberal government pledged to carry it through was dependent on Redmond's support. Did not this mean victory at last?

The Third Home Rule Bill was introduced into the House of Commons on 12 April 1912. Redmond at the summit of his parliamentary reputation enjoyed an immense triumph. He was well aware of the limitations of the bill, but it seemed that it was the principle that mattered. A National Convention, at which Redmond was enthusiastically received, welcomed it in the spirit in which it was offered. When Asquith visited Dublin three months later the only reminder of unpleasant things was an implement, described as a scythe by Asquith's biographer and as an axe by Redmond's, which was hurled at the Prime Minister riding in an open carriage by an English woman suffragette who had specially crossed from Holyhead for the purpose.

The note of rejoicing, however, was altogether premature. Redmond, so it seems in retrospect, had so concentrated his attention on removing the known obstacle to Home Rule, namely the House of Lords veto, that he considered too little other and less impersonal factors. High among these must be rated the rising political temperature in England. It was reflected in a change in the leadership of the Tory party. In the autumn of 1911 Balfour bowed to the BMG, 'Balfour must go', campaign and the choice of successor seemingly lay between two conflicting claimants, Walter Long who represented traditional interests and Austen Chamberlain of whom Churchill remarked 'he always played the game – and he always lost it'. Nothing could have suited Redmond better. But neither Chamberlain nor Long was chosen. The third man, as so often happens in politics, in the person of Andrew Bonar Law, a Canadian of Ulster Presbyterian descent, secured the prize. Many years later standing by his tomb in Westminster Abbey, Asquith spoke of Bonar Law as the Unknown Prime Minister. As leader of the Unionist party, however, he was unknown neither to Asquith nor to Redmond. Elected because he was reputed to be 'a first-class fighting man', Bonar Law in his first speech as leader lived up to that reputation. He spoke of the government as 'artful dodgers' dealing in treachery and cant, and going down the steep place like the Gadarene Swine. Instinct and background led him to select Ulster as the vulnerable joint in the armour of Home Rule. With the avowed intention of killing Home

Rule altogether he threw the whole weight of the Unionist party behind Ulster opposition to the bill.

As Redmond had foreseen, the Home Rule Bill passed the Commons, was rejected by the Lords and under the Parliament Act of 1911 would become law in 1914 unless the Unionists by constitutional or unconstitutional pressure could secure its withdrawal. Bonar Law, unlike Balfour, cared little for the distinction between the two and so in the next three years England witnessed the astonishing spectacle of the Unionist party, the party of law and order, advocating, inciting, assisting an Ulster revolt against the authority of Parliament.

The aim was to make Home Rule impossible. This was not a situation which either Asquith or Redmond were well qualified to meet. Redmond, who on principle kept himself aloof from social contacts with English party leaders in London, when in Ireland withdrew to the seclusion of his Wicklow home. He was not therefore in as close touch with political feeling in London as his long residence there might lead one to expect and he was out of touch with opinion at home. He was moreover by temperament inclined to underestimate opposition. In the summer of 1913 he was saying that the 'argumentative opposition to Home Rule was dead, that all the extravagant action, all the bombastic threats are but indications that the battle is over'. Right down to 1914 he continued to assure Asquith that Carson and the Orangemen were bluffing. This was a simple and a sanguine interpretation which was emphatically not shared by members of the Irish Volunteers or by Sinn Féin. It encouraged a policy of wait and see, to which in any event the Liberal Prime Minister was only too well disposed. It left the initiative very largely in the hands of Redmond's opponents. They did not fail to seize it.

1913 was a year of manoeuvre; 1914 the destined year of decision under the Parliament Act. The tide in 1913 had turned perceptibly against Redmond. Paradoxically enough the Unionists strengthened their position as they moderated at least in private their claim. That a small minority in north-east Ireland should seek to impose a veto on the democratically expressed wishes of more than three-quarters of the Irish people was so obviously indefensible as to be a source of weakness. But the claim of a minority, vehemently expressed, to opt out of the jurisdiction of a Home Rule government was something Liberals on their own principles were bound to consider more seriously. They did so; and under pressure from them in 1914 and as the 'extremest limit of concession' Redmond was prepared to contemplate the exclusion by plebiscite of the north-eastern counties of Ulster from the operation of the Home Rule Bill for a limited period if it satisfied Carson and his followers. It did not. They rejected scornfully the Liberal concession, as 'sentence with a stay of execution'. They demanded a clean cut. Redmond responded by saying that any compromise deserved consideration provided always that it recognized that

Ireland was a unit. The two-nation theory he described as 'an abomination and a blasphemy'. But the prospect of Home Rule with unity was fading fast.

In the spring of 1914 the Curragh Mutiny and the gunrunning at Larne further undermined faith at home in the efficacy of Redmond's parliamentary tactics and he himself, hitherto suspicious of the Irish Volunteer movement, now took over its nominal leadership. This was a sign not of strength but of weakness. It was tantamount to an admission on the part of the leader of the Irish Parliamentary party that no parliament but force or at least the display of force would be the final arbiter.

It was to avert the dread catastrophe of civil war that in July 1914 King George V summoned a conference of party leaders, including Redmond, to Buckingham Palace. But the conference failed to reach agreement on the two points of the nature of the exclusion and of the area to be excluded from the jurisdiction of the Dublin Parliament. The first indeed was never fully discussed because of disagreement on the second. Then war came. The Home Rule Bill was indeed placed on the statute book after its outbreak but it was coupled with an Act which suspended its operation till after the cessation of hostilities and was made conditional upon an amending bill which would determine the extent of its application. The goal was reached – but only on paper.

The war ushered in the last phase in Redmond's career. At its outset he enjoyed one more parliamentary triumph when on his own responsibility he pledged Ireland's support to the allied cause, saying that all troops could be withdrawn from the country. It would, he said, be guarded by its own sons and for that purpose the armed Catholics of the South would be only too glad to join with the armed Protestants of the North. It was a generous gesture inspired by a sense of outrage at the German invasion of Belgium, and by the hope that united in a common cause and in the common defence of Ireland, National and Ulster Volunteers would help to heal the divisions of the country. Though the immediate response was favourable it may well be that Redmond would have been wiser to have consulted with his colleagues, with the leaders of the National Volunteers and most of all with the War Office before he spoke. He was, however, a parliamentarian and his sense of a parliamentary occasion perhaps swayed his judgement. The outcome was for Redmond a tale of much frustration. The War Office refused to recognize the Volunteers and turned down most of Redmond's ideas about the recruitments, an Irish division and the distinguishing insignia its members should wear. 'From the very first hour', he complained in October 1916, 'our efforts were thwarted, ignored and snubbed. Everything almost that we asked for was refused and everything almost that we protested against was done.' Asquith spoke of 'dreadful mistakes' and 'most regrettable blunders', Lloyd George of stupidities that 'looked like malignities'. But for Redmond the damage by then was done. Yet he never repented of the decision he made in 1914; and of all the brave men who died on the Western Front fighting as they believed in the cause of human liberty none better deserves recall than his brother Willie Redmond. I remember a discussion in a Cambridge Combination Room about the most eloquent speaker in living memory. Many famous men had been mentioned when a London professor who had heard them all observed that none had ever moved him as had Willie Redmond. But his brother's death in action in 1917 was a blow which came to John Redmond when his world was crumbling round him. Constitutional methods themselves were on their last trial between 1911 and 1914. They failed and the party which so long had championed them was the almost unnoticed victim of the Easter Rising in 1916. One thing Redmond was spared – he did not live to see the general election two years later when the party was scornfully swept aside and thereafter only in Waterford which he had represented so long was the Redmondite cause still cherished.

Arthur Griffith condemned the policy of the Irish Parliamentary party as 'useless, degrading and demoralizing'. His verdict, widely accepted, lies heavily upon the reputation of the party's last leader. For John Redmond was a parliamentarian and as such – politically – he must be judged. He was a skilful parliamentarian, a shrewd tactician, and an eloquent speaker in the traditional manner. He was, and was known to be, an honourable man. It was his destiny to try for the last time to secure Home Rule by constitutional means. He would like to have been the Irish Botha and the Liberals encouraged by the success of their South African policy hoped he would be: but there was to be no Irish Botha. This, I think, was due principally to circumstances beyond the control of Redmond and perhaps even of Asquith. But it may be too that Redmond showed himself at some critical moments lacking in political resource. He was content to stand, as he said in welcoming the Third Home Rule Bill, 'precisely where Parnell stood'. But a quarter of a century had passed and it had brought many changes. The passage of time in particular had not lessened but intensified Unionist hostility to Home Rule. Redmond took account of it only under pressure. Might he not have been wiser to have sought agreement within Ireland perhaps on federal lines, which, as he knew from his travels, had made unity possible in Canada under more difficult circumstances (because a difference in language was added to the differences in religion), before the Home Rule Bill was introduced? At the worst would he not thereby have given conclusive evidence of his readiness to make all concessions consistent with unity at the very outset? But be that as it may there is certainly evidence that Redmond and many of his colleagues during their long sojourn at Westminster had become dangerously detached from their own people. Nor was this true simply in the political field, as was apparent during the pre-war Dublin strikes. There were new problems and new forces whose nature Redmond did not wholly comprehend. Yet at the last, one comes back simply to this. Redmond was faced with a problem which has not yet been solved. Self-government and unity has not yet come to Ireland. His successors using very different means have achieved a greater independence than Redmond aspired to and a partition he refused to contemplate in any lasting form. Not all problems after all are susceptible at a given moment of a happy solution. And if Redmond in retrospect seems in seeking that solution to have lacked some final felicity of judgement did he not also lack that element of luck, which, as Napoleon confessed, decides most battles? In the end as surely as the doomed Serbian patriot Mihailovitch thirty years later Redmond was carried away 'in the gale of the world' and his name no more held in high esteem among his countrymen. Succeeding generations mete out a rough justice and such is often the penalty of failure when it lacks some indefinable quality of greatness. In his principal purpose Parnell also failed; and the contrast in contemporary reputation between the chief and his political heir who in all things so faithfully followed him is something that makes one ponder again the divers destinies of men.

4

THE PRELUDE TO PARTITION:
Concepts and Aims in
Ireland and India*

'In this matter, when among other voices the voice of manifest right cries out against us to Heaven, I must acknowledge that never in my life have I suffered pangs like these, that I feel shame to show my face.'[1] The writer was the Empress Maria Theresa; the recipient her Chancellor Kaunitz; the occasion the first partition of Poland in 1772. Posterity remembers the Great Frederick's cruel gibe about the Empress who wept while she took, but remains little mindful of her foreboding that untold suffering would come to later generations because of a partition urged upon her for reasons of state. '*Placet*', she said in yielding to them, 'since so many great and learned men will have it so: but long after I am dead it will be known what this violating of all that was held sacred and just will give rise to.'

The eighteenth-century enlightenment was affronted by the perpetration of so cynical an act. '*On partage savamment les royaumes, comme autrefois on divisait les sermons*', protested Horace Walpole to Madame

---

*The 1976 Commonwealth Lecture. This was part of the Memorial in Cambridge to Field Marshal Smuts – a former student at Christ's College, who after the Second World War was elected Chancellor of the University. A Smuts professorial chair and a lectureship were also founded and the author was the first Smuts Professor of the History of the British Commonwealth (1953-70). Later he was invited to give this lecture.

[1] *Cambridge Modern History*, Vol. VI, *The Eighteenth Century* (Cambridge, 1925), p. 630.

du Deffand,[2] and he might have added, what the perpetrators of the partition well understood, that kingdoms, like sermons, were the more digestible when divided into three parts. Partition itself became a pejorative term, the *Annual Register* in 1807 being unable to postulate any more damning interpretation of the Tilsit agreement than that it constituted a partition of Europe itself, carved out between Buonaparte and Alexander, in which the latter 'fell into the snares of the Italian, with an imbecility bordering on insanity'.[3] In more recent times the word itself suffices to stir resentment among liberals, and antagonism among Nationalists – other than those for whom a partition is, or has been, a condition of their separate statehood.

In any enquiry into the nature of partition the point of departure must needs be the word itself. In political parlance it has no single, or simple, connotation. In the case of Poland, it meant the partitioning of an ancient kingdom in three phases into three parts, each part being absorbed into the polity of a powerful and predatory neighbour; for the Turkish Empire before the First World War it meant chiefly, as it may in South Africa,[4] progressive partition from within through the re-emergence of nationalities, Greeks and Bulgars, Romanians and Serbs, long subjected by conquest to alien rule; while the 'partition of Africa', a phrase that is itself to be used with some caution by historians – Professor Sanderson's 'The European Partition of Africa',[5] is more indicative of what happened – meant historically the division, not of a political, but of a geographical entity by powers either actually or by derivation, e.g. the South African colonies and republics, external to it.

The phenomenon of partition in this century has had two further manifestations both international in origin and consequence. The first was particular, namely the partition of Palestine to make possible the re-creation of a Jewish state; the second a product of great-power tensions, namely the partition of states along what came to be known after the First World War as the international frontier, and which after the Second World War ran through Korea, Vietnam and Germany.

While set in this wider background, the scope of this enquiry is limited to what, by contrast with the international, may be described as a domestic

---

[2] Letter of 13 April 1773. See *Supplement to the Letters of Horace Walpole,* ed. Paget Toynbee (2 Vols: Oxford, 1918), Vol. 1, p. 213. The passage in the letter continued *'et l'on massacre le peuple avec autant de sang-froid qu'on les ennuyait. Voilà un siècle de lumières'.*

[3] *Annual Register, 1807,* pp. 271–3.

[4] The distinguishing feature in the South African case is the contemplation of partition as an objective of government policy; see the exposition of the purposes of the Promotion of Bantu Self-Government Act 1959 by government spokesmen, notably Dr Verwoerd, in the South African House of Assembly Debates 1959, Vol. 101, Cols. 6001–8, 6018–9 and 6214–27.

[5] *Journal of Imperial and Commonwealth History,* Vol. III, No. 1 (1974).

i.e. within a single polity, dimension. Within such a classification two kinds of partition may be identified. The first is to be seen when states once separate then unified – for example, Belgium and Holland, Sweden and Finland, Sweden and Norway – again pulled apart. In such cases clearly there is a form of partition, but in so far as the pulling apart is related to previously existing and distinct historical, linguistic or ethnic identities, the term itself is infrequently applied,[6] the reason being that it subsumes the existence of a partitioner and when division is by domestic accord, albeit deriving from domestic discord, that role remains unfilled. It is not so, however, in the second case, that of partitions which arise when dependencies unified either previous to, or under, imperial rule divide, or are divided, in the process of becoming once more independent. In such situations, the withdrawing imperial authority, short of unconditional abandonment, as by the Portuguese of Angola, must in the last resort, and may much earlier, decide to whom power is to be transferred; and if it be to more than one successor authority, then it must in so doing assume at the least some measure of general responsibility for the consequent partition. In such an eventuality the outgoing imperial power, by necessary constitutional enactment providing for transfer,[7] must also make provision for partition. In law, therefore, there is a partitioner and the term partition is consistently used of the outcome.

The partition of Ireland and of India belong to this last category. At the time of partition both countries were within a single polity, the British imperial system, and in each case the partition took place coincidentally in time with a transfer of power, albeit limited in the Irish case, to indigenous authorities. The common denominator was thus more than partition: it was partition and a transfer in a triangular political context. My principal purpose is to consider the interplay of ideas and forces in such a triangular setting with particular regard to the extent to which the setting itself may have influenced the tactics, conditioned the responses or limited the range of options open to the three parties or protagonists, irrespective of, or superimposing upon the otherwise great differences in the histories and circumstances of the countries so partitioned.

In the two instances under consideration the triangle had as its base a nationalist majority, who cherished the theory of one nation and sought to restore, or establish, its independence as a unit; as one side a minority who, when faced with the prospect of rule by the majority community,

---

[6] This is also true of Pakistan, geographically divided since its inception in 1947, and partitioned in a political sense with the constitution of a separate state, Bangladesh, in East Bengal, in January 1972.

[7] See the Government of Ireland Act 1920 (10 & 11 Geo. V c. 67), the Irish Free State Constitution Act 1922 (13 Geo. V c. 1, session 2) and the Indian Independence Act 1947 (10 & 11 Geo. VI c. 30).

formulated a two-nation theory, or its near-equivalent; and as the other, the imperial power predisposed to holding the balance, but only for so long as that might be to its own advantage, within the limits of its resources and consistent with its image of its world rôle. The political strategy pursued by each party to the triangle was designed to ensure the fulfilment of its conceptual aim, itself conditioned in varying degree by assessment of economic or other interests, and the more closely in any particular case that strategy was tied to literal realization of concept, the less flexible it became. Theory and practice in such circumstances were apt to be more closely intertwined than essays in detailed historical reconstruction, with their discounting or neglect of the ideological, often allow.

In respect of the first party in the triangle, the concept was one of restored independence to a country long under alien subjection. In Ireland after 1916, and more especially after January 1919, the goal was symbolized in a particular constitutional form – the republic; in India the aim was more generally expressed first as Swaraj, and later as Purna Swaraj, i.e. the complete independence on which the Congress resolved on 22 March 1940. The freedom sought in each case was for a country deemed, like Mazzini's beloved Italy, to have been endowed by Providence with its own irrefutable boundary marks. In Ireland throughout the period of frustrated demand for self-rule that ran from Parnell to Pearse,[8] from the exponent (and exploiter) of constitutionalism to the protagonist of physical force, none among nationalists abated the claim to coincidence of nation, state and island – that best mannered of parliamentarians, John Redmond reacting to a suggestion of partition by denunciation of it as 'an abomination and a blasphemy', while uncompromising revolutionaries believed with Pearse that it were better for a man that he had not been born than that he should sacrifice one iota of a national claim that rested upon the foundation of its territorial integrity. In India, the All-India National Congress, which, as Gandhi succinctly put it to the Round Table Conference in 1931, claimed 'to represent the whole of India',[9] were the exponents of that self-same one-nation theory, a nation that in their case stretched from the Himalayas to Cape Comorin, possible partition being equated with outrage, or, in Gandhian phraseology, with 'the vivisection' of Mother-India. The principle of a united India, Maulana A. K. Azad, the President of the Congress, and Jawaharlal Nehru told Sir Stafford Cripps in the course of his Indian mission early in 1942, was one for which they were prepared

[8] By happy coincidence each has been the subject of a biography of unusual interest since this lecture was delivered, i.e. F.S.L. Lyons, *Charles Stewart Parnell* (London, 1977), and Ruth Dudley Edwards, *Patrick Pearse: The Triumph of Failure* (London, 1977).

[9] *Indian Round Table Conference* (2nd session), 7 September–1 December 1931, *Proceedings of the Federal Structure and Minorities Committee*, Cmd 3997, p. 390.

to go to almost any length[10] – the qualifying 'almost' indicating an attitude less rigid than the Irish and foreshadowing (if that is not reading too much into a word) Congress acquiescence on 3 June 1947 in partition as the price of independence, though it is right to recall that in the resolution approving such acquiescence the All-India Congress Committee declared: 'Geography and the mountains and the seas fashioned India as she is, and no human agency can change that shape or come in the way of her final destiny . . . when the present passions have subsided, India's problems will be viewed in their proper perspective and the false doctrine of two nations in India will be discredited and discarded by all'.[11]

There was a gap between enunciation, however eloquent or uncompromising, of the concept of one independent nation-state and its realization. In the way there came Ulster; there came Muslim India; there was, not as a constant but as a variable, its actions in no small measure conditioned by the balance of its own domestic political forces, the imperial power. There was also the complexity, itself deriving from the triangular setting, that while the concept was singular, its realization was conditional upon attainment of two goals, independence and unity. The first predicated armed revolt or at the least political pressure upon the imperial power, i.e. a militant stance – Conor Cruise O'Brien has noted how even in Parnellite days *United Ireland*, the party's journal, used the vocabulary of warfare to describe parliamentary debates, Nationalist MPs sharing in 'the exultation of battle' and engaging in 'eager man to man conflicts with the foe';[12] the second a conciliatory tone. In theory the two were reconcilable; in practice as the majority lined up behind their leaders an exhilarating mood of militancy was easily, only too easily, in part deflected to others, who by detachment from, or opposition to, nationalist aims appeared to be providing the arguments and the obstacle most likely to frustrate their attainment. The pursuit of autonomy without prejudice to unity was not, and is not, psychologically an easy assignment, as many others in Europe,[13] Asia and Africa were also to learn.

It is often suggested, or implied, that both the Irish and Indian national movements had a choice between seeking to conciliate the minority community by recognizing its deep-felt need for safeguards and attempting to impose upon it the will of the majority by rigid insistence on the fact that after all it was the majority. Theoretically that may be so, but the exercise of that choice in practice either way was so fraught with risk that there was bound to be ambivalence and reservation in the making of it.

---

[10] N. Mansergh and E. W. R. Lumby (eds), *India: The Transfer of Power 1942–47* (London, HMSO 1970–), Vol. 1, No. 496.

[11] Quoted in V. P. Menon, *The Transfer of Power in India* (Bombay, 1957), p. 384.

[12] C. C. O'Brien, *Parnell and His Party 1880–90* (Oxford, 1957), p. 81, n. 2.

[13] Cyprus is in mind especially.

Historically, however, the outline of the answers given was clear enough. Faced with the problem of recalcitrant minorities, the majority nationalist parties in Ireland and India sought, as part of their campaign for self-government, to organize and demonstrate electorally their overall representational strength. In Ireland, Parnell, that master of tactics, embarked on a policy of electoral invasion, intended to consolidate support for Home Rule in the North and to convey the impression of its inevitability. The policy was crowned with significant success. Of the eighty-nine contested Irish seats in the election of November 1885, the Nationalists won eighty-five with Ulster returning eighteen Nationalists as against seventeen Unionists. Here, if required, was convincing and conclusive evidence that there was no question of a united Northern province resisting Home Rule. The Congress victories in the provincial elections in British India in 1937, based upon a well-organized mass movement, seemed to point to a similar conclusion – there was no natural or historic area where the electorate was unitedly opposed to the national demand, the potentially separatist Muslim League under the leadership of Mahomed Ali Jinnah in fact not coming near to having a majority in any province, and, overall, winning only 108 out of 482 Muslim seats.[14] There were only two forces in India, Jawaharlal Nehru had claimed in the course of the election campaign – British imperialism and Indian nationalism – and when Jinnah had retorted that there was a third party, the Muslims, Nehru dismissed out of hand the notion of the Muslims in India as 'a nation apart'.[15] Did not the results of the elections go far to vindicate that dismissal?

But here there intervened a familiar paradox in politics. In India, as earlier in Ireland, overwhelming electoral victory significantly reinforced the claims for autonomy or independence. But in terms of unity the exact opposite was the case; there nothing failed like success. By giving the appearance of the mobilization of a seemingly external threat; by the militancy of their posture, their language on the hustings, their ballads or songs – *Bande Mataram* was deemed by some 'a hymn of hate against the Muslims'; by post-election attitudes and actions, the Congress going so far as to organize a 'mass contact' movement among Muslim peasants and workers on the argument that 'even the Muslim masses' looked up to the Congress 'for relief';[16] by their emphasis upon the link between culture and nationality the majority parties contributed significantly to the closing of anti-Home Rule ranks in Ulster and to the Muslims' resolve to mobilize

---

[14] H. V. Hodson, *The Great Divide* (London, 1969), p. 62. There were special factors bringing about the result, by no means least the League's sense of being an elitist grouping, not a popular mass movement, which accounted for its not contesting all the Muslim seats, but they little diminished the impression given.

[15] Sarvepalli Gopal, *Jawaharlal Nehru: A Biography* (London, 1975), Vol. 1, pp. 223–4.

[16] *Ibid*, p. 225.

behind the League lest they be reduced to 'mere pages' at the footstool of a Hindu Congress. In both instances the leaders of the minority dramatized the threat – Carson by organizing one great demonstration for Easter Tuesday, 1912, two days before the introduction of the Third Home Rule Bill, and others for the signing of a Solemn League and Covenant pledging resistance to Home Rule, on 28 September that year; Jinnah, reacting sharply to the Congress 'mass contact' campaign, by organizing a mass movement based on the cry, 'Islam in danger',[17] followed by the proclamation of a day of national rejoicing when the Congress provincial ministries resigned shortly after the outbreak of war, and later by Black flag days, culminating in a call to the 'Muslim nation' to direct action 'to achieve Pakistan' on 16 August 1946, a sequel to which was the 'Great Calcutta Killing', reliance being placed throughout on sentiment at the grass roots, the more inflamed because it, too, as in Ireland, stirred the embers of centuries old religious antagonisms.

Thus it was; might it have been otherwise? Before following along a road signposted with familiar and facile speculation, it is well to underline firstly that the leaders of the majority parties were overridingly preoccupied with autonomy, or national independence, and secondly that they had no certainties as to the dimensions of the minority question. It is then instructive to consider the nature of the constraints upon majority strategy operating within triangular confines. If one poses first the hypothesis that the majority nationalist parties had followed policies of conciliation, at critical times, what assurance was there on one level that this would not have been interpreted by the faithful as tantamount to abandonment in the face of minority recalcitrance, or menace, of some cherished, even integral, parts of their concept of nationality and, on another level, that it would not have led step by step to the de facto recognition of the existence in Ireland, and in India, at the very least of the semblance of a second nation?

If one looks closer for illustration to clothe the issue in concrete terms, one might ask what would have been the consequences in Ireland had John Redmond, leader of the Irish Parliamentary party before the outbreak of war in 1914, not only yielded, as he did, step by step to pressure to concede the veiled exclusion, i.e. exclusion for a period of years, of some parts of Ulster, but further, bent on conciliation of the minority, had accepted a clean cut, or the naked (to use the terminology of the time) exclusion of all of the province's nine counties, as was proposed by Sir Edward Carson on 21 July 1914, the first day of the Buckingham Palace Conference, and by him commended to Redmond and his principal associate, John Dillon,

---

[17] See Percival Griffiths, *The British Impact on India* (London, 1952), p. 340, for the impressions of a contemporary observer.

on the ground that the total exclusion of Ulster was in the interest of the earliest possible unity of Ireland, opinion in the nine counties being so evenly divided that exclusion on such a territorial basis would almost certainly prove short-lived?[18] The answer seems all too clear. The man who by irresolution, most of all on partition, was destined to discredit constitutionalism, destroy the Parliamentary party, leave a name that became a by-word for political credulity, would have been not only politically ruined overnight, but would then and there have handed over the leadership of the national movement to men who, like Carson – to whose aims they were violently opposed but whose methods they much admired – held policies of conciliation in contempt.

The parting of the ways between conciliation and majority self-assertion is conventionally deemed to have come to the Indian National Congress in the form of a more explicit choice at a given moment in time. The provincial elections of 1937, already alluded to, led, after protracted disputation about governors' powers, to Congress acceptance of invitations to form governments in provinces in which they emerged as the majority or largest party. Were they in provinces either with substantial Muslim populations or where special factors existed, as in the United Provinces,[19] to be single-party governments? Or were independent Muslims to be invited to serve? Or were Congress–League coalitions to be formed (as would indeed have been in accord with the general instruction given to governors) to ensure so far as possible that representatives of minorities should be included in provincial governments? The Muslim League entertained insecurely grounded expectations of the last, i.e. coalitions in which they would be partners. But, in fact, though a few individual non-League Muslims were, Muslim League members were not invited to serve, save only on humiliating conditions, one being that of becoming full members of the Congress. They were deeply offended. But they had not been invited, immediately because the League had fared poorly in the elections, but fundamentally because of the Congress conviction that it represented, and should act as if it did represent, all India. Had not the elections gone a long way to confirming this? Were there not Congress Muslims? (There were, but they were noticeably thin on the ground, despite Nehru's election claim that there were Muslims in the Congress who 'could provide inspiration to a thousand Jinnahs'.[20]) Why should the Congress not take power? What English party that had won a decisive electoral victory would invite its defeated opponents to share in the responsibilities of government?

---

[18] Redmond Papers' National Library of Ireland, Dublin. Redmond kept a note of the proceedings of the conference which are not on official record.

[19] See Gopal, *op. cit.*, pp. 225–7.

[20] *Ibid.*, p. 224.

Why form coalitions, notorious for their instability, when there was no need to do so? It was not reasonable to expect it: the Congress leaders did not feel it to be so. In the retrospect of more than twenty years, I went over the ground with two of them, Rajendra Prasad and Jawaharlal Nehru. Prasad, who played a key role in Bihar and Orissa,[21] remained clear in conscience – though also still mindful of the claims to office of the party faithful – and satisfied that he could have done no other, without running contrary to the spirit of parliamentary democracy and majority rule on which the Congress concept of a future unitary India rested; while Nehru, more sensitive, even troubled about the possibility of an opportunity of Congress–League working cooperation seemingly missed, and largely, as one of his colleagues later alleged, on his responsibility,[22] for ever, was still convinced no other course had been practicable, in principle warranted or even prudent, given the vanity, the personal ambition and the disruptive aims of Jinnah. Others were not so persuaded. The Congress, commented Sir Penderel Moon, 'passionately desired to preserve the unity of India. They consistently acted so as to make its partition certain'. And in their rejection of coalitions he discerned the *fons et origo malorum*.[23] His judgement, thus forcefully and felicitously phrased, is widely endorsed both in this particular and in its general formulation.

Historically neither can be viewed in isolation. In seeking to assess the consequences of a particular Congress action – repudiation of coalitions – it is as well also to bring into the reckoning the likely consequences of Congress acceptance of them. Over against the gain in Muslim goodwill

---

[21] There is a detailed explanation of what happened and why in *Rajendra Prasad: Autobiography* (Bombay, 1957), pp. 442–7. He goes so far as to write: 'appointment of Muslim Leaguers as Ministers in provinces where the Congress had been returned in a majority would have been unconstitutional'. This would, indeed, have been the case where no Muslim Leaguers had been returned, the relevant provisions of the Government of India Act 1935 (26 Geo. V c. 2), Part III, Chapter II, Section 51(2) laying down that ministers had to be members of the provincial legislature save for the first six months after appointment. Since, however, it was Congress policy to appoint single-party governments irrespective of whether there were Muslim League, or, indeed, non-Congress Muslim members or not, any such gloss would have been disingenuous. More probably Prasad was thinking only of convention since he later comments that he was convinced the Congress committed no constitutional impropriety in terms of the British precedents to which they sought to adhere.

[22] Maulana Azad considered that Nehru's advice against inclusion of more than one Muslim League minister in the United Provinces to have been a major error attributable to Nehru's 'theoretical bias'. See A. K. Azad, *India Wins Freedom* (Bombay, 1959), pp. 160–2.

[23] *Divide and Quit* (London, 1961), p. 14. Sir Percival Griffiths' conclusion (*op. cit.*, p. 340) was that the Congress was fully within its rights, but had made 'a grave tactical blunder'; V. P. Menon's that it was 'a factor which induced neutral Muslim opinion to turn to the support of Jinnah' (*op. cit.*, p. 56).

there would then have had to be set the price to be paid for a concession of all-India principle. Coalitions in the provinces would have implied a coalition when the time came to form a responsible government at an as yet non-existent responsible, representative centre. Would such a coalition have enhanced the prospect of a unitary independent India? And what might have been the effect overall of such concession upon the unity of the Congress party itself? Might not conciliation of the minority have had to be paid for in division within the majority? The fact that such questions arise suffices in itself to indicate that, in this as in most other cases, it may be unrealistic to assume that had one thing been different all else would have remained the same. It is in fact improbable. The leadership of constitutional, or quasi-constitutional, national movements is at all times peculiarly vulnerable to allegations by sea-green incorruptibles to its left of retraction from the concept of the independent, unitary nationhood it is there to realize. In Ireland there had been the protagonists of physical force, in India there were the Hindu communalists, as those who were mindful of the later twenties had reason to recall, waiting in the wings. Redmond made some concession of nationalist principle which rested upon majority rule and he fell: the Congress none and they remained and with them the constitutionalist control of the national movement, albeit precariously, survived.

Sir Penderel Moon's more general judgement upon the course of Congress policy might also *mutatis mutandis*, but with qualification, be pronounced upon Sinn Féin. With at least an equal passion, they desired unity and intermittently rather than consistently acted so as to prejudice its attainment; the greater in particular their insistence upon the Catholic–Gaelic foundation of Irish nationhood, the more acute the Northerners' feeling that they were, and indeed were deemed to be, alien to it. In both countries the majority well understood that liberty must needs be won by sustained effort and a readiness, in both cases impressively forthcoming, for sacrifice in the national cause. But unity in each case, more deeply grounded as it was in concept than in history, was apt to be assumed. Parnell's most recent biographer tells us that the idea 'that Ireland might possibly contain two nations, not one, apparently never entered his head',[24] while as we have seen, that same possibility in respect of India was summarily dismissed by Nehru in 1937. From such assumptions of unity may have derived many of the insensitivities which confirmed partition. But how far did they cause it?

Or to put the question in another way, is there evidence in Ireland or in India to suggest that either at such critical junctures as have been considered or over an extended period of time, greater sensitivity reflected in

---

[24] Lyons, *op. cit.*, p. 623.

more conciliatory attitudes on the part of the majority would in fact have produced a different outcome, as distinct from a different and a less, or more, blood-spattered road to the same outcome? To answer that – and it is a question of cardinal importance – one must consider the aims of the second party and then in each case try to assess how far those aims may have imposed constraints upon minority action and reaction, such as may themselves have precluded unity by understanding and peaceful political process.

In both Ireland and India the minority community belonged to a ruling, or a former ruling, race. This was socially in terms of land ownership, economically in terms of control of the levers of industrial power as well as politically a self-evident reality in Ulster; in India it was a legacy, overlaid by nearly two centuries of British rule, but with reminders of one-time dominance in the Princely States, the ruler of the greatest of them, Hyderabad, being a Muslim holding sway over a preponderantly Hindu population, and, immediately of more importance, the social standing of the landowning Muslim leadership in the United Provinces and the Punjab. In both Ireland and India this ruling past was psychologically important in that it created a presumption on the part of the minority at least of non-subordination when imperial rule ended. There was a second, and a fundamental factor. Neither Ulster Protestants nor Muslims shared the religion, tradition or, in the case of the Muslims in north-western India, the literature or any of the languages of the majority community. They did not have the same heroes or folk-memories, nor yet the same inner allegiance. To that extent they did not instinctively feel themselves to be part of one nation, their attitude being rather one of aloofness, even in days of quiescence and settled imperial rule.

But were they more than minority communities? The imperial power did not so treat them in governmental terms. Dublin Castle administration, whatever may be thought of it – and James Bryce, as Chief Secretary in 1906, was depressed by the 'intolerable defects . . . which made its working inconceivably troublesome and harassing'[25] while Sir Warren Fisher, when, as head of the civil service, he had a look at it in its last phase, summed up his impressions in a sentence, 'the Castle administration does not administer'[26] – was for the whole of Ireland; and, while the map of India was a mosaic of princely States and British–Indian provinces with concessions made to minorities in the latter by way of electoral weightage,

---

[25] Bryce to Goldwin Smith, 16 June 1906, quoted by Patricia Jalland in 'A Liberal Chief Secretary and the Irish Question: Augustine Birrell 1907–1914', *The Historical Journal*, Vol. 19, No. 2 (1976), p. 421.

[26] Report of Sir Warren Fisher, 12 May 1920. Quoted in Charles Townshend, *The British Campaign in Ireland 1919–1921* (Oxford, 1975), p. 78.

unity was the basis and oft-proclaimed goal of British rule – though there was conflict, reflecting part subconscious ambivalence, between unitary profession on the one hand and preoccupation with the development of provincial self-government on the other, it having been persuasively argued[27] that progressive devolution of power to the provinces on the scale on which it took place, while marking an advance towards self-government, also in corresponding and necessary measure eased the way to partition. But while making allowance for such part-contradiction between profession and practice, the overall position remained that the structure of imperial administration subsumed that, if power were to be transferred, it would be in India, as in Ireland, to a central and single successor authority with the carry-over, or addition, of safeguards for minorities. And what was implicit in patterns of government was explicit in terms of economic, social and political realities. Were they to be disregarded, as disregarded they must needs be, were division to succeed to unity? Was Derry to be cut off from its Donegal hinterland, the jute mills of Calcutta from the jute of East Bengal? How did you disentangle Protestant from Catholic in Northern Ireland, Muslim from Hindu in Bengal or Muslim from Hindu and Sikh in the Punjab? Were the services and police, the personnel of government and even the office furniture to be divided? The answer to all of these questions including the last – civil servants were much interested in the fate of the furniture and the files[28] – was to be in the affirmative which *inter alia* underlines the fact that historically the issue was no more determined by such considerations than it was by the structural implications of imperial administration. On the contrary it was brought to the point of decision in long-range dialectics – the demand of the majority for self-government, or independence, for the whole of Ireland or India being met by the counter-claim of the minority that, by reason of differences in race, community or nation, division should succeed to the unity that had prevailed under imperial rule – with the rhetoric which is so compulsive an element in the appeal of nationalism[29] accentuating the disassociating protest of a counter-nationalism.

---

[27] By Professor R. J. Moore in *The Crisis of Indian Unity 1917–1940* (Oxford, 1974), p. 316, where he concludes categorically 'There can be no doubt that . . . the method and timing of the devolutionary process exacerbated divisions within India. Britain's no freedom without unity principle placed freedom beyond early reach. The enlistment of Muslim collaborators through the concession of autonomous communal provinces enabled Muslims to entrench themselves in their majority provinces'.

[28] I am indebted to Dr J. McColgan for information on this point in his unpublished dissertation, 'The Irish Administration in Transition 1920–22' (UCD, 1976) and to personal impressions in respect of India. See Azad, *op. cit.*, p. 201 for an indication of the problems relating to files.

[29] Pearse, writes his most recent biographer, was convinced that 'it was rhetoric not steady organizing by faceless men that would bring the host of the true Gaels from

In both Ireland and India the contention of the smaller community came
to be that it was to be regarded not as a minority but as a distinct and
distinguishable entity, and, therefore, not properly to be subjected to the
will of the majority. Beyond that, however, there was an important difference. In Ulster the positive Unionist claim was not that the Ulster
Unionists constituted a separate nation – though that also was sometimes
adumbrated – but rather that they were, and wished to remain, part of
another nation. They were in Ireland but not unreservedly of it: of Britain,
again with qualification, but not in it. They believed that the Union had
been economically beneficial, remained politically and strategically realistic,
its continuance moreover being for them something in the nature of a
psychological imperative. Far, therefore, from its being their wish to secede,
it was their militant intent to remain a part of the United Kingdom. It
was 'our cherished position of equal citizenship in the United Kingdom'
that 100,000 Covenanters in September 1912, 'this time of threatened
calamity', pledged themselves, Carson at their head, to defend by the use
of 'all means which may be found necessary to defeat the present conspiracy to set up a Home Rule Parliament in Ireland'.[30] And there they
took their stand, with this qualification that while the preservation of their
'cherished position' in the United Kingdom remained a constant, their initial and peculiarly Carsonite (and English Unionist) purpose of defeating
Home Rule – the maintenance of the Union in its integrity Carson termed
'the guiding star of my political life' – gave way to the more modest and
realistic aim, throughout entertained by the province's indigenous leader,
James Craig, and adopted by Bonar Law, the New Brunswicker of Ulster
descent who, in November 1911, succeeded Balfour in the leadership of
the English Unionist party, of excluding the province of Ulster, or some
part of it, from subjection to a Home Rule Parliament in Dublin dominated
by those they regarded as hereditary foes. Either way, it was a case of a
minority resolved not to submit to majority rule, but not a case of a
minority that conceived of itself as embodying a self-sufficient separate
nationhood. To that extent, therefore, the two-nation theory fitted the contention of the minority in Ireland, but only with qualifications such as
were not to apply in India. There the counter-assertion to majority claims,
when it came effectively in the years 1936–40, was unequivocal. It was that
there were two nations, both within the subcontinent and both aspiring

---

(*Note 29 cont.*) all the corners of Ireland', Edwards, *op. cit.*, p. 160. History has shown
his conviction to have been well founded but the more successful such rhetoric was
in giving emotional appeal to abstract concept, the more sharply it marked off those
who did not entertain the concept.

[30] The text of the Covenant is reprinted in Paul Buckland (ed.), *Irish Unionism*
(Belfast, Northern Ireland PRO, 1973), Document No. 119.

to independence. It is to Jinnah, as more than leader in a conventional political sense, of the Muslim League, accordingly and, in the circumstances logically, that one must look for the classic exposition of the two-nation theory.

In his address to the Lahore Conference of the Muslim League in March 1940 Jinnah began with an emphatic repudiation of what he described as a simplistic Hindu and British notion that the differences in India were of a communal character, such as might be resolved by concessions, by safeguards within a unitary state, by giving a more substantial measure of devolution to the provinces or, alternatively, in a federal system with a centre vested, if need be, with minimal powers.[31] On the contrary, in Jinnah's words, it was 'a dream that Hindus and Muslims can ever evolve a common nationality . . .'; they 'have two different religions, philosophies, social customs, literatures. They neither intermarry nor even interdine. Indeed they belong to two different civilizations'. The notion of majority rule in such countries was an irrelevance and a geographic concept of nationhood meaningless. Yet it was not, however, in this rhetoric, as I believe, that Jinnah was formulating the essence of his case. It was rather in the quiet assertion: 'The problem of India is not of an intercommunal character, but manifestly of an international one and must be treated as such'. By international he meant literally as between nations. From this contention he was not to retreat. In the autumn of 1944, the Viceroy, reporting to the Secretary of State on the causes of the breakdown of recently concluded Gandhi–Jinnah talks, entered into in an attempt to bridge the gulf between the Congress and the League, noted: 'Jinnah adhered to "two nations" theory according to which Moslems are separate nation from Hindus though intermingled with them. He pressed acceptance by Gandhi of the Moslem League's Lahore resolution of March 1940 and made it clear that he would accept nothing less than sovereign Moslem States . . . and demanded . . . relations between Moslem States and the rest of India should be by treaty as between equal and independent powers. Gandhi denied "two nations" theory'.[32] The Governor of the United Provinces added the further gloss that in the talks neither Jinnah nor Gandhi had abandoned their former ideas, Jinnah emphasizing the two-nation theory and Pakistan more strongly than before and clearly wanting 'this question finally decided before the British leave; Gandhi, though he camouflages his position as usual, aims at a Hindu Raj and adheres to the view that independence must come before a settlement'.[33] Gandhi himself retrospectively confirmed the

---

[31] The address is reprinted in N. Mansergh (ed.), *Documents and Speeches on British Commonwealth Affairs* (2 Vols., Oxford, 1953), Vol. II, pp. 609–12.

[32] N. Mansergh and Penderel Moon (eds.), *India: The Transfer of Power 1942–47*, Vol. V, No. 30.

[33] *Ibid.*, No. 33.

correctness of his diagnosis in replying to a question posed by Tej Bahadur Sapru, 'Quaid-i-Azam [Jinnah] would have nothing short of the two nations theory and therefore complete dissolution . . . It was just here that we split'.[34] The heart of the matter was in that last brief sentence. Maulana Azad – and who was better, or more painfully placed to pass judgement than the minority President of the majority national movement? – confirmed that this was so. 'Mr Jinnah's scheme', he wrote in a submission to the British Cabinet in April 1946, 'is based on his two-nation theory. His thesis is that India contains many nationalities based on religious differences. Of them the two major nations, the Hindus and Muslims, must have separate states. When Dr Edward Thompson once pointed out to Mr Jinnah that Hindus and Muslims live side by side in thousands of Indian towns, villages and hamlets, Mr Jinnah replied that this in no way affected their separate nationality. Two nations, according to Mr Jinnah, confront one another . . .'[35]

Jinnah in formulating the concept of two nations, as against two communities in India, had a practical, over and above a dialectical point to establish. Nations, unlike communities, negotiate as equals, irrespective of size. That is what he wanted to happen *before* power was transferred. And with a lawyer's logic and his own resolute refusal to concede anything inconsistent with his concept of a Muslim nation in India, he built up by stages a position in which at conferences and later in government, the Muslim League demanded and obtained virtual parity[36] with the Congress, the representatives of the minority with those of the majority, on the implicit assumption, at all times repudiated by the Congress, of the separate nationhood of Muslims and Hindus – the Congress nomination of its own President, the Muslim, Maulana Azad, as one of its representatives to the Simla Conference 1945 being, in Jinnah's phrase, a 'symbolic affront' to which he retorted by publicly refusing to shake hands with the Maulana, an incident in itself indicative of the constraints deriving from concepts, in this case from the concept that the League represented *all* Muslims, and therefore by logical derivation that Muslims could represent only the League. But while such strict adherence to the implications of a two-nation theory may have been a handicap in negotiations, it did provide at once a rationale for intransigence and a base from which to withstand Congress and British pressures for concessions. A more

---

[34] *Ibid.*, No. 344, annex.

[35] Azad, *op. cit.*, p. 143.

[36] In the Interim Government formed on 15 October 1946 the six members nominated by the Congress included by agreement a representative of the Scheduled Castes; the Muslim League being entitled to nominate five without restriction. See Menon, *op. cit.*, pp. 315–16.

consummate master of the art of political negation even than Carson,[37] Jinnah sought and succeeded, by negation, in ensuring that a transfer of power could take place only on the basis of a two-nation concept.

What validity did the concept possess? Were there two nations in India? Or, for that matter, in Ireland even though there the doctrine was at no point formulated in all its uncompromising bleakness? Politics, not being a science, offers no answers demonstrably correct. But the questions none the less may be worth posing, if only for their implications. If it were proven, as it cannot be, that in either, or both cases, there were two nations, then, given the temper of twentieth-century nationalism, it would be reasonable to infer that there existed an inbuilt presumption of partition. If, in turn, that were so, then, to come back to a question posed earlier, it would be reasonable also to conclude that more conciliatory policies, or more understanding attitudes, on the part of the majority, were unlikely to conjure that second nation out of existence. If, on the other hand, it could be demonstrated that there existed not two nations but only majority and minority communities, then partition assumes the guise of an unnatural or contrived division and the burden of responsibility resting on all parties, and on the third by no means least, is correspondingly greater.

The position of the third party, the imperial power, differed from the first and second in one very evident respect – it did not seek, it controlled, the levers of power. Prima facie in the exercise of that control it had, in accord with Tacitean precept, an interest initially in becoming and then in continuing to be a third party, i.e. in creating a situation with partition potential – though by no means necessarily in partition since, when such control was about to be demitted, the balance of advantage might well incline otherwise and towards the constitution of a united, well-disposed successor state. For that, among other reasons, it is less than realistic to look for a consistent pattern of imperial policy, even in one particular triangular situation. An imperial government, unlike a national movement, is not primarily concerned to advance a cause, or bring about the realization of an ideal, but rather to guide and direct affairs in the light of its own pragmatic judgements upon its own best interests. The limitations upon its freedom of action, while very real, are thus ordinarily of a material kind, such as were imposed upon British governments by considerations of security in the Irish and of the world balance of power in the Indian cases; in both by the limits of Britain's military and economic resources; and by obligations assumed, or assurances given, as well as by past actions which had foreclosed otherwise possible options.

---

[37] It is possibly not altogether coincidental that both were lawyers and that both made their early reputations as members of a minority, outside their later community homelands, Carson at the Irish Bar and as MP for Trinity College Dublin, Jinnah in Bombay.

But ordinarily also an imperial power is not wholly free from constraints of an ideological or conceptual nature. In the British case, two such constraints may be mentioned. The first, general in its application, was Britain's commitment after the First World War to the idea of a Commonwealth of free and equal nations which progressively tended to limit, or preclude, courses of action inconsistent with its character or advancement. This was evident in the Irish and, of first importance in the Indian case. The second was altogether particular to the Anglo-Irish triangular relationship. It derived from an incident in domestic politics, the association of Whigs and Radicals with the Tories in order to defeat the First Home Rule Bill in 1886. That association was continued thereafter within the folds of a Unionist party, predominantly Conservative, yet embracing those on the right and the left who had seceded from the Liberals on Home Rule. It was a party which, however adaptable in its responses to changing interests in other fields, had implicit in its very being one unchanging element – support for the Union. That was, in effect, written into its constitution, by virtue of its being the very occasion and bond of its existence. Since the party, with the aid of its inbuilt majority in the Lords, was in a position to determine Irish policy negatively, when not positively, from 1886 down to the Anglo-Irish settlement 1920–1, its conceptual commitment to Union imposed a rigidity upon policy rare in the annals of modern British history.

Overall the third party, more particularly as the time of transfer – unwilled by it in the Irish but willed in the Indian case – approached, like the first and the second, one way or another also had limited grounds for manoeuvre – more limited, if I may anticipate my own conclusion, than Prime Ministers, Secretaries of State or Viceroys in the more spacious of their utterances liked to suggest, their critics to suppose or historians in their later judgement to imply.

Beyond this, one might venture a general comment. In a triangular pre-transfer of power situation there is, all affinities supposed or actual apart, a tendency for the second and third parties, the minority and the outgoing imperial power, to be drawn together in resistance to the demands of the first, the majority Nationalist party.[38] Indeed it is close to a law of politics. In part it may be explained in terms of near-coincidence in immediate interest, despite the difference in long-term aims. The imperial power, over and above an inbuilt and non-rational reluctance to depart, will almost certainly prefer, having rational regard to the safeguarding of its interests, a phased withdrawal, while the first aim of minority parties must be to delay the imperial departure until assured of the realization of their own concepts of their own future. All of these aspects were apparent, with one evident qualification, in the Anglo-Irish and Anglo-Indian situations.

---

[38] This was evident also in Cyprus.

In Ireland the association between the second, minority, party and the third, which for convenience is here termed the imperial power,[39] was manifestly a political factor of first importance, broad community of interests being reinforced by the bonds of kinship. It was not, however, a unifying factor in domestic politics, but, on the contrary, a source of deep party division, one of the great English political parties, the Liberal party from Gladstone to Asquith, being committed as a matter of principle to Home Rule for all Ireland – Asquith affirming in 1912 that 'Ireland is a nation, not two nations, but one nation'[40] – the other, the Unionist party, to the maintenance of the Union and by necessary inference, to the defeat of Home Rule.

When in November 1911 Bonar Law took over the leadership of the Unionist party, he reaffirmed this purpose, asserting specifically that he was not interested in the exclusion of Ulster, or some part of it, from the jurisdiction of a Dublin-dominated Home Rule Parliament, but with defeating Home Rule in the interests of the unity of Kingdom and Empire. He could imagine no lengths of resistance, so he declared in a long-reverberating, declamatory utterance at Blenheim on 29 July 1912, to which Ulster could go in such a cause, which he would not be prepared to support. But even in the passionate temper of pre-war politics, and despite the party's ideological commitment to the Union, the English Unionist leadership had perforce to recognize that the claim of a settler minority in north-east Ireland to impose a veto upon the constitutionally expressed wishes of more than three-quarters of the Irish people over an indefinite period of time was so obviously indefensible on ordinary democratic reckoning as to be a source of electoral weakness. With no little equivocation, the party leadership accordingly moved towards a more limited objective – that of ensuring that the minority in the North was excluded from the jurisdiction of a Home Rule Parliament, a course the more easily acquiesced in by reason of an assumption not confined to Unionists that, without Ulster, Home Rule was not viable and that therefore, through such exclusion, the Union might still be preserved. Under pressure of Covenanting campaigning, the threat of armed revolt in Ulster, backed by unrelenting English Unionist pressure, the Liberal government yielded step by step and by the outbreak of war conceded the principle of exclusion for a period and for an area yet to be determined. The concession ensured the realization of the Ulster, but not of the English, Unionists' conceptual aim, the Ulstermen, having therewith implicitly established their contention that in Ireland they were not to be treated as a minority but a

---

[39] In Irish debates of the Asquith-Lloyd George era 'Imperial' Government (or Parliament) were terms in general use in this context.

[40] Roy Jenkins, *Asquith* (London, 1964), p. 279.

community apart without thereby, however, in any way weakening, indeed if anything strengthening, the demand for Home Rule elsewhere in Ireland.

The postwar Government of Ireland Bill 1919, by making provision for a settlement on the basis of Home Rule for two parts of a divided Ireland, lent statutory substance to this concept of separateness. 'The new policy', noted Captain Wedgwood Benn in the debate on its second reading, 'is that Ireland is two nations.'[41] Lloyd George equivocated, observing 'Ulster is not a minority to be safeguarded. Ulster is an entity to be dealt with . . . I am not now going to enter into the question of whether there is one nation or two nations . . .'[42] The basis of the bill, however, was that Ireland was not one nation. For Ulstermen that sufficed. They had attained their immediate goal and their campaign against subjection to a Dublin-based Home Rule was crowned with success. Unqualified English Unionist backing of their cause at critical moments had been a condition of it. Indeed, it has been claimed that the outcome was, in a particular sense, the handiwork of one man, the Canadian, Andrew Bonar Law. But for his fundamental commitment to Ulster, concludes his biographer, Northern Ireland would not have assumed the form it did.[43] In its own important but limited sense, this is a reasonable contention. Nor is it unfitting. Bonar Law had backed Ulster for itself over and above the Unionist party's wider purpose – defeating Home Rule – which Ulster's resistance was thought to serve; and though 'diehards' continued to feel bitter resentment at the abandonment of the Union as a whole even to safeguard the position of a cherished part, his was the decisive influence in persuading the main body of Unionists to see as a worthwhile end what had erstwhile been thought of as a means to an end. But form is not substance and the separation of the north-eastern counties from the rest of Ireland is hardly to be thought of as susceptible of explanation in personal terms.

The principle of division accepted, important subsidiary questions remained still open to debate. Chief among them were the area to be excluded and the period of its exclusion. The two were interrelated.

In respect of area, the whole province of Ulster constituted a historic unit, but it held out no assurance of a settled Protestant majority. Equally, however, so Carson had protested in the aftermath of the 1916 Rising, the Ulster Unionists did not want 'bits of counties here and bits of counties there, a tessellated pavement with a bit in and a bit out', such as partition determined district by district by majority local allegiance would certainly have brought about. On the contrary they demanded a coherent, compact

---

[41] H. of C. Deb., 29 March 1920, Vol. 127, Col. 1020.

[42] *Ibid.*, 31 March 1920, Col. 1333.

[43] Robert Blake, *The Unknown Prime Minister* (London, 1955). See especially his verdict on p. 531.

area of six counties. Earlier still, in 1912, an even more compact area of four counties had been proposed and the debate on the Government of Ireland Bill 1919 showed that this possibility had not been altogether forgotten.

Late that year, 1919, the Cabinet reviewed all of these possibilities – the exclusion of the whole of Ulster, of the six counties, or of an area more narrowly defined. But while such was the theoretical range of options before them, there was also the limiting factor that only the Ulster Unionists were willing, or in a position, to run the local, devolved administration that was contemplated in the draft bill. They had their own conditions for running it. Those conditions were firstly lasting exclusion and secondly, to ensure that, a strong preference, conveyed to the Cabinet in December 1919, which was tantamount in effect to a further condition, that the devolution scheme should be applied to what were termed the six Protestant counties, no more and no less.[44] That preference reflected, as Captain Craig later phrased it, an Ulster Unionist conviction that the best way to safeguard Ulster was 'to save as much as we knew we could hold. To try to hold more . . . would seem an act of gross folly on our part'.[45] The Cabinet, despite some lingering glances at the possibility either of excluding all Ulster or of plebiscites, acceded to Ulster Unionist wishes. The upshot was the partitioning of Ireland in such a way that the exclusion of the Unionist minority from an all-Ireland polity created a new Nationalist minority, much smaller in total certainly, but near-identical in its one-third proportion to that Unionist minority which was now to become a majority.

About this Lloyd George made two points in the course of the later negotiations on the Anglo-Irish Treaty. The first was on area: 'The real unit', he told the Irish delegates, 'was Ulster. It was an old province and a recognized unit . . . but it was felt to be handing over a large Catholic population to the control of the Protestants. There was almost an agreement for the partition of Ulster. Therefore we had to get a new unit . . . on the whole, the six county area had been acceptable to the Nationalists as preferable to a new delimitation of Ulster. True, if you took a plebiscite of Tyrone and Fermanagh, there would be a Catholic majority . . . The alternative would have been a Boundary Commission. There would then have been a more overwhelmingly Protestant majority. In order to persuade Ulster to come in there is an advantage in her having a Catholic population.'[46] The second was on the attitude of the Cabinet to partition. 'We stand neutral', he said. 'That would be useful', retorted Gavan Duffy, 'if you had not created a partition Parliament.'

---

[44] Cab. 27/68 (15 and 19 December).

[45] H. of C. Deb., Vol. 127, Col. 992.

[46] Thomas Jones, *Whitehall Diary*, ed. K. Middlemas (3 Vols., Oxford, 1969–71), Vol. III, p. 131.

On the first point made by the Prime Minister one may reflect that the Ulster Unionists understood better what they had caused to be done than Lloyd George who did it; on the second, one may note that it elicited a realistic comment from a representative of the first party on the advantage to the second of getting matters settled before the withdrawal of the third. So it was that, in the case of Northern Ireland, Jinnah's dream – divide and depart,[47] in that order with the frontiers settled in accord with minority views – was realized. By way of even better measure, as an inducement to the minority to acquiesce in an all-Ireland superstructure, there was acceptance of the principle of parity of representation between minority and majority on the proposed Council of Ireland, a fact which, as Asquith noted, was calculated in itself to weight the scales against the unity the Council was ostensibly designed to promote. And yet, underlying the settlement, there was an assumption in which Jinnah could not have acquiesced. It was, that seems clear from Cabinet records, that partition, in the majority Cabinet view, was a temporary expedient rather than a lasting division, it being expressly recorded therein that the unity of Ireland was the long-term aim.[48] That was not consistent with a concept of two nations, but rather of one that was temporarily divided. The definition of the Irish Free State as initially co-terminous with the whole of Ireland in the subsequently negotiated Anglo-Irish Treaty indicated the same line of thinking.

The first part of the Irish settlement, the Government of Ireland Act 1920, was determined by two sides of the Irish triangle, the British and the Ulster Unionists, the second at one remove so to speak, there being in Lloyd George's later excusing phrase no one to negotiate with on the third, the Nationalist side, with Sinn Féin in revolt. In December of the following year the second part of it, the Anglo-Irish Treaty 1921, was negotiated again by two of the three, but a different two, Sinn Féin and the British government. The former knew what they wanted, an all-Ireland republic, but had not defined, short of that, what they might settle for; the latter had obtained in Northern Ireland one long-standing objective, the safeguarding of the position of the minority to which they were committed and with it the substance of their own security interest. For the rest, despite much that has been written in praise of Lloyd George's dexterity and statesmanship, they relied amid many postwar preoccupations upon repression and improvisation. A dominion settlement emerged; it did not, however, as might reasonably be, and often is, inferred, represent the fulfilment of a settled British policy. Far from it: members of the Cabinet long

---

[47] In the Irish case it was the Dublin Castle administration that departed; the sovereignty of Westminster, despite devolution, remaining unimpaired in the six counties.

[48] Cab. 23/18, C. 16 (19).

continued to contemplate a Home Rule settlement on the basis of the 1920 Act. When they were informed in December 1920 that very little was known about the provisions of the 1920 Act in the area described in that Act as Southern Ireland, they found themselves in general agreement that steps should be taken to remedy this by giving it the widest possible publicity there.[49] Since the only hope of a settlement with Sinn Féin was to let assuaging oblivion close over the provisions of an Act which had partitioned Ireland, fell far short of dominion status, and indeed conceded rather more modest powers than earlier Home Rule bills to the parliaments it proposed to constitute, this unconscious essay in irony, while undermining Cabinet credibility, serves more importantly to dispel illusions of calculated Georgian (or other) dominion design. The historical evidence, indeed, suggests that, not for the first or last time in Irish affairs, events shaped policy; not policy the sequence of events. All important in that unfolding story was the fact that the course pursued involved warfare, at once of a seemingly self-defeating kind – the advice tendered by the British Commander-in-Chief in Ireland, Sir Neville Macready, to his political masters having as a recurrent theme: 'Whatever we do we are sure to be wrong'[50] – and of a character that psychologically ran counter to the concept of Commonwealth. Both were by 1920–1 unacceptable to opinion at home where popular British conviction, almost irrespective of party, of the outstanding success, first in peace and then in war, of a Commonwealth deriving from classical liberal approaches to Empire,[51] in fact propelled the man, who had dismissed Asquithian notions of a dominion settlement in Ireland with 'Whoever heard such nonsense?', towards a dominion settlement. It was not Lloyd George who changed the contours of the Irish question, but the widening contours of the Irish question that changed Lloyd George.

In the springtime of 1921 when Lloyd George became so suddenly converted to a dominion status solution, he had reason to be sensitive to dominion views on the Irish question, as also to dominion precedents. There was an Imperial Conference about to foregather in London and its first meeting was held in the Cabinet Room at 10 Downing Street on 20 June.[52] It was there, too, on 14 July 1921 that Lloyd George had his first meeting with de Valera. His secretary had never seen him so excited, 'bringing up

---

[49] Cab. 23/23, 81 (120) 30 December 1920.

[50] Quoted in Townshend, *op. cit.*, p. 178.

[51] Austen Chamberlain's (leader of the Unionist party during Bonar Law's illness) sharing of it was of particular importance in the course of the Irish negotiations.

[52] The conference continued in session till 5 August 1921. Had it still been in session in December the climax of Anglo-Irish negotiations might have been otherwise in character, if not in substance.

all his guns', as she put it, with a big map of the British Empire hung up
on the wall, 'great blotches of red all over it'. When de Valera came in,
Lloyd George pointed with studied deliberation to the chairs around the
table at which the dominion leaders sat at the Imperial Conference – there
were Hughes and Massey from Australia and New Zealand; there was
Meighen, the representative of English and French united in one dominion; there was Smuts symbolizing the reconciliation of Boer and Briton
within the Union. Lloyd George then looked long and fixedly at the remaining chair. De Valera remained silent, so Lloyd George had to tell him
the chair was for Ireland. 'All we ask you to do is to take your place in
this sisterhood of free nations.'[53] By December, after protracted negotiations, invitation had been superseded by insistence, backed by the threat
of force, on free association.

With the dominion settlement of 1921, Unionism in England, though
not in Ulster, had lost its *raison d'être*. Conservatism re-emerged as ex-
Unionists ensured that Lloyd George never should. Even so, it now appears
that Lloyd George, as Liberal leader of a predominantly Unionist Cabinet
and sensitive to the Unionist majority in Parliament, overestimated the
rigidity of their views on Union – or, alternatively, underestimated his own
freedom of manoeuvre in negotiation. He was not only a prisoner, as he
was apt himself to say, of the Coalition, but also in some measure, as were
many of his colleagues, constrained by memories of the passionate pre-
war Anglo-Irish past.

In respect of substance, the 1920–1 Anglo-Irish Settlement had one
aspect, so evident as to be deserving of comment, only because in subsequent years it was apt to be glossed over. It was that no reduction in the
number of parties involved was achieved as a result of it. They remained
as before, their conceptual approaches fundamentally unchanged, though
now there were two sovereign states and a subordinate government, where
there had been a sovereign state, a national movement and a minority resist-
ant to it. The imperial government retained unimpaired in all respects its
sovereignty in one part of Ireland. With demission of power to an Irish
state there had not, therefore, come demission of all its Irish responsibility – but, on the contrary, the contingent possibility of its again becoming
exacting in yet another triangular context.

In terms of negotiating procedures and priorities the Treaty has two
points of interest. To those who entertained the concept of Ireland as a

---

[53] The arrangements for the meeting are recorded in extracts from Miss Stevenson's
diary reprinted in Lord Beaverbrook, *The Decline and Fall of Lloyd George* (London,
1963), pp. 85–6. The account of the interview, at which Miss Stevenson was not present, is much later recollected by President de Valera. He seemed retrospectively well
pleased at not having asked the question expected of him!

nation, there ought not to have been, as there was not, a third party to negotiations for an Anglo-Irish settlement. For them third-party presence would have been a liability, and as such was to be avoided, as a matter of tactics. 'Nothing', de Valera told General Smuts on 6 July 1921, 'could come from a conference of the three parties.' The two principals should discuss their differences, including Ulster, and then treat with the minority. In a sense he had his way. The Ulstermen were off-stage during the negotiations that led to the Treaty, but as they already had in substance what they wanted their presence might only have served to reopen negotiations on what they had obtained. From the Irish point of view, therefore, the negotiating advantages of the absence of a third party, in this context the Ulster Unionists, was counterbalanced by the practical disadvantage of their having obtained prior settlement of their claims.

De Valera's misgivings about triangular exchanges were shared to the full by Gandhi, though the Gandhian and Valeran notions of the third party – the party that was *de trop* – differed, the British filling that unenviable role in the first instance, the Ulstermen in the second. The difference was accounted for by the fact that, whereas de Valera thought of an Anglo-Irish settlement as something to be negotiated overall between Britain and Ireland, Gandhi believed that the British should first quit India, leaving it to the Congress, the League, the Princes and representatives of other minorities to make a settlement thereafter.

Behind such differences in tactical approaches, however, and in part explaining them, was the fundamental difference in the position of the imperial power in Ireland and in India. In the latter, as distinct from the former, it was their declared, though far from universally credited, intent to go. What had to be decided was the nature and timing of their departure – both important matters certainly, but not quite on the same plane of importance as intent. On timing, Gandhi's view ran counter to that of successive British governments, which was that the British should defer departure until agreement had been reached between parties, communities and classes in India. In the thirties, when the diehards in opposition to the Government of India Bill, itself essentially a temporizing device behind its impressive federal facade, apparently saw little inconsistency in championing the cause of the minorities, the illiterate masses and the outcasts, while at the same time seeking to muster a 'solid phalanx of Rolls Royce rajahs'[54] as a barrier, first to the advance and then to the entrenchment of a Congress raj, attitudes uninhibitedly taken up by, but by no means confined exclusively to, the extreme right, seemed to indicate, and not only to Gandhi, that an interpretation might be placed on British responsibilities, which would afford reason for them to stay for ever. In the Congress–British

---

[54] The phrase is used by Moore, *op. cit.*, p. 137.

dialectic of the early war years a situation thus developed in which Gandhi became the more insistent that the departure of the British, the third party, was an essential condition precedent to settlement with the second; whereas in the predominant British view agreement within India remained a condition of Indian political advance – the Secretary of State, Lord Zetland, in February 1940 advising his Cabinet colleagues, 'we must insist on an agreement of all the parties concerned as an essential condition of progress'[55] of which he [Lord Zetland] in constitutional terms declared himself to be in favour. It was, however, a condition which rendered such progress unlikely, since it made any advance on the part of the majority dependent upon the concurrence, not only of the Muslims, but of other and smaller minorities as well. Moreover, not quite all members of the Cabinet entertained the Secretary of State's notion of the conciliatory role properly to be played by the third party. On the contrary, the First Lord of the Admiralty commented that he 'did not share the anxiety to encourage unity between the Hindu and Moslem communities', their communal feud being 'a bulwark of British rule in India'.[56]

Some two years later the First Lord, now Prime Minister and at the pinnacle of his power and prestige, in an extempore outburst startled a distinguished Indian representative to the War Cabinet, Ramaswami Mudaliar, coming to London hopefully to hear about 'progress', by telling him that he [Churchill] was not in the mood to conciliate Indian nationalism, but rather to tell the world of the benefits of imperial rule.[57] For eighty years, he continued, while America had a civil war, Russia its revolutions, China had been torn to pieces, India, thanks to British rule, had had uninterrupted peace and even now, he concluded in a splendid climax, 'an Indian maid with bangles on can travel from Travancore to Punjab all alone without fear of molestation . . . in this country today . . . our Wrens and Waafs cannot go two miles with the same feeling of safety'. The Viceroy found Mudaliar's report of the conversation 'most entertaining'. He could afford to. Delhi was seven thousand miles from Downing Street – and even so his successor, Wavell, had cause to develop sensitivity to Churchillian reverberations resounding over the wires from the remote source of imperial authority. Close at hand, in the War Cabinet, the prospect of them, so L. S. Amery as Secretary of State allowed, sufficed to discourage all large discussion of India's future.

When set out in more temperate terms the essence of the matter, as seen by the third party from Whitehall, differed in one important respect, that

---

[55] Cab. 65/5 30 ((40) 4 2 February) 1940.

[56] *Ibid.*

[57] *India: The Transfer of Power 1942–47*, Vol. III, No. 2. By contrast with Churchill, Amery felt himself to be a man of liberal views on Indian policy. Not many in India shared that opinion.

of intention to go, as Churchill himself was soon perforce to acknowledge, but not greatly in regard to the rôle of the communal factor in determining the time of departure. 'The political deadlock in India today', the Secretary of State in a major submission on policy to the War Cabinet had noted in January 1942, 'is concerned, ostensibly, with the transfer of power from British to Indian hands. In reality it is mainly concerned with the far more difficult issue of what Indian hands, what Indian Government, or Governments are capable of taking over without bringing about anarchy or even civil war.' In February that year, however, C. R. Attlee, feeling that such negative analysis no longer sufficed, recommended the sending out to India of some person of high standing to negotiate a settlement. 'There is', he said, 'precedent for such action. Lord Durham', he continued in a judgement which little accords with the opinions of some younger historians (to which I am not among the rush of converts), 'saved Canada to the British Empire. We need a man to do in India what Durham did in Canada.'[58] Cripps was chosen or chose himself – it is not quite clear which – to fill that role and he took with him to India two months later a draft declaration which indicated, first, that the War Cabinet was working within a Commonwealth concept and, secondly, and not only to Congress, that by conceding the right of non-accession and the formation, should provinces seizing advantage of that right so desire, of a separate Union, they were opening the way to partition before the transfer of power. R. A. Butler remarked upon the impression created by the declaration, 'the unity of India – the goal of British policy hitherto – must be set aside',[59] while Field Marshal Smuts, in whose memory I am honoured to give this lecture, the theme of which I venture to believe would have been of much interest to him, mindful of earlier events which fell within the astonishing range of his experience, immediately seized upon the significance of what was apparently about to be conceded. 'Express opening left for partition', he cabled Churchill, 'may be taken as a British invitation or incitement to partition . . . It may be argued that Irish tactics of partition is [sic] once more followed . . .' and he expressed his misgivings lest this should prejudice prospects of settlement with the majority.[60] For once he was vouchsafed no reply. But Churchill found further occasion to remind another dominion war-leader, Mackenzie King of Canada, that the question to be resolved was not one between the British government and India but between different 'sects or nations' in India itself: 'the Moslems, a hundred millions, declare they will insist upon Pakistan, i.e. a sort of Ulster in the North'.[61]

---

[58] *Ibid.*, Vol. I, No. 60.

[59] *Ibid.*, No. 255.

[60] *Ibid.*, No. 244.

[61] *Ibid.*, No. 346.

There was in any case no reassurance to be given to Smuts since, if British governments continued, as they did, to abide by the view that agreement between the first and second parties was a condition precedent to their own departure, they could not, if indeed they were to go, continue to exclude the one condition, partition, on which the second, minority party, expressed willingness to come to an agreement with the first party. That was the third party's dilemma – none the less so for being of their own making. Their freedom of action was restricted by the commitments into which their predecessors had entered and themselves endorsed. In view of those commitments they felt they could not honourably, had they wished – which they did not – and all other considerations aside, contemplate a transfer of power to the majority without minority concurrence.

On the failure of the Cripps mission Churchill was well content to let the problem rest precisely at that point – and when in 1944 the Viceroy proposed a less passive rôle, the Prime Minister delivered the magisterial rebuke: 'These very large problems require to be considered at leisure and best of all in victorious peace'.[62] Peace came and Churchill went. What further action within possible limits was to be taken? The British raj was running down; the higher echelons of its services were disillusioned and dispirited – this was a recurrent theme of Wavell's reports as Viceroy – the time had come when it was in British interests, over and above being in conformity with Britain's long-declared intent, to go. The Australian, Richard Casey, for a time Governor of Bengal, with a fresh eye on the scene, was an early advocate of departure in accord with a fixed timetable such as was subsequently adopted by Attlee's Labour administration. Transfer power to one successor, he urged, but if that is not possible, then to two.[63] The advice he tendered stemmed from a conviction that 'the demands of Hindus and Muslims have now crystallized into irreconcilability – an All-India unitary Government on the one hand and the two-nation theory on the other – centripetal, and centrifugal . . . I fail to see how we can influence the outcome one way or the other . . . We can give the Indians independence but we cannot give them unity. I would believe that we have to be completely neutral as between All-India on the one hand and Hindustan and Pakistan on the other'. 'Neutral' – the very word used to describe the position of the imperial government on the self-same issue by Lloyd George to the Irish delegates in 1921.

But in the event it was questionably so. First the Cabinet mission sent to India by the Labour government, in a statement of 16 May 1946, commented upon and expressly rejected the proposal which the League had submitted to them for 'a separate and fully independent state of

---

[62] *Ibid.*, Vol. V, No. 111.
[63] *Ibid.*, No. 91.

Pakistan'.[64] This elicited its inevitable sharp reaction from the League and its leader. Muslims had no intention, so the League declared, of substituting Caste Hindu for British domination. Any attempt to impose majority rule, threatened Jinnah in March 1947, while the leaders of post-colonial Asia were foregathering at the Asian Relations Conference in Delhi, would lead to the bloodiest civil war in the history of the continent. It was a possibility few at the Conference were disposed to discount. With seemingly no peaceful alternative to partition thus remaining, the prospect of it had perforce to be faced and a territorial basis for partition to be determined. Here the League's own arguments for the partition of India, on the grounds of the existence within it of two nations, were turned against it by Lord Mountbatten, the last Viceroy, with the consequence that the Pakistan of Jinnah's initial territorial claims, namely of the whole of Muslim-majority provinces, the majority of whose Muslims opted for Pakistan – a curious contention this – was excluded and in its place there was to be a Pakistan with frontiers in the Punjab and Bengal to be determined by boundary commissions in the light of the 'nationhood' of the population. This meant a Pakistan confined to Muslim-majority areas, or what a Governor of the Punjab had indeed earlier described as 'true' as distinct from 'crude' Pakistan,[65] but what Jinnah had hitherto discounted as 'truncated' or 'moth-eaten' Pakistan, but which none the less, if only by reason of the conceptual realization of aim which it represented, he was in no position to reject.

Partition in India even though on the basis of delimitation by district was bound to, and did, bring into existence new minorities. By some, such minorities had been thought of as assurances of good behaviour. If there are to be separate Muslim states, Chaudhri Khaliq-uz-zaman, the local Muslim League leader, had earlier told the Governor of the United Provinces, they must have plenty of Hindus in them to provide an insurance against the Muslims of Oudh being maltreated by the majority community there.[66] In cruder terms the minorities were spoken of as hostages: in the crudest the phrase was murder for murder. Out of this sentiment of 'hostages and retaliation' which he thought 'barbarous' there flowed, in Azad's opinion, 'the rivers of blood' that followed upon partition.[67]

Important in the contriving of the Indian settlement was accord in the last phase between the first and third parties, i.e. the Congress and the British – an accord which reflected something more than mutual understanding at the highest level during the period of the Mountbatten

[64] Reprinted in Mansergh (ed.), *Documents and Speeches on British Commonwealth Affairs*, Vol. II, pp. 644–52.
[65] *India: The Transfer of Power 1942–47*, Vol. VI, Nos. 29 and 51.
[66] *Ibid.*, No. 327.
[67] Azad, *op. cit.*, p. 198. See also, p. 210.

Viceroyalty, though it may be that even the staunchest of Congress leaders were that much the more ready to hold the cup of conciliation to the lips of high station. Its all important outcome was the recognition, painful on the part of Congress, regretful on the part of the British Cabinet and Viceroy, of the absence by that time of a practical alternative to the partitioning of India. The consequence was partition effected with the assent of the majority party, Gandhi on a day of silence indicating his acquiescence,[68] Vallabhbhai Patel allowing 'whether we liked it or not, there were two nations in India', Maulana Azad being left alone in counselling deferment in the hope, albeit forlorn, of unity;[69] as well as of the minority party, Jinnah being committed by the concept he had advanced and the tactics he had otherwise so successfully pursued, to accept the truncated Pakistan he had a year previously deemed non-viable. The basis for the transfer of power once again was dominion status, but by free choice of those to whom power was being transferred, coupled with a sense on the British side of satisfying realization of their view of a right post-imperial relationship.

The rôle of the third party in Ireland and in India indicates near-identity in the issues demanding policy decisions of it and some marked discrepancies in its making of them. Thus, in respect of Ireland the tactical decision was taken to make a settlement with the minority before making one with the majority; in India the settlement was made with majority and minority leaders simultaneously, i.e. an overall settlement as against one in two stages. In Ireland the boundaries of the area to be excluded were determined in accord with the wishes of the minority, the possibility of reference to a Boundary Commission (which met but proved abortive) being extended later; in India by boundary commissions making recommendations in the light of the 'national' allegiance of the inhabitants by district, and not by province as desired by the minority, at the time of transfer. In both cases the settlement was in principal part, or wholly, on a dominion basis; but in the one case acceptance was obtained under threat of renewal of military action, in the other by free volition of the parties concerned.

In all of these matters it may at first sight appear that the imperial government adopted different courses, in the second, Indian, case because of awareness of the unsatisfactory nature or vulnerability to criticism, as reflected in Smuts's comments in 1942, of that pursued in the first, the Irish. No doubt there was the element of experience gained, or lessons learned. But more important were the constraints of past commitments or political circumstances determining the outcome, chief among them being the fact that in India the British government was itself pledged to withdraw, whereas in Ireland it had such intent only in a qualified Home

---

[68] A. Campbell-Johnson, *Mission with Mountbatten* (London, 1951), p. 101.

[69] Azad, *op. cit.*, pp. 183-90.

Rule form, and with one party backing. Yet what was most important applied to both, it was a lack of commitment to majority rule, counterbalancing in its binding force the commitments to minorities.

In this lecture I have sought to approach large and debatable historical questions not, as is traditional, in terms of unity forfeited or federation failed – and even federations that failed appear to have an irresistible fascination for many imperial or Commonwealth historians almost as though they carried an inbuilt presumption or even entitlement to success – but rather in the conceptual contexts in which partition was effected. In those contexts, there is a sufficiency of features in Irish and Indian experience to suggest that in a triangular situation with partition coincidental in time with a transfer of power, there is something in the nature of a partitioning paradigm, with the strategy and tactics of each party in each case in significant, though not uniform, measure conditioned by it. This would seem to suggest that conventional assessments of the interplay of men and events, and of the extent to which there was freedom of manoeuvre as the climax neared, may need downward adjustment. By contrast, such comparative analysis suggests that the importance of concepts in the determining or predetermining of policy needs to be revised sharply upwards. There were in varying degrees conceptual imperatives for all of the parties concerned in Ireland and in India, which, once formulated and receiving popular sanction, imposed rigorous constraints upon the freedom of action even of the most powerful of political leaders. This was especially true of majority parties with their twin objectives of independence and unity and who, in India as in Ireland, when the moment of choice came opted for independence. Yet the outlook of both was conditioned by their sense that partition was not a political device but a moral wrong, to Redmond a 'blasphemy'; to Gandhi a 'sin'.[70] Were concessions to be made, recognition to be given to what was iniquitous? – for twentieth-century nationalism thought in such terms where the eighteenth-century enlightenment, affronted by the cynicism of a great power partition, condemned a lapse below what was permissible by civilized standards of international behaviour. But the determining influence of concept applies no less forcibly to minorities who rightly, or mistakenly, are persuaded that their very survival is threatened by subjection to what Jinnah termed the will of a 'brute' majority, not of their own, but of those they deem to be an alien people, and their only safeguard to be found in the uncompromising affirmation and reaffirmation of their separate identity.

How and why such concepts of community or nation came to be expressed and popularly endorsed in the forms in which they were, thus becomes something of enhanced historical importance and something also

---

[70] *India: The Transfer of Power 1942–47*, Vol. VII, No. 47.

which may be illumined by comparative analysis over and above study in isolation. Did they spring spontaneously from the authentic aspirations of peoples? Or were they in the first instance, at any rate in their more forceful formulations, tactical devices, of which later their devisers became prisoners?[71] That is one question that arises, and to answer it requires a study of both policy motivation at a high level and also case studies in the evolution of regional and local opinion, especially in rural Ireland and in the million villages of the Indian subcontinent, where causes once adopted might be held to with a tenacity little understood by sophisticated dwellers of the capitals. Another question is the nature of the influence, whether inevitably by reason of the circumstances, or deliberately, exercised by the imperial power either over a long period in the bringing into being a situation in which partition becomes the only road out or, in a later phase, in determining how and to whom power should be demitted on its withdrawal. In our own age in a Rhodesian setting, imperial policy was formulated in terms of no independence before majority rule, NIBMAR. But in Ireland and in India the formulation of policy was otherwise – it was in effect NIBMIR, no independence before minority rule or, to be exact, self-rule was assured. Did the difference reflect only differences in circumstances? Or was there also in the light of intervening Commonwealth experience a change of mind?

Behind these particular questions lie others of wider relevance and likely to arise in all areas where majority rule, developing minority nationalism, or the purposes of devolution are living issues. They relate to the nature of nationhood itself and allow of specific formulation. Is there, in respect of nationhood, such a thing as a geographical imperative? How is a second nation within what has been a single state to be identified? How is the authenticity of its nationhood to be established? Can the third party in this analytical enquiry, the imperial power, by its policies and actions, nourish a second nation into existence? Can the first party, the Nationalist majority, by understanding and restraint – or for that matter by force – conjure or frighten it out of existence? Or does its life come from within? Contention and polemics have been a setting in which such questions, understandably emotional in their context, have been approached. But analysis, sparing in judgement, may also have a contribution of its own to make. After all for many men and women it has been a matter of life and death that the answers to all such questions should be as nearly right as lies in human power to give them. While it has been the case that from most partitions the 'untold' sufferings which an Austrian Empress

---

[71] See Dr Anil Seal's comment on Jinnah 'hoist with his own petard of Pakistan' in *Locality, Province and Nation: Essays in Indian Politics 1870–1914*, ed. J. Gallagher. G. Johnson and A. Seal (Cambridge, 1973), p. 24.

forecast[72] of one of them have followed, yet there have been perceptible differences in degree and statesmen may do well to study the signposts leading to partition, and the actual timing and process of past partitions, the better to mitigate the consequences of such as may not by understanding or foresight be averted. More particularly in that category of partition of which this lecture treats, it seems that the time of choice comes early, while two communities stand side by side and, despite illusions that continue to be entertained, is likely to be past, short of the use of force, once they stand face to face.

---

[72] Diderot in St Petersburg in November 1773 in his *Entretiens avec Catherine II* shared Maria Theresa's forebodings, observing that '*nous ne doutons pas que le partage de ce mouton ne devienne un jour la source d'une longue querelle entre les trois loups* . . . .' but mindful no doubt of his imperial patroness, went on to express the reassuring view that it was Austria that would pay the price. *Oeuvres politiques*, ed. Paul Vernière (Paris, 1963), pp. 261–2.

5

THE GOVERNMENT OF IRELAND ACT 1920:

Its Origins and Purposes –
The Working of the 'Official' Mind

Professor Lyons, in his recently published history, *Ireland since the Famine*, describes the offer implicit in Lloyd George's Government of Ireland Bill 1919 as being 'totally divorced . . . from the realities of political life in Ireland'.[1] It is not the purpose of this paper to weigh that verdict but to pose a question peripheral to it. The question is this: if it be accepted that the bill was 'totally divorced' from the realities of political life in Ireland, was it then in whole, or in part, an essay in political fantasy? Or was it related to other realities, namely the realities of political life in war and postwar England? This paper seeks to isolate and elucidate the second and inherently more probable of these alternatives by reviewing some of the important discussions in Parliament, and more especially in Cabinet, which preceded Cabinet agreement in 1919 to sponsor what was in effect the fourth and last Home Rule bill.

The bill was first formulated by a committee of the Cabinet appointed for this purpose in 1919 and then, in draft, its principal provisions and purposes were discussed and debated first in Cabinet and then in Parliament. The thinking of the Cabinet was largely derivative, as was inevitable on a matter already so much deliberated upon, and it is the purpose of this paper to trace its development over what seems to be a natural and meaningful period of time. It may, of course, be objected at the outset

---

[1] F. S. L. Lyons, *Ireland since the Famine* (London, 1971), p. 412.

that to speak of the 'thinking' of a Cabinet, and still more of a number of Cabinets, even though with overlapping personnel, is otiose – that there were *per contra* only the thoughts of individual members. Clearly there is force in this contention, but it may be urged on the other side that any such committee, or succession of committees, engaged upon a common undertaking or enterprise is apt either to develop an outlook that is more than the sum of the outlook of its members or else to disintegrate, at any rate, psychologically. Disintegration, actual over and above psychological, appeared indeed to be the likely destiny of Asquith's Coalition in the summer of 1916 on Irish policy, but the succeeding Lloyd George Coalitions achieved sufficient sense of common purpose to embark upon common action. In the light of their composition and of the controversies of the recent past this was in itself sufficiently remarkable to deserve enquiry as to how it came about. The essential source material for such an enquiry is to be found in the records of Cabinet or Cabinet committee discussions and conclusions.[2]

It is, of course, the case that opinions, as expressed in Cabinet, or for that matter in Parliament, were rarely spontaneous and that more often than not they reflected a conclusion or consensus or compromise reached after individual or party exchanges of view. That is certainly important, especially to biographers and students of English politics, but from the broader perspective of Anglo-Irish relations – something apt to be lost sight of in dramatic reconstruction of personal and party in-fighting in the Coalition era – what mattered was the extent to which there was a convergence of English political opinion at the highest level upon a particular, and *per se* improbable and, as it proved, inadequate panacea for the problem of Anglo-Irish relations.

The interest of such an analysis of the evolution of opinion on Irish policy that preceded the enactment of the 1920 Act is enhanced by reason of the fact that it took place in three successive Coalition Cabinets of a steadily increasing Unionist and steadily diminishing Liberal proportionate content – that of Asquith, formed in May 1915, that of Lloyd George's War Cabinet formed in December 1916 and finally that of Lloyd George's postwar administration formed in January 1919. This meant, given party attitudes to the Third Home Rule Bill, a presumption in each case, not of agreement, but of difference on Irish policy within each succeeding Cabinet. Yet by 1920 there had emerged, if not agreement upon, at least acquiescence in a particular settlement. One necessary condition of its emergence was Unionist preparedness to abandon Union and to accept the view that Home Rule, not merely with partition, but with two

---

[2] *The Records of the Cabinet Office till 1922* (London, HMSO 1966), pp. 3–17, provide a helpful guide to the material available.

parliaments in Ireland, was the best practicable solution of the Irish question in terms of British interests; and another was that Coalition Liberals, who after 1916, and more especially after 1919, were not necessarily the most reputable of Liberals, should be persuaded that there was recognition, at least in principle, of the concept of the unity of Ireland to which earlier they had been committed by their support for the Third Home Rule Bill. By what processes of argument, pressure of events or personal power of persuasion were these ends achieved? A. J. P. Taylor would have us believe that credit, if that is the right word, is to be attributed to the last, as exercised by Lloyd George who 'devised an arrangement of fantastic complexity, the Government of Ireland Act (1920): the United Kingdom, United Ireland, a separate Ulster, all mixed together'.[3] But while Lloyd George certainly placed his *imprimatur* upon the Act, not least by his parliamentary exposition of its purposes,[4] the level at which it may be said to have been of his devising is another matter. An explanation of so complex an outcome to so controversial an issue in personal terms may appear at first sight somewhat oversimple to be satisfying.

The remoter landmarks on the road that led to the formulation of the 1920 Act need only brief recall. There was no provision for the partitioning of Ireland in any of the Home Rule bills, though the possibility of special treatment for Ulster had been considered and rejected by the Cabinet before the introduction of the third. On the first day, however, of the committee stage, 11 June 1912,[5] two young Liberal members, Agar-Robartes and Neil Primrose, moved an amendment making acceptance of a Home Rule Parliament conditional upon the exclusion of the four north-eastern counties, Antrim, Armagh, Down and Derry from its provisions, Agar-Robartes explaining that the amendment was intended to remove the chief stumbling block to Home Rule, which was, in his judgement, the attempt to achieve the impossible, the fusing together of two incongruous elements in one polity and the corresponding failure to recognize that Ireland was not one but two nations. This argument commended itself neither to the Liberal government nor to the Unionists, Bonar Law, however, saying on behalf of the Unionist party that he would vote in favour of the amendment, not because he was the less opposed to Home Rule for the rest of Ireland, but because it would make a bad bill less bad.[6] 'We do not', said Carson, 'accept this Amendment' – which he described as the most vital which probably could be moved – 'as a compromise of the question. There

---

[3] *English History 1914–1945* (Oxford, 1965), p. 156.

[4] H. of C. Deb. 22 December 1919, Vol. 123, Cols. 1168–75.

[5] H. of C. Deb. Fifth Series, Vol. XXXIX, Col. 771.

[6] *Ibid.*, Col. 779.

is no compromise possible.'[7] And because that was so there ought to be no Home Rule. But he noted also that he would never leave out Fermanagh and Tyrone. From another standpoint the amendment was dismissed by the Prime Minister as the most self-stultifying he had known. No wonder it had not been moved by any of the representatives of Ulster itself. 'Are these chivalrous champions of the rights of the Protestant minority', he asked 'going to take shelter . . . in this oasis, or Alsatia . . . in which they are a majority, in which they are exposed to no kind of hardship or injustice . . .?[8] Lloyd George also opposed the amendment on the significantly different ground that if four counties were to be excluded, 'there ought to be an overwhelming demand for it', and clear agreement about which counties were to be excluded. He saw no evidence of either; on the contrary the Ulster Unionist demand was not exclusion for a given area but 'the right to veto autonomy to the rest of Ireland',[9] and as such to be discounted and dismissed. If, however, there were such a demand from Ulster, the government, of course, should give it serious consideration.

The Buckingham Palace Conference, 21–23 July 1914, conveniently reflected the next stage – that reached at the outbreak of the war. There were two essential points at issue at the conference – the nature of the exclusion, i.e. open or veiled, temporary or permanent, and the extent of the area to be excluded – and neither was settled. Indeed the first was never discussed because there was no agreement on the second. What happened was that Asquith, presuming that there was no possibility of profitable discussion of a settlement other than on the lines of exclusion of some sort, identified the two serious outstanding points as area and time limit, and urged that the former should be discussed first. Carson, Bonar Law, Lansdowne and Craig argued strongly for the reverse.[10] Redmond, however, protested saying it was impossible to consider the question of time limit until that of area had been disposed of. His view prevailed and the question of area was thereupon discussed. Carson, according to Redmond's typescript notes of discussions which had no official rapporteur, urged the exclusion of all Ulster, commending it to Redmond and Dillon with the argument that if a smaller, more homogeneous area were to be excluded, reunion of the whole of Ireland would be delayed. The contention had force but acceptance of the conclusion was 'quite impossible' for Redmond. Carson then demanded, as a minimum, 'a clean cut' excluding a *bloc* consisting of the six counties of Antrim, Down, Armagh, Derry, Tyrone and

---

[7] *Ibid.*, Cols. 1065 and 1068.

[8] *Ibid.*, Col. 786.

[9] *Ibid.*, Col. 1126.

[10] *Redmond Papers*, National Library of Ireland, Dublin, 21 July 1914.

Fermanagh, including Derry city and Belfast,[11] all to vote as one unit and to remain under the Imperial Parliament, but with administrative responsibility for their own affairs.[12] The debate, however, was for the most part focused on detailed delimitation by district and the submissions made by Redmond were in direct line with those examined by the Boundary Commission ten years later. More generally a study of Redmond's records indicates the shift of emphasis from the 1912 amendment. The premise of debate was now the exclusion of six *not* four counties, with the nature of the exclusion yet to be explored – a fact which had its bearing on the 1916 negotiations.

At the outbreak of war, or to be more precise, in October 1914, a Home Rule Act[13] was placed on the statute book, coupled with an Act[14] suspending its operation till a date to be determined 'not being later than the end of the present War' and with an understanding that Parliament would then have an opportunity of passing an amending bill making special provision for Ulster or some part of it. But, in effect these were paper transactions placing on record the political equipoise in August 1914. Essentially their intention was to put the Irish question 'on ice' for the duration. The first Coalition imperilled the balance of political forces on which such a possibility depended and the Easter Rebellion destroyed it, not merely in rather obvious political terms, but also at a deeper psychological level. It was not so much that the Dublin Castle system had been exposed as inadequate on a particular and momentous occasion as that it was felt in Cabinet, and most of all by the Prime Minister, that in itself and in what it represented, it no longer provided a possible basis for the administration and government of Ireland.

It is in this context that the Memorandum which Asquith submitted to the Cabinet in two parts on 19 and 21 May 1916[15] on his return from Ireland, may be taken to mark the unfreezing at that level of the Irish question. Asquith, on his visit, had formed two distinct impressions. The first was that despite the prudence and discretion of the military command, there had been incidents which had aroused 'a good deal of uneasiness and sympathy in many people in Dublin and elsewhere in Ireland who lent no countenance to the outbreak' with the rebels and the second that there

---

[11] The counties listed were referred to as the six 'plantation' counties. But historically this is not warranted. Six Ulster counties were planted under the 1609 'articles of plantation' but Cavan and Donegal were included in that number and Antrim and Down were not.

[12] Redmond Papers, 23 July 1914.

[13] Government of Ireland Act 1914, 4 & 5 Geo. V, C. 90.

[14] Suspensory Act 1914, 4 & 5 Geo. V, C. 88.

[15] Cab. 37 / 148 / 18.

did not seem to be 'any general or widespread feeling of bitterness between the civil population and the soldiers'. He himself 'went one day on foot partly through a considerable crowd and was received, not only without disrespect, but with remarkable warmth'. These impressions would seem to have reinforced his natural predisposition to think yet again in terms of the classical Liberal solution of self-government as a step not to estrangement but to closer and more harmonious relations.

But, classical Liberal solvents of imperial–national relations were apt to subsume that if there were majority–minority tensions, they too, were susceptible to similar panaceas. In Belfast, Asquith was reminded that there existed quite different possibilities. The Lord Mayor of Belfast, 'a level headed and public spirited man', told him that during the early autumn of 1915 'a sort of atmospheric wave' overspread Protestant Ulster. 'We had sent' (such was or became the prevailing opinion) 'the best of our manhood to the front; the Catholic[s] of the South and West have contributed substantially less; if we were now to allow what remains of our available men to recruit, we shall be left defenceless against a possible, even probable, Nationalist invasion of our province; and our wives, our children, our homes, our industry, our religion will be at the mercy of our hereditary foes. From that day to this recruiting in Ulster has practically ceased; and so long as this belief, and the temper which it engenders, persists, not only will there be no effective recruiting for the Army, but there will be a determined resistance to any attempt on the part of the State to disarm those who remain at home.'

Ulster leaders confirmed to the Prime Minister that what he had been told was a correct interpretation of the state of mind of the vast majority of the Protestant population of Belfast and industrial Ulster and that nothing could dislodge such feelings from their minds. Those feelings rendered domestic disarmament, however desirable, impracticable. What then remained? One or two repeated to Asquith the old formula of resolute government but the large majority 'were clearly of [the] opinion that the only way to escape was by prompt settlement of the whole problem. . .' It was, said Campbell, the Attorney-General, 'a case of now or never'. But what did such a settlement require? The answer came clear – Home Rule with an amendment of the Home Rule Act 1914 such as would adequately safeguard the future of the Ulster Protestants, and that was deemed to mean the permanent exclusion of Ulster or some part of it.

The Prime Minister acquiesced reluctantly in this conclusion. It appeared to him to be 'the duty of the Government to do everything in their power to force a general settlement'. By that means alone could arms be controlled and it was all important that this should be so, lest otherwise the two armies of North and South should be held in leash 'for a final spring at one another's throats when peace was declared'. In 1914 the possibility of a settlement on such lines had broken down on the problem of the area to be excluded but, now, Asquith was by no means sure that the Nationalists (apart from the O'Brienites in Cork from whom he had received a deputation) would not 'be disposed to prefer the total exclusion (for the time being at any rate) of Ulster' to the continued withholding of Home Rule from the rest of Ireland. If, however, the ultimate solution was to be thought of on Home Rule-cum-partition lines, there had to be wartime transition arrangements and there Asquith contemplated the disappearance 'of the fiction' of a Chief Secretary, the appointment of no successor to the Lord Lieutenant – the Viceroyalty having become 'a costly and futile anachronism' – and single British ministerial control of Irish administration operating with the help of an Irish advisory council.

The Asquith memorandum of 19 – 21 May led on naturally to the Lloyd George negotiations, undertaken at the Prime Minister's invitation at the end of the month. Asquith spoke in the House of Commons of a bold effort on fresh lines that might lead to an agreed settlement between those representing different interests and parties in Ireland and told members that the Minister of Munitions, Lloyd George, at the unanimous request of his colleagues had undertaken to devote his energies to the task.[16] But while there may have been occasion for boldness, there was little opportunity for freshness and, as might confidently have been predicted, Lloyd George sought to manipulate familiar formulae with the one overriding purpose of obtaining a settlement if not by agreement, at least with a semblance of agreement. This was easy in respect of negotiating method, for Lloyd George, unlike Cripps in India in 1942, was bound by no Cabinet declaration, for the good reason that the Coalition Cabinet in 1916 would not have been able to reach agreement upon its terms. His task, accordingly, realistically viewed, was not merely to secure the assent, however reluctant, of the Nationalist and Ulster Unionist leadership to a 'prompt' settlement, but having done that to persuade the Cabinet collectively to accept it.[17]

It was later an allegation of Lloyd George's Unionist critics that there was on the Cabinet side a 'blue print for negotiations', namely Asquith's memorandum. The point was put by Lansdowne in a paper circulated to the Cabinet on 21 June,[18] in which he wrote that 'while it would have been unwise to fetter Lloyd George with meticulous restrictions' it was understood in Cabinet that Lloyd George in negotiations would not go

---

[16] H. of C. Deb. Vol. LXXXII, Cols. 2309–11.

[17] For an account of the negotiations that followed as recalled by Lloyd George see *War Memoirs*, 2 Vols. (London, 1938), Vol. 1, pp. 418–25, and as interpreted by Asquith's biographer, see Roy Jenkins's *Asquith* (London, 1964), pp. 397–402.

[18] Cab. 37/150/11.

beyond the lines of the memorandum.[19] In view of the transitional arrangements there outlined he [Lansdowne] had no idea that anything so far-reaching as the terms of Lloyd George's reported discussions with Irish leaders was in mind. In particular, Asquith had concluded that the Home Rule Act could not take effect till after the war and by implication, so Lansdowne considered, this conclusion had received public affirmation in the Prime Minister's speech at Ladybank on 14 June, when Asquith had said that at the end of the war 'the fabric of the Empire will have been refashioned, and the relations not only between Great Britain and Ireland but also between the United Kingdom and our Dominions will of necessity be brought under close and connected review'. In reply Lloyd George, in fact, conceded that he had not been authorized to bind the Cabinet, but he deemed none the less that he had been authorized to deal with the Irish leaders on the assumption that Home Rule might be brought into immediate operation. He had thus clearly conveyed to the Irish leaders the impression that he was not merely, in Lansdowne's phrase, 'gathering up' their opinions, but was in a position to and had in fact made them a firm offer.

On 23 June Long echoed Lansdowne's complaints about the scope of the discussions. The Irish business was, he wrote, 'unhappily involved in mystery and the consequence is that a great deal of deplorable misapprehension has arisen'. Both Carson and Redmond appeared to have misinterpreted the Prime Minister's reference to the breakdown of the existing machinery of Irish government, as meaning that the whole form of government under the Union had failed and that Home Rule was the only alternative. But in his memorandum the Prime Minister had written that the Home Rule Act could not come into force until the end of the war. Moreover, alleged Long, Lloyd George had been commissioned to undertake *confidential* negotiations and to report results to the Cabinet before any public announcement was made. The first was obviously unrealistic, since Irish leaders had to consult and persuade their respective supporters, but there may have been more substance in the second, in view of Lansdowne's further complaint in the House of Lords on 29 June that the Cabinet were still insufficiently seized of all the points involved in the negotiations.[20]

To the Unionists' sense of grievance about the conduct of negotiations was to be added their protests in Cabinet at their content and direction. The two, inevitably, were not readily to be disentangled and on one point Lloyd George seemingly attached more significance to the Asquithian adjective 'prompt' than Asquith himself, for he moved with remarkable speed towards a settlement formulated by the end of May, the basis of which

[19] Cab. 37/150/15.
[20] H. of L. Deb. Vol. XXII Col. 506.

was the application of the Home Rule Act as soon as possible, with acceptance of a Nationalist modification to the effect that the number of Irish
members at Westminster should remain unaltered at 103 instead of being
reduced, as contemplated in the 1914 Act, to 42, and of a Unionist demand
that the six 'plantation' counties of the north-east should be excluded from
the jurisdiction of the Home Rule Parliament and directly administered
by a Secretary of State responsible to the Imperial Parliament for the period
of the war, with the longer term resolution of the Irish question to be referred to a postwar Imperial Conference. But such an overall settlement could
win Irish acceptance only by ambivalence in personal presentation and from
that Lloyd George was not one to shrink. He assured Redmond, and this
is very familiar ground, that the arrangements, including exclusion, should
in fact be temporary, i.e. for the period of the war, and in his own words
he had 'placed his life upon the table and would stand or fall by the agreement come to', while to Carson he wrote, 'We must make it quite clear
that at the end of the provisional period, Ulster does not, whether she wills
it or not, merge in the rest of Ireland'. The contradiction, which allegedly
alone enabled Carson to persuade the Ulster Unionists to renounce three
of the Ulster counties on plea of permanence, and actually enabled Redmond to persuade a majority of his party to acquiesce in what he deemed
to be a temporary – though clearly open to perpetuation on any reckoning – partition, has been regarded as of critical significance.[21] But four
points are to be noted, the first three in passing and the fourth for fuller
consideration. The first is that without Lloyd George's negotiating dexterity – the historian is well advised to refrain from semblance of moral
judgement – there was no prospect whatever of a 'prompt' settlement. The
second is that in essence Lloyd George was employing a procrastinating
device, since the issue of transient or lasting exclusion would in legislative
terms be deferred till the end of the war, and the third that in fact the difference, as Devlin surmised, between temporary and permanent exclusion
was, politically as distinct from psychologically, minimal or even non-
existent, since what the Ulster Unionists had obtained and enjoyed they
would assuredly not have abandoned after a period of years. The fourth
– and this is a tangled skein that needs to be more deliberately unravelled
– is that the Cabinet would have been divided, to the point of partial disrup-
tion, had the attempt been made to give effect to the proposed heads of
settlement, not only because of the Ulster question but also, and immediately more so, because of Home Rule and the nature of it, for the rest of
Ireland.

Lansdowne's objections on this second point certainly lacked nothing

---

[21] The story is told in Denis Gwynn, *History of Partition* 1912–25, (Dublin, 1950),
Chap. V. Lloyd George's letter to Carson was dated 29 May 1916.

in directness of statement. 'Is this', he asked, in his memorandum of 21 June, 'the moment for imposing upon the country, in the guise of an interim arrangement, a bold and startling scheme which at once concedes in principle all that the most extreme Nationalists have been demanding, viz the disappearance of Castle Government and the establishment of an Irish Parliament with an Irish Executive responsible to it? The triumph of lawlessness and disloyalty would be complete. We may delude ourselves by saying that this arrangement is purely provisional, but the capitulation will be palpable and its significance will not be diminished by the exclusion of Ulster or part of the province.' Sinn Féin would not be conciliated and, he proceeded in a passage that foreshadowed the evolution of Southern Unionist sentiment that received public expression at the Convention a year later: 'I have always thought that any measure of Home Rule which presented to the World as a new Irish nation, an Ireland from which Ulster or any part of it was excluded, would be a deplorable and humiliating confession of failure; and if Home Rule is to come I should prefer a measure embracing the whole of Ireland, with safeguards for the minority wherever found'.

In a less cogent paper of 23 June, Long supported Lansdowne specifically on the point that Home Rule during the war was not, as alleged by Lloyd George, an imperial necessity but would prove an imperial disaster. The following day, however, a Unionist of quite different intellectual calibre, A. J. Balfour, countered with a memorandum circulated to the Unionist members of the Cabinet.[22] Balfour took as his starting point an assertion by Lord Selborne, a vehement critic of the proposed settlement, to the effect that there was no guarantee he [Selborne] was not prepared to give that a Home Rule Parliament be established immediately after the war, but that he would rather resign than see it set up a moment earlier. Balfour's feeling was rather the other way. If Home Rule there had to be 'let us at least exclude from its operation as much of Unionist Ulster as possible'. Were Lloyd George's scheme to be carried through 'the six Ulster counties would have permanently secured to them – by consent and without bloodshed – their place in the United Kingdom. Will anybody assert that, if the settlement of their fate be deferred till peace is declared, terms equally good could be obtained without a dangerous struggle?' He had always held that rather than submit to Home Rule, Ulster should fight and Ulster would be right, but equally he had no illusions about the price in terms of civilized society and damage to property this would entail. 'Very strong therefore', he argued, 'must be the arguments which would induce me to run the hazard of civil war, when we have offered to us voluntarily all that successful civil war could give.' He did not think the arguments were strong. An Irish government was unlikely to countenance a suicidal policy of assisting Germany and were they to

---

[22] Cab. 37/150/17.

prove as incapable of government as Mexicans, why then Home Rule would perish never to be revived. But he did not himself entertain such ideas, nor did he believe that Redmond and his friends would tolerate Sinn Féin notions of an Irish republic dependent on Germany any more than 'we can tolerate it ourselves'. Therefore, concluded Balfour, 'the war supplies no sufficient justification for neglecting the unique opportunity now offered for settling peacefully and permanently the problem of Ulster'.

Ironically enough Balfour's memorandum was written the same day as a report from General Maxwell, also circulated to the Cabinet, which might have been thought to knock from under it the principal prop on which it rested.[23] People in Ireland, noted Maxwell, 'think Sinn Féinism and patriotism are synonymous terms'. Home Rule was again being discussed and that in itself was evidence that rebellion paid. Redmond and his party were discredited, the North was quiet only because the Unionists had the arms and they knew they could defend themselves and the only conclusion was that the Irish question would never be settled in Ireland.

Lord Robert Cecil followed with a paper on 26 June,[24] to express disagreement with Balfour partly on these same grounds, but further alleging that, of the triumvirate by whom a Home Rule administration would be principally directed, Redmond had no administrative experience and had given no evidence of administrative ability, that Dillon had always been a convinced enemy of 'this country', that Devlin had announced that his first act would be to free all 'rebel' prisoners and that none – and this was clearly the telling point – would have the authority of popular choice. Sinn Féin on the other hand would, and its two principal tenets were: (i) 'vehement rejection' of any proposal for the division of Ireland, (ii) profound mistrust of the Irish Parliamentary party. Sinn Féin would not be conciliated by the proposals in debate. To withdraw the offer of Home Rule would be equally dangerous, Carson having warned that to withdraw the proposals now 'would throw Ulster into a ferment and convert the rest of Ireland into "hell"'. So what did Lord Robert suggest? Something perhaps a little devious for so high-minded a man – for the duration of the war, martial law with symbolic Home Rule, i.e. if the necessary amending bill excluding the six counties were passed, a Home Rule Parliament could meet, elect a Speaker and then adjourn till the end of the war!

The Cabinet met on 27 June and Asquith reported to the King that despite the hardly won concurrence of Carson and Redmond to the settlement, Lansdowne on grounds of concession to rebellion and risk of encouraging further rebellion, especially in view of the terms of Maxwell's report, and Long on grounds of lack of a genuine acceptance of the basis

[23] Cab. 37/150/18.
[24] Cab. 37/150/21.

of it by the Nationalists, could accept no responsibility for it; Cecil advanced in the English interest his symbolic Home Rule cum suspension of executive power till the end of the war stratagem; Curzon feared defeat in the Lords, with the consequent risk of an election and newly elected fresh members 'of a revolutionary tinge being returned'; but Crewe and Grey on the Liberal side strongly supported the settlement and Bonar Law on the Unionist side, who wondered what was the alternative to the proposal, said he would recommend his party to ratify it at their meeting the next day.[25] But, according to Asquith, it was Balfour who 'delivered the most effective pronouncement in the long conclave'. He dissociated himself entirely from Lansdowne and Long and far from believing the proposed settlement 'a concession to rebellion', he thought 'it might be far more fairly represented as a Unionist triumph', the exclusion of the six Ulster counties having been the maximum demand of the Unionist leaders at the Buckingham Palace Conference. 'With unanswerable logic', he [Balfour] proceeded to point out the absurdity of the contention that the establishment of a Home Rule Parliament at a distance of six or eight, and more probably twelve or eighteen months could seriously embarrass action in the war, stressed the importance of not alienating United States opinion and declared himself a wholehearted supporter of the policy of Carson and Bonar Law. Clearly the moment of truth was approaching. But before it came Lloyd George intervened. He suggested the appointment of a small committee of the Cabinet to consider further safeguards, which might avert the resignation of Unionist members of the Cabinet. Curzon and Chamberlain agreed, Lansdowne acquiesced, Long held out to the last. The proposal was adopted and the committee (the Prime Minister, Lloyd George, Cecil and the Attorney General, F. E. Smith) appointed to consider and formulate such additions as seemed to be necessary. By this means, Asquith observed, a series of resignations, with the consequent possible dissolution of the government, which 'would not only be a national calamity but a national crime', had been averted. What he did not tell the King – perhaps he did not wholly understand – was that some resignations were the price of settlement. Even a week later, on 5 July (when the Cabinet met to receive the report of the committee it had set up) when Lansdowne spoke of his dilemma, 'either horn of which seemed to promise danger if not disaster', as between a settlement he disliked and distrusted and the risk of political chaos 'which might necessitate the worst of evils – a general election', and Long of his position as a 'cruel' one, Asquith found cause for much satisfaction in the fact that both decided to remain and that Selborne's was accordingly the only resignation. He contended that this had amply justified the delay which had obviated

---

[25] Cab. 37/150/23. See also Jenkins, *op. cit.*, pp. 399–401.

'premature and precipitate decisions'.[26] But on 11 July in a speech in the House of Lords which, as Asquith wrote to Crewe, gave the 'greatest offence to the Irish',[27] Lansdowne made it brutally clear that his continued membership of the Cabinet was on the basis of 'permanent and enduring' exclusion of the six counties together with continuing British wartime control over defence dispositions in the twenty-six regardless of the existence of a Home Rule administration of which his mistrust was ostentatiously displayed.[28]

The headings of the settlement as outlined by the committee and preliminary to the drafting of legislation were laid before the Cabinet on 17 July. They provided principally:

(1) that the Government of Ireland Act 1914 should be brought into force as soon as possible subject to certain modifications;
(2) that the Act was not to apply to an excluded six counties area, which was to be administered by a Secretary of State;
(3) that the Irish representation in the House of Commons was to remain unaltered at 103.

To reassure critics, special safeguards were included to protect British military and naval interests. The Act was to remain in force for twelve months but the period could be extended and a permanent settlement considered after the war at an Imperial Conference concerned with closer cooperation of the dominions with imperial government.

The submission of the outline of legislation which did not foreclose the Ulster options provoked renewed Unionist opposition. Cecil, Lansdowne and Long all returned to the charge. It was essential, argued Cecil, that exclusion should be definite until the excluded areas wished to return.[29] Equally it was impossible for the Unionist party to support a settlement unless Irish representation at Westminster were diminished – the one boon of Home Rule – since otherwise Ulster would be at the mercy of eighty Irish Nationalist members. It was impossible, therefore, to proceed with the experiment, though he allowed that something had been gained in that Unionist leaders were now definitely pledged to Home Rule for the south and west of Ireland and the Liberal party had conceded that six Ulster counties could not be included in a Home Rule Ireland without their consent. Lansdowne argued that the Ulster Unionists had 'notoriously' accepted the settlement only on the assumption of permanent

---

[26] Cab. 37/151/8. See also Jenkins, op. cit., p. 401.

[27] Quoted in ibid., p. 402.

[28] H. of L. Deb. Fifth Series, Vol XXII, Cols. 645–9.

[29] Cab. 37/151/37.

exclusion,[30] while Long, supporting Landowne's demand for a structural change in the Home Rule Act to exclude the six counties, enquired further whether it was right to divert attention from the war.[31]

On 19 July Asquith reported to the King that he could not assent to further postponement, but that the Cabinet after much discussion of the draft bill agreed (i) that Carson's claim for the definitive exclusion of Ulster could not be resisted, (ii) that the Nationalists should be told that after the Home Rule Parliament had been set up, Irish representation in the imperial House of Commons must be reduced, with the proviso that it should be restored when an amending Irish bill was introduced.[32] This was to make an already dangerously disadvantageous compromise impossible for the Irish Nationalist leaders and thus destroy, as intended, the basis of the settlement. When a bill with such provision was introduced on 25 July Redmond declined to support it and on 27 July, by which date Redmond, for whom the negotiations had disastrous consequences, was extricating himself finally from them, Asquith reported to the King: 'It was agreed that for the immediate future in Ireland the simplest and least objectionable plan would be to revert for a time to the old system of Lord Lieutenant and Chief Secretary'.[33] What it must have cost him to pen those words!

What conclusions may be drawn from the complex and abortive negotiations of the summer of 1916? The first and most important in general terms was that the options before any composite Coalition Cabinet were extremely limited. Hard-core English Unionist opinion, reinforced by the most highly placed spokesman of the Southern Unionists, would not acquiesce in Home Rule, even with six-county exclusion, in wartime, short of safeguards which would render Home Rule meaningless, despite the readiness of the new leadership in the persons of Bonar Law and F. E. Smith, and the old in the person of Balfour, to contemplate imminent Home Rule, given permanent exclusion for the six counties; the Liberal leadership, including presumably Lloyd George, though he remained a negotiator without personal commitment, desired Home Rule forthwith, acquiescing in the exclusion of the six counties as a necessary condition of it, but with such exclusion decently veiled in deference to the concept of unity, to which their allegiance was already bespoken; the Irish Nationalist leadership, in a position of nominal strength with a Home Rule Act on the statute book and the special treatment for the north-eastern counties still to be decided, but politically altogether insecure at home, were neither willing nor able to

---

[30] Cab. 37/151/38.
[31] Cab. 37/151/42.
[32] Cab. 37/152/1.
[33] Cab. 37/152/22.

negotiate on the basis of a lasting partition, but had, however, shown themselves prepared to acquiesce in the temporary exclusion of six counties – the possibility of four now being discounted and disregarded – as the price of immediate Home Rule; the Ulster Unionists, having in effect twice diminished their pretensions, by abandoning first, for the period of the Lloyd George negotiations, their objection to Home Rule in principle and second their claim to the whole province of Ulster, had little more to concede short of conceding all. Within this complex clearly something had to give or to be sacrificed and in 1916 what gave in general terms was Liberal, more particularly, Asquithian resolution in the face of aristocratic Unionist opposition to Home Rule in wartime on the basis of a divided Ireland.

But such a general conclusion in isolation is insufficient. Why precisely did the 1916 negotiations fail? To argue that this was to be attributed to Lloyd George's dexterity, or duplicity, does no more than push the question back two stages further. Why in the first instance did he feel compelled to resort to a negotiating gamble with the odds on premature and damaging revelation so obviously against him? The answer is that in no other way could he hope to take even a first step towards a settlement. And then secondly, was it because of Lloyd George's conflicting assurances that the settlement collapsed? To this long-standing assumption A. J. P. Taylor gives a categoric negative.[34] The objection, he writes of Lansdowne, Long and other hard-core Unionists, was over Southern Ireland, not over Ulster. The first was certainly so. But it was not their only objection, as emerged very clearly in July with reiterated demands for permanent exclusion of the six counties. Would Asquith indeed have made the concession to a 'little aristocratic clique'[35] which finally wrecked the proposals, had it not been for the additional demands for a reduction in the number of Irish members and for a structural alteration in the 1914 Act, voiced publicly by Lansdowne in his speech of 11 July in the Lords, and both assured of broadly based Unionist support precisely because they were designed to safeguard the 'plantation' counties? The truth would seem to be that, in the initial stages of the controversy, the opposition was to wartime Home Rule in the rest of Ireland, but as it progressed, demands for a reduction of Irish members and structural amendment of the Home Rule Act indicated that it was the future of Ulster that was fundamental. Moreover, unless the view is taken that Asquith was deliberately misleading Redmond, that was the purport of a letter to him dated 28 July 1916 and marked 'for you *alone*'. 'I say nothing', wrote the Prime Minister, 'as to the responsibility of this person

---

[34] Taylor, *op. cit.*, pp. 71–2, Note B.
[35] Quoted in Trevor Wilson, *The Downfall of the Liberal Party 1914–1935* (London, 1968), p. 74 from *Manchester Guardian*, 26 July 1916.

or that' [for the breakdown of the negotiations] but 'I am sure you agree that the actual breaking point was not the figure at which the Irish members should be retained in the Imperial Parliament. This could easily be arranged by some form of compromise . . . The real point is the future of the Excluded area. Carson (naturally) wants safeguards against 'automatic inclusion'. You (with equal reason) desire to keep open, and effectively open, the possibility of revision and review – at an early date.'[36]

Asquith told Redmond in that same letter of 28 July that the important thing was to keep the negotiating spirit alive. It was superfluous advice – neither could stop negotiating and in the end it helped to bring disaster to both. Lloyd George, who displaced Asquith in December, was also a negotiator, but he negotiated for appearance as well as for ends. The Irish Convention, of which Professor McDowell has written the detailed story,[37] was his grand essay in the art. It is to be noted, however, that Lloyd George's own first choice, as set out in his letter to Redmond of 16 May 1917,[38] was not for a Convention at all, but for a Home Rule settlement with the exclusion of the six counties, subject to reconsideration by Parliament after five years and with a Council of Ireland composed in equal numbers of delegations from the two parts of Ireland with powers to extend or to initiate the ending of the area of exclusion. It was only in view of its rejection that Lloyd George reverted to the South African Convention precedent which loomed so large in the minds of most Liberal and some Unionist leaders. The Convention indeed took place, but it was the proposal that was discarded that foreshadowed the future, including not only partition, but the notion of a Council and the idea of parity as between majority and minority in the membership of that Council. The changes that took place in 1919–20 marked in fact a further retreat from the concept of unity in as much as the five year initial period of exclusion adumbrated in 1917 was to disappear and the Council to be restricted in respect of the initiatives open to it.

Lloyd George's letter to Redmond reinforces other evidence to the effect that within a few months of his accession to the highest office Lloyd George was probing for a solution along the lines of exclusion for the six counties, increasingly thought of in quasi-permanent terms and Home Rule for the twenty-six. 'I saw Lloyd George two or three times in Paris', wrote T. P. O'Connor, 'on 10 May, 1917; so far as I could gather he was still on his absurd "clean cut" proposition.'[39] There is a certain ring of conviction

---

[36] Redmond Papers.

[37] R.B. McDowell, *The Irish Convention 1917–18* (London, 1970).

[38] Cd 8573 and also reprinted in *Report of the Proceedings of the Irish Convention* Cd 9019, pp. 50–1.

[39] Redmond Papers.

in Lloyd George's repeated comments, as on 7 March 1917, on the differences between North and South – the inhabitants of the former being 'as alien in blood, in religious faith, in traditions, in outlook – as alien from the rest of Ireland in this respect as the inhabitants of Fife or Aberdeen'.[40] This was the view made explicit in the Agar-Robartes amendment in 1912 and while the majority of Liberals may be thought to have stood firm by the principle of unity, there was evidently a minority of them who felt that self-determination, preferably on the basis of county option for the north-eastern counties, at the least was not inconsistent with their principles. It is true that at the Convention the Ulster representatives had reverted to their all Ulster exclusion demand as the price of Home Rule but, vulnerable though he was to Unionist pressures in Parliament and Cabinet, Lloyd George was well placed to discount claims which no longer commended themselves to much influential English Unionist opinion.

In early 1918 two questions compelled attention – the first the follow-up to the Convention and the second, in its Irish context, the manpower shortage. The Coalition Cabinet, aware that they were separate issues, decided to treat them as though they were not and as a result produced a package deal – Home Rule and conscription to be extended to Ireland as near-simultaneously as was practicable – on the argument that, since there was no prospect of agreement on either separately, objections to each might cancel out if they were taken in conjunction. The one positive result was that the Cabinet *appeared* to have a policy in respect of Ireland, which was important in its English political context, but which, in its Irish, may well have been worse than having none. Inevitably, in such circumstances, the composite policy was pursued with an almost total lack of conviction.

On 28 March 1918, the Cabinet, without waiting for the final report of the Convention, decided to extend conscription to Ireland as soon as that report was received.[41] It was an abrupt decision on a matter long debated in a desultory way and the decision taken was against the weight of official opinion over a period of time, Duke, on his appointment as Chief Secretary, having assured Maxwell (September 1916) that 'from my knowledge of English politics and all I could learn of the Irish situation an extension of the Military Service Act to Ireland must be regarded as impracticable', and Maxwell in a memorandum circulated to the Cabinet a month later having questioned whether, in 1916, such a policy were not already too late, adding that it would, however, 'please militant Sinn Féiners and Unionists, the former because it would play into their hands . . . the latter because they consider what is good enough for England is good for Ireland, but the motive imputed to them would be their desire to kill Home

---

[40] H. of C. Deb. Vol. XCI, Col. 459.
[41] Cab. 23/14. 28: 3: 18.

Rule'.[42] Duke reiterated his strong objections to conscription in Ireland on 20 and again on 29 March 1918,[43] i.e. immediately after the Cabinet decision. Why then was it taken? The answer is first and fundamentally because of a near-desperate shortage of men on the Western Front, with gloomy forebodings even in the highest circles about the stopping of the German offensive short of Calais – there had been for the same fundamental reason earlier conscription crises in Australia and Canada; second, the pressure of opinion in Parliament and country upon the Cabinet demanding equality of sacrifice, the more insistently with the age of conscription about to be raised from forty-five to fifty. Embedded in the demand was doubtless the feeling, expressed very characteristically by Lansdowne in 1916, who had then forecast that the government would be eventually driven to conscription,[44] that 'nothing in the end would be more beneficial socially to Ireland than to pass the bulk of her young men through the army' since it would mean that they 'would return to ordinary life with ideas of duty and discipline', not otherwise to be acquired. But it was the added inducement of a package deal that persuaded the majority of the Cabinet, including Curzon, Smuts and Lloyd George, whose attitude on Ireland was evidently hardening, as Hankey noted[45] in April 1918, to line up with Milner and Balfour on this issue. Smuts's reasoning is of some interest. In the event of the Convention agreeing on a report, and indeed in any event, he thought the passage of a Home Rule Bill and conscription, while in effect simultaneous, should be so timed that Home Rule would come 'first on the ground that this would remove the Irish sense of historic wrong and satisfy United States and Dominion opinion on Home Rule'. Evidently he attached importance to these, in one respect surely altogether misconceived, views for the record of what he said is amended and extended.

There was a full-scale discussion on Ireland at a Cabinet conference on 3 April,[46] at which the Viceroy, Lord Wimborne and Duke and Robinson[47] were present. Wimborne said compulsory service before settlement of the Convention 'would be to cause an explosion in Ireland'. Milner deprecated 'playing with conscription'; once entered upon, it would have to be 'seen through'. The majority, however, remained in favour of

---

[42] Cab. 37/155/8 and 37/155/40.

[43] Cab. 24/5.

[44] Cab. 37/157/8.

[45] Thomas Jones, *Whitehall Diary*, ed. K. Middlemas, Vol. I (London, 1969), p. 57 and Vol. III, p. 4. See also D. G. Boyce, 'How to settle the Irish question: Lloyd George and Ireland 1916–21' in A. J. P. Taylor (ed.), *Lloyd George – Twelve Essays* (London, 1971), pp. 143–5 and generally.

[46] Cab. 23/14.

[47] Sir Henry Robinson, President, Local Government Board for Ireland.

taking both together. Smuts thought now was the right time to do so. Bonar Law, having regard to the danger of an explosion in Ulster, guardedly assented, saying that the government would have to stand or fall by both bills. Robinson thought firmness essential, since weakness would provoke resistance to the death and while agreeing with Wimborne on the need for contemporaneous action, none the less expected general opposition from Unionists and Sinn Féin, were the two measures to be introduced in conjunction. 'However strange it might appear', commented Milner, 'an attack from both sides would not be a bad thing.' He felt also that an Irish settlement must needs be imposed. The fundamental point was the war, remarked Balfour in gloomy philosophic reflection, and the question was whether they would be stronger if they got a few men from Ireland at the risk of disturbances or did nothing. He laid down two policies – all or none. If the second were adopted it would be difficult to persuade England to accept the decision. 'We would have to state' he concluded, 'the naked truth that Ireland is a sheer weakness, but it would be a greater weakness if we did something than it was if we did nothing.'

The package policy was announced in the House of Commons on 9 April[48] with a Military Service Bill on the one hand which, while not extending conscription forthwith to Ireland, empowered the government to do so by Order in Council and an invitation to Parliament to frame a measure of self-government for Ireland. Carson commended conscription but without concession on the ground that it was either good or bad in itself; the Nationalist members were united in passionate protest against it and next day Lloyd George thought the Irish 'were trying to work themselves up into a frenzy', Tom Jones as a result rather missing 'the buoyant, cheerful note' so characteristic of him.[49] The Cabinet appointed another committee to draft another Irish bill, the chairman being Walter Long, and Curzon, Smuts, Cave, H. A. L. Fisher and Duke being among the members. The first meeting was held on 15 April. On 20 April, Tom Jones, after a long discussion, told Hankey that he thought the government's Irish policy was 'a mad one'.[50] On 9 May Chamberlain at a meeting of the Irish committee was contending defensively that 'to withdraw from compulsion was to surrender the unity of the Imperial Government' in face of a challenge from Irish Nationalists and he did not see how the government could remain in office if that were done, while Smuts with the agility for which he was renowned conceded that 'in abstract principle' Chamberlain was right, 'conscription and Home Rule were conjoint, associate measures' but Home Rule might mean 'letting loose forces of

---

[48] H. of C. Deb. Vol. 104, Col. 1364.
[49] *Whitehall Diary*, Vol. I, p. 56.
[50] *Ibid.*, p. 61.

civil war when we are fighting for our life' and should therefore be held over anyway as 'a big imperial question' – presumably he was already thinking in terms of a dominion solution – and conscription, also carrying its own civil war risk, should be likewise deferred.[51] On 14 June the Irish committee reported it was impossible to give effect to the dual policy. Conscription was tacitly dropped and in Churchill's retrospective verdict the government was left with 'all the resentment against compulsion and in the end no law and no men'.[52]

The constitutional discussions in the Irish committee were somewhat more illuminating. The committee, it is true, had here one essential purpose – to play for time. But its members were less than content with so self-denying a rôle. They looked for a more specific *raison d'être* and found it by seeking to fulfil one avowed object of their being, namely the drafting of a bill. But they ran inevitably into difficulties both of principle and of detail. The chairman, not unreasonably perhaps, wanted a bill that might pass through Parliament and he felt that the only hope of achieving this was by drafting the provisions in such a way that they would be consistent with federation of the British Isles. He had strong initial support from Austen Chamberlain, who said on 16 April that powers might be given to an Irish Parliament so far as was compatible with a federal constitution. 'I do not exclude federal reconstruction of [the] United Kingdom – that is the real test for the Irish Bill'.[53] In a later memorandum he developed the argument, contending that all past attempts at Home Rule had failed, not because of the incapacity of governments, but because of the impossibility of finding a solution within the limits they had set themselves.[54] But were the context to be widened the problem would become more manageable. He himself believed that, because of the complexity of the issues and the revolutionary ferment that would arise after the war, it would have to be in any case, since one imperial government and Parliament could no longer deal with everything, but would find it necessary to devolve a part of its responsibilities on other bodies to set itself free for the work which it alone could do. If such a scheme of federal devolution were not applied, he surmised, 'We shall be in grave danger of revolution before many years have passed'. Devolution, therefore, was as necessary in English as in Irish interests and the two problems should be run together. That would change the context of the Irish question because while it would, for example, be possible to think of customs and

---

[51] Cab. 27/46 and *Whitehall Diary*, Vol. I, p. 63.

[52] Cab. 27/46 and W. S. Churchill, *The World Crisis: The Aftermath* (London, 1929), p. 281.

[53] *Whitehall Diary*, Vol. III, pp. 5–6 and Cab. 27/46.

[54] Cab. 24/5, 14 July 1918.

excise in the hands of a Home Rule government, it would be impossible in a federation to conceive of them except in the hands of the federal government. So the Chamberlainite moral was, cease to think of the Irish question in isolation, but enlarge the setting, bearing in mind that the problem of decentralization of government was a general not a particular problem.

The argument was not without consequence on the longer term but it carried only modest conviction in a disillusioned committee, from which Cave wished to resign because he thought it was ploughing the sands and in which Curzon saw no line of advance.[55] An answer of a kind was later given to Chamberlain's contention in a letter from Lord Hugh Cecil. He recognised, even while deploring, the fact of Irish nationality and he argued that federalism and nationality were contradictory and mutually fatal. 'The truth is', he wrote, 'that colouring *federalism* with nationalism is like painting a rat red; it kills the animal.'[56] But while he drew no such inference himself, presumably the federal notion remained relevant where there was no such national sentiment. The strange conclusion that he did draw was that by a process of elimination, nationality and federalism alike having revealed their impracticability, the Irish might eventually be driven towards Union with provincial devolution.

In December 1918 a new balance of political forces emerged to face a new situation. The general election resulted in an overwhelming victory for the Coalition, which returned 478 members on the Coalition coupon, as against 29 Liberals, 59 Labour, and no less than 48 Conservatives without it. The Coalition membership of 478 was made up of 333 Coalition Unionists as against 135 Coalition Liberals.[57] There was, because of Sinn Féin abstention, no organized Irish Nationalist vote in the House of Commons, but the Ulster Unionists remained. Unionist predominance in the House was reflected in a Cabinet where Lloyd George continued as Prime Minister, with immense prestige, but little personal following; Bonar Law was Lord Privy Seal; Balfour, Lord President; Curzon, Foreign Secretary; Birkenhead, Lord Chancellor; Milner, Colonial Secretary and Churchill, still it is true a Liberal in allegiance, at the War Office. Much, perhaps too much, has been made, by way of explaining the Cabinet's Irish policy, of Lloyd George's isolation, of his comparative impotence as the prisoner of the Coalition.

More important than the change in the balance of political forces at Westminster was the change in the legislative situation. There was now a

---

[55] *Whitehall Diary*, Vol. III, pp. 5–6.

[56] *Ibid.*, p. 12.

[57] The results of the election are reviewed in Taylor, *op. cit.*, pp. 125–8 and Wilson, *op. cit.*, pp. 89–198. Because of difficulties in identifying allegiance in a few cases, the figures do not exactly coincide.

time factor tantamount to a time limit. The Home Rule Act was on the statute book and it was scheduled to come into force automatically when hostilities formally concluded with the signature of the Peace Treaties. The Coalition Cabinet, as the Unionists realised, was no longer playing for time but constricted by time. Either the Home Rule Act, as amended to meet the assurances to Ulster Unionists, was given effect or there was a new Act repealing and replacing it. The Coalition Cabinet decided upon the second course and as a result, the last section, 76(2) of the 1920 Act was to read, 'The Government of Ireland Act, 1914, is hereby repealed as from the passing of this Act'. A condition of such enactment, however, had been prior Cabinet consensus on Irish policy and if it was reached comparatively quickly that would seem to have been, first because of the statutory need for prompt action, secondly because of the growing realization on the part of party leaders of how few were the options in English political terms, let alone Irish, open to them and last, and probably least, because of Lloyd George's ingenuity in negotiation.

The first consideration of policy was left to yet another Irish committee, under the chairmanship once again of Walter Long. On 4 November 1919 the committee in a first report urged that the Cabinet should make 'a sincere attempt to deal with the Irish question once and for all'.[58] They further reviewed and reached conclusions upon three possibilities. The first to have regard for the conclusions only, was that exclusion from a Home Rule Bill on a basis of county option was unworkable; the second was that the idea of an Irish Parliament, at best doubtfully consistent with pledges of non-coercion given by the Prime Minister to the Ulster Unionists, was vitiated, as indeed was county option, by the assumption that it was within the power of the Imperial Parliament to impose unity upon Ireland; the third was that if alternatively Home Rule were established, not for all Ireland as a unit, but for both parts of Ireland, that would provide for the complete withdrawal of British rule from the whole of Ireland in the sphere of domestic government, be consistent both with the fact that there was a majority in Ulster, as opposed to Dublin rule, as there was a Nationalist majority opposed to British rule in the rest of Ireland and with pledges already given, and finally would 'enormously minimize' the gravity of partition, since there would then be no Nationalists under (direct) British rule and both North and South would enjoy immediate state rights with a link between them.

In the course of subsequent Cabinet discussions on the broad issues of policy on 11 November and 3 December one part of these conclusions especially came in for criticism.[59] While it was accepted that the Ulster

---

[58] Cab. 27/68.
[59] Cab. 23/18.

Unionists could not be coerced and that their separate status should be recognized, it was urged on 11 November, first, that Ulster had always taken the standpoint of retaining the same position as Great Britain and not, as the committee contemplated, of being placed under a different régime; second, that the remaining provinces would obtain rather less than under the Home Rule Act and that it was therefore not likely to be acceptable to them, and third, that the three remaining provinces were overwhelmingly in favour of Sinn Féin and that the first action of Sinn Féin in power would be to declare an independent republic unless this was provided against in the bill in some way. It was, however, also accepted that it was impossible to retreat, that a mere repeal of the Home Rule Act or postponement was probably not acceptable to Parliament and very undesirable from the point of view of the United States and the dominions. The committee, taking these views into account, was invited to submit further and more detailed proposals.

At the Cabinet meeting on 3 December discussion centred mainly on three propositions submitted by the committee for consideration: first, that there should be a Parliament for the south and west of Ireland, but that the six counties should be allowed to vote in favour of remaining part of the United Kingdom for all purposes; second, that there should be a Parliament for the south and west and a Parliament for the whole of Ulster, and third, that there should be a Parliament for the south and west and a Parliament for the six counties.[60] In favour of the first proposition, that is the six counties remaining an undifferentiated part of the United Kingdom, was a clear basis of principle – so it was claimed – namely that of self-determination to be applied if necessary by plebiscite; against it the assertion that the 'Covenanters' would be opposed, because they had bound themselves to treat Ulster as a unit, that the Nationalists would likewise be opposed and also all moderate elements in the South and West, with the result that the prospect of the eventual unity of Ireland would be 'greatly diminished' by the exclusion of the six counties. There were also practical difficulties.

In the light of objections and difficulties, the Cabinet then ruled out the continued inclusion of the six counties for all purposes in the United Kingdom. There followed an interchange of opinion on policy and while views were expressed in favour of keeping either Ulster or the six counties separate, the general feeling was that the ultimate aim of government policy in Ireland was a united Ireland with a separate Parliament of its own, bound by the closest ties with Great Britain, but that this must be achieved with the largest possible support and without offending the Protestants in Ulster; in fact as Sir Edward Carson had put it, 'Ulster must be won by kindness'

---

[60] Cab. 23/18. The committee's proposals were attached to the minutes as Appendix 1.

and this ultimate aim could only be achieved by something like general consent in Ireland.

The assertion of principle did not, however, affect concentration on immediate solutions, which might seem to have rested on the assumption that the longest way round would prove the shortest way home. The reasons for and against a separate Parliament for Ulster or for the six counties were explored in some detail. They were not dissimilar. A significant argument for a six-county area was the already higher rate of increase among Catholics, with the danger that in the course of time the Protestants would be 'swamped' if the whole province were the unit. But like so many statistical forecasts this was no sooner advanced than it was refuted. A more acceptable argument for the six-county area was the advantage of having people under a Northern Ireland Parliament as homogeneous as possible. Against this, once again, were the sentiments of the 'Covenanters' for the province of Ulster and also its superiority as an administrative unit. In the upshot the Cabinet agreed that the bill should be drafted on the basis of a Parliament for Ulster, but reconsidered if it were later found that a six-county area was more acceptable. In accord with a recommendation of the committee, it was further agreed that there should be a Council of Ireland with power to bring an Irish Parliament into being and that it should consist of equal numbers of representatives, twenty, from each Parliament.

The most important statement in the records of the meeting of 3 December was the enunciation of ultimate aim – a single Parliament for a united country. It came in for subsequent questioning. A week later, on 10 December 1919, when the draft bill[61] was before the Cabinet, it was stated that lifelong Unionists would prefer that there should not be a single Parliament. But it was reiterated that one of the principal aims of government policy was to produce a good effect in the dominions as well as the United States and that this could not be done except by a measure paving the way to unity, if and when both the North and the South were willing to accept it. The general trend of Cabinet opinion remained in favour of adhering to the original statement.[62] In a predominantly Unionist Cabinet this was of importance, despite implicit qualifications. At the same time another issue was foreclosing. It was reported that opinion among responsible Ulster politicians was in favour of limiting the excluded area to six counties 'since the idea of governing three Ulster counties which had a Nationalist majority was not relished'.[63] It was noted that such a solution would fit in with any scheme for the creation of a federal system.

---

[61] Paper C.P. – 266.

[62] Cab. 23/18.

[63] *Ibid.*

On 15 December accounts of further conversations on this, superficially still open, issue with Ulster leaders confirmed doubts as to whether the Northern Parliament would be able effectively to govern the three Ulster counties where there was a large Nationalist majority. Those leaders, it was reported, 'greatly preferred' that the scheme should be applied only to the six 'Protestant' counties. Sir James Craig had further suggested, in a personal conversation with Sir Laming Worthington-Evans, the establishment of a Boundary Commission to examine the distribution of population along the borders of the whole of the six counties and to take a vote in districts on either side where there was a doubt about allegiance. This proposal was commended as being in accord with the practice and principles adopted in the Peace Treaties and referred to Long's Irish committee for consideration.[64]

When the Cabinet met on 19 December for the last time before the government's policy was outlined in Parliament, the Prime Minister reported that he with some colleagues had had a long conference with Sir James Craig that morning and that Craig had expressed his strong opinion in favour of confining the Northern Ireland Parliament to the six counties.[65] He was reported to have expressed himself strongly in favour of the proposed Boundary Commission and to be prepared to try to work the new Parliament. One more extended discussion followed in which again it was urged that if the ultimate aim of the government's policy was a united Ireland, it would be better that the jurisdiction of the Northern Parliament should extend over the whole of Ulster, which included both Roman Catholics and Protestants, both urban and rural districts, and by its size was more suited to possessing a separate Parliament. In favour of the six-county scheme was that the Ulster leaders were prepared to work it and that in turn might help towards unity with goodwill, while against the all-Ulster scheme was the difficulty for the government of trying to force through something unacceptable to friends and critics alike. It was better, such was the general view, to have something theoretically less perfect, if thereby it would secure more general acceptance. The idea of an immediate Boundary Commission, however, met with considerable favour. Its purpose would have been to advise on the precise Boundary to be included in the bill. It was urged, however, that enquiries would produce unrest and the idea was not pressed.

---

[64] Cab. 23/1. The accepted view has been hitherto that expressed by Denis Gwynn, *op. cit.* (p. 202): 'There had been no question of a Boundary Commission . . . until the suggestion was put forward tentatively to Arthur Griffith by Mr Tom Jones on 8 November [1921]'; Craig is alleged to have found it 'odious'. Lyons. *op. cit.*, p. 432.

[65] Cab. 23/18, 19: xii: 19.

The issue of area was not quite finally disposed of when Lloyd George outlined the Cabinet's Irish policy in the debate on the adjournment on 22 December 1919[66]and the reason was that the Cabinet, partly because of its own uncertainty of mind, desired to leave itself some small freedom of manoeuvre. Lloyd George, who went out of his way once again to underscore heavily the differences between the north-eastern counties and the rest of Ireland – 'a fairly solid population, a homogeneous population – alien in race, alien in sympathy, alien in religion, alien in tradition, alien in outlook from the rest of the population of Ireland . . .' – said that in respect of area there were four possibilities: (a) the exclusion of Ulster as a whole, (b) county option, leaving large minorities outside the excluded area, (c) the exclusion of the six counties, and (d) the six counties with subsequent adjustments. Policy in fact oscillated between the first and the last two, an excellent device for ensuring attention or, if need be, extracting concessions. But the great concession of separate status was assured in statutory form and Carson, after an initial rhetorical flourish of denunciation, showed his appreciation. Of two cardinal facts mentioned by the Prime Minister, Carson recognized but deplored the first, namely that the Home Rule Act was on the statute book, but welcomed the second, namely that this was to be the first bill admitting 'Ulster's right to be treated as a separate entity'.[67] Even in respect of the separate Parliament for which Ulster had not asked there was the attraction of security. 'You cannot knock Parliaments up and down as you do a ball, and, once you have planted them there, you cannot get rid of them.'[68] The matter of area was not finally disposed of till 24 February 1920 when the Cabinet decision, after an interposition on the part of Bonar Law for the exclusion of the whole of Ulster, came down finally in favour of the six 'plantation' counties as a block, without consultation with the inhabitants on a county or other regional basis. Nor was any Boundary Commission established, all of which was reasonable on the basis of temporary, unreasonable on the basis of permanent, separation.[69] In Cabinet terms, however, the Buckingham Palace Conference debates, the 1916 negotiations and the 1918–19 discussions had in effect demonstrated that settlement on such lines was the only outcome consistent with semblance of Coalition Cabinet consensus and parliamentary viability. The exclusion of a larger area would have offended some Liberal and doubtless Labour sentiment, the exclusion of a smaller – as contemplated by the Agar-Robartes amendment – would

---

[66] H. of C. Deb. Vol. 123, Col. 1171.

[67] *Ibid.*, Col. 1197.

[68] *Ibid.*, Col. 1202.

[69] *Whitehall Diaries*, Vol. III, pp. 104 and 106.

have been unacceptable to the English over and above the Ulster Unionist leadership. But the argument for exclusion of the larger area in the interests of ultimate unity received no convincing answer from any quarter.

The relation between area and form of government was not, however, so clear. The importance of the federal concept, either in its purer form or watered down to devolution, is often overlooked, but was certainly important in some Unionist thinking and in giving shape to the 1920 Act. Federalism in its classic form presupposes the existence of coordinate authority as between the centre and the constituent units, not the subordination of the latter to the former. In that form the federal idea was not pursued. The Act of 1920 states explicitly (s. 75) that 'notwithstanding the establishment of the Parliaments of Northern and Southern Ireland . . . the supreme authority of the Parliament of the United Kingdom shall remain unaffected and undiminished over all persons, matters and things in Ireland and every part thereof'. So long as that section remains on the statute book it is, therefore, otiose to talk of a federal, or even quasi-federal, system. On the other hand the federal concept transmuted into the devolutionary idea, examined by the Speaker's Conference on Devolution in 1919, still carried with it the idea of a separate though subordinate legislature and administrative institutions. To that extent it played an important part in rationalizing the notion of a separate provincial government for the six counties and in so doing had a perceptible influence on the question of area. It was possible to conceive of Ulster as a whole remaining part of a United Kingdom wholly governed from London, but unrealistic to think of it sustaining a separate Parliament on so precarious a balance of political opinion. Equally once the notion of subordinate parliamentary institutions was adopted, it was unrealistic to think of a four-county area sustaining them. There was, therefore, a closer correlation between area and form of government than is apt to be recognized. It was implicit but never, so far as I can trace, made explicit in Cabinet discussions.

There is a further point to be noted and this also was clearly a condition of the Cabinet consensus. The partition of Ireland was effected within or upon a concept of continuing unity. The establishment of separate Parliaments in Section 1 of the Act was, on paper, in part counter-balanced by the constitution of the Council of Ireland in Section 2. 'A fleshless and bloodless skeleton', Asquith termed it and he appreciated more clearly than any other critic the implications of parity as between North and South, as between minority and majority in the composition of the Council of Ireland. 'It is left', he said, 'to an Ulster minority for all time to veto, if it pleases, the coming into existence of an Irish Parliament.'[70] None the

---

[70] H. of C. Deb. Vol. 127, Cols. 112–13.

less this symbolic deference to unity, for what it was worth, was also a condition of Coalition consensus and it, too, derived from 1914, 1916 and post-1917 Cabinet or Irish committee discussions.

Finally, and here I return to the quotation from Professor Lyons with which this paper opened, Cabinet consensus was conditional upon the ignoring on paper of the political realities, not in the whole, but in the greater part of Ireland. Cabinet discussions, beyond the periphery of and therefore not examined in this paper, make it perfectly clear that most members understood that a limited Home Rule measure would not be acceptable in what was termed Southern Ireland any time after 1916 and the reaction to conscription underlined the message for those who had not hitherto received it. More and more there are allusions to dominion status, coupled with a disturbing awareness that dominion status was likely to mean republicanism in two stages instead of one. This was very evident in the debate on the 1920 bill in the House of Commons, those Labour members who appealed to the principle of self-determination, when confronted with the question – would not self-determination mean a republic? – shrinking from an affirmative and taking refuge in federalist generalisations.[71] If, therefore, the Cabinet had sought to conform to Irish realities, it would at once have ceased to conform to those of English politics and in particular those on which two Coalition Cabinets had rested. 'Indirectly', writes A. J. P. Taylor, 'the Government of Ireland Act ended the troubles.' In so doing he had in mind chiefly that it made possible the new initiatives implicit in the King's Speech at the opening of the Northern Ireland Parliament. But his comment has meaning at a deeper level. The enactment of the bill made possible the consideration of a settlement with Irish nationalism because, and only because, by taking account of English political realities it had reopened options in respect of Irish policy, otherwise foreclosed.

Lloyd George was Prime Minister and Bonar Law the leader of the Unionist party, the one without and the other with strong views on Ulster, but it is a misconception to think of the Act of 1920 as being in any fundamental sense their achievement or the product of Lloyd George's dexterity and still less of his devising. It was on the contrary fashioned in Cabinet committee and carried the unmistakable marks of successful committee searching for compromise. It was also and more importantly the outcome of the continually narrowing range of choice, which had confronted each successive British government since the outbreak of war, because of the opinions, prejudices and fears – and there was within the ruling establishment great fear of revolutionary forces, social as well as

---

[71] H. of C. Deb. Vol. 127, see speeches by Wedgwood Benn, cols. 1017–28 and Clynes Cols. 944–56.

nationalist – of a succession of secondary figures, Long, Lansdowne, Cecil, Cave, Worthington-Evans, who with an inflexibility deriving from and dependent upon the groundswell of conservative parliamentary and public opinion,[72] were able to deprive even the most powerful of Cabinets of the freedom of manoeuvre that is usually an essential condition of the statesmanslike resolution of complex and intractable issues.

[72] D. G. Boyce, 'British Conservative Opinion, the Ulster Question and the partition of Ireland, 1912–21' *Irish Historical Studies*, Vol. XXII, pp. 89–112 provides a valuable analysis of developments in Conservative opinion down to the Anglo-Irish Treaty 1921.

6

IRELAND AND THE BRITISH COMMONWEALTH OF NATIONS:
The Dominion Settlement*

Lost causes seem to be my lot! In the Thomas Davis lectures on *The Shaping of Modern Ireland* my theme was John Redmond and the Third Home Rule Bill; tonight it is Irish membership of the British Commonwealth, a cause not only lost – well lost many may think – but also, in the context of the dramatic events of forty years ago, dull. Yet at the time Ireland's status as a dominion within the Commonwealth aroused emotions, the intensity of which succeeding generations find it increasingly hard to comprehend. And surely contemporaries were right to feel so strongly. Dominion status was the substance of the settlement; the purpose and the life-force without which the Treaty was meaningless. Dull it may be; indispensable to understanding it none the less remains.

The factual record is concise and clear. Ireland became a dominion on 6 December 1921. The first article of the Treaty stated that she should have the same constitutional status in the community of nations known as the British Empire as the Dominion of Canada, the Commonwealth of Australia, the Dominion of New Zealand and the Union of South Africa. The second and the third articles of the Treaty defined the Irish position more closely by saying that her relation to the Imperial Parliament and government should be that of the Dominion of Canada and that the Governor-General should be appointed in like manner as the Canadian

---

* First broadcast as a Thomas Davis lecture by Radio Éireann.

Governor-General. The fourth article prescribing the terms of the oath, which Lord Birkenhead regrettably enough may *not* have described as 'the greatest piece of prevarication in history', made particular reference to Irish membership of the group of nations forming the British Commonwealth of Nations. In sum these provisions left no room for doubt about the fact that the Irish Free State was to be a dominion. But they invited two larger questions – why dominion status for Ireland? And what was a dominion? Let me try to offer some answer to each in turn.

Why dominion status for Ireland? There is a simple answer. It was imposed by the British. It was accepted by the Irish plenipotentiaries following upon an ultimatum – the word is Churchill's – and on pain of a resumption of immediate and terrible war – the phrase is President de Valera's. But is it a sufficient answer? Hardly. In so far as it implies that dominion status was altogether objectionable to the Irish and altogether acceptable to the British it is misleading. It was neither.

The problem central to the whole negotiations was indicated in Lloyd George's question – how might the association of Ireland with the community of nations known as the British Empire best be reconciled with Irish national aspirations? The answer, in the Irish view, was not by dominion status. On this, so far as I know, the Dáil Cabinet were unanimous in the summer of 1921. Their demand was for a republic, in some way externally associated, if need be, with the British Commonwealth. And it was with suggestions to this end that they sought to counter British proposals for dominion status. In respect of form the two ideas were incompatible. Republican status was inconsistent with dominion status. In one sense this was all-important. Mr Lloyd George and President de Valera, however much they might differ on lesser matters, agreed on what was fundamental. To both men it was the symbols of sovereignty that signified most. But there, of course, their agreement ended, Lloyd George never failing in his insistence that the monarchical symbolism of the Crown must be the essential feature of the settlement and de Valera resolved that the republic should not be sacrificed. In this conflict the British view prevailed, was imposed if you like, with dominion status. It was the Crown, not the republic, that was embodied in the Treaty and later, in a form as diluted as its draftsmen could devise, in the constitution of the Irish Free State. This presence of the Crown in the constitution was a distinguishing feature, common to all dominions, of dominion status. Whether on the broader view it was the most important feature was a matter on which men were, and no doubt long will be, deeply divided.

There was, in any case, more to dominion status than the symbolism of monarchy. There was an expanding, if still debatable, area of freedom. The dominions, Canada, Australia, New Zealand and South Africa, which had entered the First World War as British colonies, ended as separate signatories to the Peace Treaties at Versailles. They were foundation members of the new international organization, the League of Nations. They had long been wholly self-governing in their domestic affairs and by 1921 two among them at least, Canada and South Africa, were seeking to secure for themselves corresponding independence in international affairs, so that they might for example assume international obligations, or not assume them, as their own parliaments and governments saw fit, enter treaties or not enter into them as their own governments decided and generally be in no way obliged to follow British foreign policies. True, the growing practice of equality was still counterbalanced by the theory of subordination. But might not this by a concerted effort and with Irish reinforcement soon be altogether removed? True also, there was the fear, strongly voiced by President de Valera and by Erskine Childers, that in the case of Ireland geographical propinquity would mean a diminution of dominion powers. But would the overseas dominions acquiesce in any such curtailment? In sum was there not at least a prospect that in terms of independence Irish national aspirations might be reconciled with membership of the community of nations known as the British Commonwealth through dominion status? Did it not in its own way provide much of the substance of what Sinn Féin had been fighting for? Were there not assets in respect of power to offset liabilities in respect of constitutional forms? At any rate, in whatever way the balance of argument and probability was deemed to fall, here was something different in kind from Home Rule.

If dominion status was not without advantages for the Irish, it was assuredly not without objection for the British. And moreover what was especially attractive about it on the Irish side, namely the prospect of expanding freedom, was precisely what was objectionable about it to many on the British side. If Lloyd George's approach to dominion status for Ireland was unusually devious, there was at least a reason for it. He was the Liberal leader of a Coalition Cabinet dependent on the support of a great Unionist majority for survival in office. This majority may not have been made up, as was said after the 1918 election, of a lot of hard-faced men who looked as if they had done well out of the war but at any rate it was made up of men for the most part hostile, and in some few cases almost pathologically hostile, to the idea of a self-governing Ireland. They talked about Lloyd George as 'the great little man who had won the war' but in matters on which emotion ran high he was not a free agent. He was the prisoner of the Coalition, a prisoner who more than once, so we are told, thought of escape by resignation. It was not he, but his defeated and much abused predecessor Asquith who, in 1919, first formally proposed dominion status for Ireland. The proposal was received by Unionists with howls of execration. And why? Bonar Law, the Canadian Unionist

leader in the Coalition, well remembered for his pre-war assault on Home
Rule, gave one telling reason. The connection of the dominions with the
Empire, he warned the House of Commons in 1920, depended upon
themselves. If 'they choose tomorrow', he said, 'to say "we will no longer
make a part of the British Empire" we would not try to force them'. Dominion status for Ireland, therefore, might mean first secession, then an
independent republic. The very idea of dominion status must accordingly
be resisted root and branch. Lloyd George gave every appearance of doing
so. Further dominion status proposals from Asquith elicited from him the
comment 'was ever such lunacy proposed by anybody?' That was October
1920. In July 1921 he was warmly commending a dominion status settlement to Mr de Valera. This time the suggestion had not come, immediately
at least, from a British but from a Commonwealth source.

On 13 June 1921, General Smuts, then Prime Minister of South Africa,
lunched with King George V at Windsor Castle. He found the King anxiously preoccupied about the speech he was shortly to deliver at the opening of the Northern Ireland Parliament. The draft submitted to the King
by the Irish Office was reputedly 'a blood-thirsty document'. General Smuts
suggested something altogether different. He prepared a draft which he
sent with a letter to Lloyd George. In it, Smuts spoke of the Irish situation
as 'an unmeasured calamity' and 'a negation of all the principles of government' for which the Commonwealth stood. He suggested that the King's
speech in Belfast should contain a promise of dominion status for Ireland,
a promise which he felt sure would have the support of all the dominion
prime ministers. Lloyd George did not agree and the promise was not made.
But the idea of dominion status was given new point and urgency.

On 4 July dominion status was formally put forward by the British
government as a basis of settlement. True the offer was so hedged about
with reservations subtracting from it that Lloyd George was left open to
Mr de Valera's retort that the principle of the proposed pact was not easy
to determine. But none the less, from the British point of view, the offer
was decisive. It was one to which the majority of the Coalition's supporters
were instinctively opposed. Their hearts were with the Prime Minister when
he denounced dominion status as insanity; against him when he recommended it as a basis of settlement. Yet in England there was one thing
greatly in its favour.

Dominion status was an experiment which had been tried elsewhere and
had succeeded. The union of English and French in the Dominion of
Canada was thought of as a major triumph of English statemanship, while
fresh in the minds of Lloyd George, Chamberlain and Churchill was the
success of the policy of trust and reconciliation which brought into being
the Union of South Africa. Austen Chamberlain, at the time leader of
the Unionist party and son of Joseph Chamberlain, the man who had killed

the First Home Rule Bill, said explicitly that it was the success of those Liberal policies in South Africa, which brought a South African dominion into existence, that more than anything else persuaded him to break with his own cherished convictions and his party's tradition and sponsor a dominion settlement of the Irish question. In England it is much easier to take a revolutionary step if you can say 'we have travelled this road before'. But in Ireland the advance was to be by untrodden ways.

That might not have mattered quite so much but for one thing. Dominion status lacked precision. It was conceived of, not as something possessing final form at any given point in time, but as something in process of continuing development. In negotiation this was an undoubted liability. Uncertainties implicit in the status served greatly to accentuate mistrust and suspicion, the British coming to regard President de Valera as 'a visionary' likely to see mountains where they saw only molehills, while the Irish thought of Lloyd George as a master of political dexterity, not to say duplicity, who used the liberal imperial vocabulary of Gladstone to further the purposes of Castlereagh. Yet the problem at root was more than personal. Even at this distance in time, it is not easy to say concisely and with precision – and here I come to my second question – what dominion status for Ireland did involve.

In the House of Commons debate on the Treaty, Lloyd George asked himself the self-same question. What, he said, does dominion status mean? But he did not answer it. He talked instead, and not unreasonably, of the dangers of definition, of limiting development by too many finalities, of introducing rigidities alien to British constitutional thinking. He was prepared to say what dominion status did not mean. But not what it did. The Treaty, as we have seen, defined dominion status by analogy, that is, by saying that the status of the Irish Free State would be that of the other dominions which it listed by name and more particularly that of Canada. The British Prime Minister was prepared to go no further. But we can perhaps do so, without plunging into constitutional detail, by looking at dominion status through the eyes of the dominions.

In 1921 the dominions conveniently enough were debating their own status. General Smuts was foremost among those who wished to have dominion status more clearly defined. Smuts repudiated Empire; he championed Commonwealth. The dominions, he pointed out, enjoyed a large measure of equality in practice but in law and constitutional form they were subordinate to the United Kingdom. He wanted the theory brought into line with practice. In a memorandum, circulated to the British Cabinet but not published till many years later, Smuts warned that unless this course were followed the Commonwealth would be faced with other Irelands, with other examples of doing too little and being too late. At the Imperial Conference in London, in June 1921, the issue was joined. Smuts was opposed notably by Australia's Prime Minister, W. M. Hughes. Hughes did not like the idea of defining imperial relations. There was no need for it. 'The difference between the status of the dominions now and twenty-five years ago', he said, 'is very great. We were colonies, we became dominions. We have been accorded the status of nations . . . What greater advance is conceivable? What remains to us? We are like so many Alexanders. What other worlds have we to conquer?' Neither the South Africans, nor the Canadians were persuaded. There were other worlds they wished to conquer. But at that crucial moment in the summer of 1921 it was hard, if only because of this still unresolved debate, for Lloyd George, or for the Irish, or for anyone else, to forecast with certainty how dominion relations would develop – how hard you can imagine by asking yourself tonight what relations between the countries of the Common Market will be in twenty or thirty years' time.

We know now the tide of dominion nationalism was flowing too strongly to be checked. 'The fact of Canadian and South African independence', said Michael Collins in the Treaty debate, 'is something real and solid and will grow in reality and force as time goes on.' That certainly proved to be true. He was right, too, in saying, 'We have got rid of the word Empire', and that in its place there was the British Commonwealth of Nations – the term itself with its very different overtones making its first official appearance in Article IV of the Treaty. Kevin O'Higgins who, like most supporters of the Treaty, did not believe that dominion status was the fulfilment of Ireland's destiny, hoped none the less that what remained would be won by agreement and by peaceful political evolution. That, too, proved substantially true. Dominion status despite the fears of some of its critics and, perhaps even more important, despite the forms with which it was still enshrouded, conferred a substantial measure of freedom and opened the way for complete independence. I think this might have been more generally recognised at the time, but for one thing. Kevin O'Higgins, to my mind, put his finger on it when he said that the most objectionable aspect of the Treaty was the threat of force that had been used to influence Ireland to a decision to enter what he called 'this miniature League of Nations'. He went on 'It has been called a League of Free Nations. I admit in practice it is so; but it is unwise and unstatesmanlike to bind any such League by any ties other than purely voluntary ties . . . I quite admit that in the case of Ireland the tie is not voluntary . . . the status is not equal'. Ireland was forced into a free association. That contradiction, that handicap, laid upon dominion status when Lloyd George foreclosed debate on 5 December 1921, with an ultimatum, clung to it like an old man of the sea, shaken off only when dominion status itself was discarded.

Many particular objections to dominion status were, of course, raised in the Treaty debate – objections about the subordination that it might mean in respect of the Crown or its representative, the Governor-General, or the armed forces or the judiciary. But in fact such limitations upon Irish, or for that matter upon dominion sovereignty, did not very long survive. At the first Imperial Conference at which the Irish played an active part, in 1926, the process of redefining Commonwealth relations was begun. Lord Balfour, familiar forty years earlier as 'Bloody Balfour', presided in his old age 'with a smile like moonlight on a tombstone', according to Kevin O'Higgins, over the deliberations of a committee which opened the way for the last stage in the advance of the dominions to the unquestioned independence they have enjoyed since the Second World War. In 1931, with the enactment of the Statute of Westminster, what remained of the old colonial Empire had been pulled asunder and Mr Patrick McGilligan had reason for claiming in the Dáil that the Irish had played a large part in doing it. In that sense dominion status gave freedom to achieve freedom. It may not have been the goal but it had opened the way to the goal. The road to it was, however, slow and winding and in time of great transition young men generally prefer to travel by faster ways.

But if, as the historian must, one probes a little further one finds oneself looking again at the problem central to the debate in 1921 in another light. How might the association of Ireland with the community of nations known as the British Empire best be reconciled with Irish national aspirations? Canadians and Australians had advanced with satisfaction from colonial to dominion status. This was a road along which they wished to travel. They felt it was a road along which it was natural they should travel. They were countries of settlement. In Ireland there were counties of settlement – in the north-east. In a dominion their inclusion was the natural, their exclusion the illogical thing. For the rest, Ireland was not a country of settlement. It was one of the historic nations of Europe. It was not extra-European but European national symbolism to which it aspired. The republic, not dominion status, was the goal. The point was put with characteristic forthrightness by Austin Stack in the Treaty debate. 'Let us assume', he said, 'that under the Treaty Ireland will enjoy full Canadian powers. But', he went on, 'I for one cannot accept from England full Canadian powers, three-quarter Canadian powers, or half Canadian powers. I stand for what is Ireland's right, full independence and nothing short of it.' What was natural and appropriate for the existing dominions would be in effect unnatural and inappropriate, at any rate, for a partitioned Ireland. The countries that were dominions in 1921 might seek independence, but Ireland was seeking something more as well – independence and recognition of a separate national identity. Dominion status at that time might lead to the one without necessarily including the other. And to that extent dominion status was conceived, and well conceived, but for another situation. And in so far as the British believed that by conceding dominion status to Ireland, she would become a dominion psychologically as well as constitutionally they were mistaken.

And here I come back to a simple but basic fact; dominion status in 1921 was not compatible with republican status. Allegiance to the Crown was then an essential feature of it. That allegiance had to be expressed in the form of an oath. That oath was embodied in the Treaty; it was embodied in the constitution and it could not be removed (because of the fundamental status given to the provisions of the Treaty by the Constitution Act) without denouncing the Treaty and dominion status of which the oath, at British insistence, was an integral part. It was because this was so that Mr de Valera said in the Treaty debate: 'I am against the Treaty because it does not do the fundamental thing'. It did not recognize, as he claimed external association would have done, the separate, distinct existence of a republic. On the contrary, it gave away republican independence by bringing Ireland as a dominion within the British Empire and more precisely, as he said, by according recognition to the King as the source of executive authority in Ireland. Over against, therefore, the substance (in part still prospective) of freedom there had to be placed the abandonment of the symbolism which expressed national aspirations. The distinction between dominion status and external association was sharp rather than broad and that helps to explain why the division that ensued was deep and lasting. There are times when constitutional forms express things that for many men matter most and this was one of them.

It was because this was so that the debate on dominion status in Ireland – it sounds paradoxical but I am sure it is true – enlarged the experience of the British Commonwealth of Nations and will always hold its interest far beyond the bounds of these islands. The question posed in 1921 might be rephrased to read: how may national, republican aspirations best be reconciled with a monarchical, imperial or Commonwealth states system? The suggested answer on the Irish side was external association, something that would possess the substance of dominion status but replace its monarchical with republican forms. In 1921 that solution was deemed impossible of consideration, as politically it then was, by the British negotiators. India, a historic nation of another continent, later posed the same problem, coupled with an explicit wish to remain a member state of the Commonwealth as a republic. The Indians were fully familiar with the Irish background as I myself can testify, having discussed these matters in Delhi in 1946 with the members of a committee concerned with the drafting of the Indian republican constitution. Profiting by Irish experience, the problem of republican India's relations with the Commonwealth was resolved in 1949 – the formula by which India acknowledged the King as head of the Commonwealth being virtually identical with the formula proposed by President de Valera for the same purpose in Document No. 2

in 1922. The Commonwealth henceforward has had complete constitutional, as well as political, equality, its member states being monarchical or republican as they themselves desire. But by the time the British found the answer, the Irish had lost interest in the question.

7

FOREWORD TO THOMAS JONES'S
WHITEHALL DIARY

Thomas Jones's *Whitehall Diary* is enormously rich in its Irish material. This is partly because T. J. was personally so deeply involved in the resolution of Anglo-Irish differences, but even more because of the historical significance of the events which it recalls and the dramatic quality, often with overtones of tragedy, of the personal encounters of which it tells. Students of recent Anglo-Irish history, while mindful of the fact that the entries in the diaries of Irish interest form part of a larger whole, the origin and nature of which are explained in Keith Middlemas's 'Introduction' to Volume I, will warmly welcome their collection and publication in a single volume. Apart from the biography of Eamon de Valera by the Earl of Longford and Thomas P. O'Neill, which is in certain significant respects complementary within the common time-span, no work of comparable interest or equal authority on the shaping of Anglo-Irish relations has appeared for a generation. And in one respect it stands alone. It describes policies in the making when their outcome was all unknown.

The *Diary* entries, reproduced in this volume, cover the years 1918 to 1925, the first entry recording a discussion in the Cabinet on conscription for Ireland and the last the surprisingly peaceful obsequies of the Boundary Commission, the very concept of which was, and by the more perspicacious was understood to be, charged with political dynamite. Most readers will be familiar, and some very familiar, with the outline of intervening events in the stormy post-First-World-War climacteric of

Anglo-Irish relations, but even for those in the latter category there remain certain questions of outstanding interest not yet fully and finally resolved. To what extent, for example, was the Anglo-Irish settlement 1920–1, with its twin foundations in the 1920 Government of Ireland 'Partition' Act and the 1921 Anglo-Irish Treaty, conceived of at the time as a deliberate, unified policy on the part of Lloyd George and the Coalition Cabinet, as distinct from being in its second phase near-desperate improvisation in the face of a situation going out of all semblance of effective control? What really were the factors that persuaded members of the Coalition Cabinet in June 1921 to make a reversal of policy, which Churchill described as seemingly more sudden and complete than any in modern times, by seeking reconciliation with the forces of militant Irish nationalism? When and why did Lloyd George first begin to think seriously of the dominion settlement, which he had earlier so contemptuously repudiated? How nearly did members of the Cabinet in the course of Scottish summer peregrinations, which took them at the PM's behest, but with understandable reluctance, first to the Town Hall at Inverness – how graphically T. J. describes their meeting there! – and then to Gairloch, come to breaking off negotiations during those protracted exchanges between Lloyd George and de Valera, which in themselves constitute something of a classic in imperialist–nationalist dialectics? What actually happened, to pose a more particular but controversial question, about the presentation of credentials by the Irish delegates when negotiations began? What were the relations between Lloyd George and his Unionist colleagues during the negotiations and was there at any point serious likelihood of the threatened alternative diehard government under Bonar Law coming to power? Are existing accounts of how the Irish delegates were persuaded, or felt compelled, to accept dominion status with allegiance to the Crown well authenticated in all their dramatic detail? What was the post-Treaty relationship of the British government, especially Churchill, with the Irish Provisional Government, especially Collins, and is there fresh light to be thrown on allegations of undue Churchillian pressure on the latter to assert the authority of the Provisional Government by force if necessary?

It is not to be supposed that this third volume of the *Whitehall Diary* will in fact give a final answer to any one, or all, of these questions, but the entries do, in my judgement, help to supply further evidence of a kind essential to the formulation of an answer to all of them, and, indeed, to many others more personal in character or more limited in compass. They do so, essentially, because they narrow the gap between knowledge of courses adopted, or policies pursued, and appreciation of why, in what precise circumstances, in the light of what personal views and for what reasons (or lack of reasons), such policies were adopted. In so doing this volume of the *Whitehall Diary* makes its unique contribution to history.

Even though something of what the *Diary* entries contain might be gleaned from other and scattered sources, the fact remains that collectively they comprise the sort of material about which historians dream and about which their dreams are all too rarely realized. For what we have in this volume are the contemporary impressions of a man who was specially charged with the recording of discussions on Irish policy – whether in Cabinet, Cabinet committee or with individual ministers; with emissaries as eminent as Smuts; with intermediaries as elusive as Cope; with representatives of Ulster Unionism or the more flexible but still influential spokesmen of the Southern Unionists; and supremely with the Irish republican leaders, their personalities, first reflected as it were darkly in a Pauline glass through the reports of others, then coming individually on to the stage in the arrangement of the Truce (which took effect on 11 July 1921) and finally, de Valera significantly excepted, for some two months remaining there as principals at the conference table, or at less formal but no less important meetings away from it. Given the pressures that must have existed, most of the accounts are remarkable in their fullness as well as in their interest, T. J. being a compulsive recorder above all of matters bearing on Anglo-Irish relations. Nor are his *Diary* entries merely the notes of an experienced *rapporteur* on often complex and usually contentious – such being the nature of the Irish question at that time – debate; they are the contributions of a man who was himself emotionally involved and who by taking seemingly small initiatives, or by communicating rather more, or on one important occasion rather less, than he was commissioned to do, expressed his own personal commitment and made his own perhaps critically important contribution, not least on 5 December 1921, to a settlement in Ireland on a dominion basis, in the possibility of which he had become interested at a significantly early date and to which subsequently he became strongly, almost passionately, predisposed.

Chronologically the *Diary* entries fall into three principal parts. The first part, down to the Truce in July 1921, covers the period of the Anglo-Irish war and the partition of Ireland; the second, the period of negotiations culminating in the signing of the Anglo-Irish Treaty on 6 December 1921; and the third, the difficult period of transition in the working out of a new Anglo-Irish relationship. Substantially, also, the entries may be classified under three principal headings. First there are T. J.'s accounts of Cabinet proceedings, and ministerial exchanges; second, his descriptions, sometimes in great detail and in their manifold intricacies, of Anglo-Irish negotiations for Truce and Treaty; and finally, but by no means least in their interest, more personal papers including T. J.'s own correspondence with Lloyd George, Balfour, Hankey, and others, containing something of his own assessments of a developing situation, coupled with his reflections upon events and personalities.

Chronology and classification overlap at all points, but in the first chronological period it so happens that the entries under the first 'Cabinet' classification are of outstanding interest. There was a succession of discussions at Cabinet level on the Irish situation in 1920 which touched upon the foundations of British policy in Ireland – most notably those of 31 May at which members of the Irish executive were present; of 23 July (of which H. A. L. Fisher remarked that it was the first real discussion in his time in the Cabinet of the Irish question); and of 1 December. Such discussions continued in the earlier months of 1921, though focusing increasingly, as members of the Cabinet were slowly disillusioned with the prospect of pacification by repression, upon the possibility of settlement by negotiation, with the meeting of 12 May providing a significant indication of ministerial predispositions, and that of a group of ministers on 6 July, at which General Smuts reported on the impressions he had formed on his recent visit to Dublin, constituting in effect the climax to them. Of course, there exist also the official Cabinet Minutes of all these meetings, but while there is duplication in respect of outcome and conclusion, there is lacking in the latter, not only the nature and variety of personal contribution that is recorded in the former, but also any personal impression of the balance of argument, of ministerial idiosyncracy or the trifling personal incident so apt to be associated with the conclusion of momentous events. How useful, for example, it is to have Tom Jones's summarizing reflection appended to his account of the meeting on 6 July 1921 and reading: 'All through the recent discussions . . . the most irreconcilable Minister has been Balfour. Churchill has frankly acknowledged the failure of the policy of force. Birkenhead wobbles as if unwilling to break either with the P.M. or with Churchill. . . . Curzon has always been for going the greatest lengths in conciliation'.

In the second chronological period, running from the Truce to the Treaty, entries under all classifications are to be found in rich variety. So much has been published and written on the dramatic events of these six months that it would be pardonable to suppose that even T. J. had little to add. But any such presumption on the part of the reader is likely soon to be dispelled. The exchanges between Lloyd George and de Valera preliminary to the negotiations were published at the time and first-hand accounts have been given of both British and Irish attitudes reflected in them. But the reasoning in depth behind the British responses, and the illuminating contemporary detail about the making of them, has not hitherto been so freshly set out. It is interesting, for example, to read of Austen Chamberlain, in the PM's absence, reading de Valera's reply of 10 August 1921, looking 'more grave than the document itself', and later, in Cabinet, conveying 'a feeling of mild panic to his colleagues' while giving 'a palpitating summary' of the reply; and to learn how Lloyd George in his solitary attempt to undermine de Valera's republican position by appeal to the readiness of past Irish leaders to accept allegiance to the Crown, enlisted the aid of T. J. in a search for suitable quotations, a search which took him from the Library of the National Liberal Club to Austen Chamberlain from whom he hoped, in vain as it proved, to borrow Lecky's *Leaders of Irish Opinion*. But it is, of course, less to the preliminaries than to the actual negotiations that the reader's attention will be most closely drawn. While not sensibly modifying the characterization and contours of a dramatic story, the entries add a new dimension in their reproduction of the actual exchanges between the British and Irish delegates and in their revelation of how British attitudes were shaped and British policies determined from day to day – and in late November–early December from hour to hour.

The *Diary* has also something to add about the impressions made by the Irish delegation upon the British negotiators. Michael Collins had already, in May, elicited admiration from T. J., who in a letter to Bonar Law, commenting *inter alia* on the extraordinary tenacity of the IRA, had inquired rhetorically where was Collins during the Great War, adding: 'He would have been worth a dozen brass hats'. That regard deepened during the Treaty negotiations, as also did respect on the British side for the leader of the Irish delegation, Arthur Griffith. On the other hand the judgement, outlook, and personality of Irish leaders who were not present were apt to be increasingly disregarded or even dangerously discounted. T. J. was shrewd enough to foresee that Collins would one day be a candidate for 'canonization'; it does not seem to have occurred to him that de Valera might be an even stronger one. No doubt this was an almost inevitable consequence of the negotiations, tense, hard, and self-absorbing as they were, with concessions wrung by devices, some of which can be described at best as devious. T. J. was always there, an intermediary who became in the literal sense indispensable. Behind him was Lloyd George, who, T. J. noted, had framed below the bookshelves in his bedroom a text from the Book of Job: 'There is a path which no fowl knoweth and which the eye of the vulture hath not seen'. This record of Lloyd George's Irish negotiations suggests that it was well chosen.

The third chronological phase is somewhat lacking in unity. Apart from British relations with the Provisional Government during the prelude to and after the outbreak of the Civil War in Ireland, it illuminates the problems of securing British acquiescence in the provisions of the Constitution of the Irish Free State and three years later, in a world of other leaders both British and Irish, of reaching final agreement on the boundary question. Fortunately, however, a continuing element remained in the person of Tom Jones – there in his accustomed vantage point to record the circumstances surrounding the conclusion of what was, however regarded, one of the great turning points in British, Irish, and even Commonwealth history.

Part II

The Inter-War Years

8

IRELAND: EXTERNAL RELATIONS
1926-1939*

There was one dominant factor in Ireland's external relations in the period 1926–1939. It was her membership of the British Commonwealth of Nations. In 1921 the Irish Free State became a dominion. She was not, for reasons I suggested in a talk I gave on 'The Dominion Settlement' in an earlier Thomas Davis series,[1] a natural dominion. She had not, like Canada or Australia, moved gradually from colonial to dominion status; on the contrary, she had acquired a dominion status her leaders had never sought as a result, not of evolutionary, constitutional processes, but of revolutionary action. None the less having become a dominion, the meaning, development, expansion and finally the supersession of that status became the chief preoccupation of successive Irish governments in their external policies.

Broadly speaking there were two possible Commonwealth policies for Irish governments after 1921. The first was to refashion the Commonwealth in closer accord with Irish interests and outlook; the second to seek the first opportunity to unravel, or by one dramatic revolutionary stroke to sever, Irish ties with the Commonwealth. These alternatives, again speaking very broadly, were pursued in turn by President Cosgrave's government from 1922 to 1932, and by President de Valera's administration from 1932

---

* First broadcast as a Thomas Davis lecture by Radio Éireann
[1] Reprinted in Desmond Williams (ed.), *The Irish Struggle, 1916-1926* (London, 1966). [*Reproduced in this volume as Chapter 6.*]

onwards. Behind them lay different assessments of Commonwealth potentialities, of Irish interests, not least in terms of national unity, and perhaps most of all of personal temperament and political instinct.

In 1926 the time was favourable for the pursuit of the first policy – that is to say, of a policy of constructive reinterpretation of Commonwealth ties in terms more congenial to Irish ears and more in accord with Irish interests and aspirations. In the summer of that year dominion leaders gathered together in London for an Imperial Conference. The emotions and thoughts of the day were summed up in one word – status. The principal task of the conference was to consider and, if possible, to define the status of the dominions and their relations with Britain. This may sound now an exercise in political abstractions; at the time, however, it was thought of, and probably rightly, as a last chance to reconcile dominion liberties with Commonwealth unity. Before he left Cape Town, the South African Prime Minister, General Hertzog, warned that he would set the veldt on fire with a campaign for republican independence if dominion equality with Britain were not recognized. The conference, when it met, set up an Inter-Imperial Relations Committee to find a satisfying formula. Kevin O'Higgins was the Irish representative. He worked closely with the Canadians throughout and with the South Africans in the later stages. He felt that the direction was right, that substantial headway was being made and remarked that one would need to have been at the Imperial Conference of 1923 'to realize the vast change in our position'.[2] The chairman of this committee was Lord Balfour, now in his old age and with memories of Mitchelstown far behind him. In Kevin O'Higgins's memorable comment, Balfour presided over the committee's deliberations with 'a smile like moonlight on a tombstone'. But more important he produced a formula in a situation where a formula was not easy to find. The formula has passed down to history. It defined the relations of Great Britain and the dominions in these words: 'They are autonomous Communities within the British Empire, equal in status, in no way subordinate one to another in any aspect of their domestic or external affairs, though united by a common allegiance to the Crown, and freely associated as members of the British Commonwealth of Nations'.

To the Balfour formula all subscribed. But there were things contained in it which some delegates liked a good deal better than others – the Australians and New Zealanders, for example, being insistent on the opening references to the British Empire, the Canadians, South Africans and Irish placing all their emphasis on the concluding British Commonwealth of Nations. There was no doubt, however, on which side the future lay.

---

[2] Quoted in T. de V. White, *Kevin O'Higgins* (London, 1948), p. 221. See Chap. XIV generally.

Equality was proclaimed to be the root principle of British Commonwealth relations. Equality meant, *negatively* the ending of legal or constitutional inequalities as between Britain and the dominions and *positively* the opening of the high road to further advances in dominion nationalism. The Commonwealth was well on the way to becoming, in fact as well as in name, a Commonwealth of Nations. That was important for all of them but more important for the Irish Free State than for any of them. 'We have brought home the bacon', said the South African Prime Minister, General Hertzog, to the cheering burghers of Pretoria. 'Irish bacon', commented Kevin O'Higgins tersely.

The equality proclaimed in 1926 was given practical application in succeeding years. At the Imperial Conference of 1930 and in the drafting of the Statute of Westminster, the Irish played their full part. Mr Patrick McGilligan, the Irish delegate to the 1930 Conference, declared in July 1931 that, with the passage of the Statute of Westminster, the imperial system 'which it took centuries to build' was finally demolished. In its place there was a Commonwealth of Nations. It was not an Empire. It was an association of free and equal nations. And the Irish Free State was one among them. But was *it* free? Mr McGilligan's political opponents were by no means convinced. What of the Treaty, that Treaty imposed under threat 'of immediate and terrible war'? What about the hated oath of allegiance? What about the Governor-General residing in the old Vice-Regal Lodge and symbolizing the presence of the Crown in the Constitution? What about Irish neutrality with the Treaty ports in British hands? What about the right of secession itself? All these questions were asked; they were the coin of contemporary political controversy. And some at least of them were soon to be put to the test. The second wave of Irish revolutionary nationalism sweeping Mr de Valera into office early in 1932 ensured that – and a good deal more besides. The period of Irish refashioning of the Commonwealth ended before it had really begun.

To understand what followed in the second phase of Irish policy it is necessary to pause and reconsider some things from the past. The first article of the Treaty had declared that the Irish Free State should have the same constitutional status as the Dominion of Canada, the Commonwealth of Australia, the Dominion of New Zealand and the Union of South Africa, and the third article more particularly defined Irish status by reference to that of Canada, the oldest dominion. The Treaty as a whole was vested with the force of fundamental law, both the Constituent Act and the Constitution declaring that if any provision of the Constitution, or of any amendment thereof, or any law made thereunder was in any respect repugnant to any provision of the Treaty, it was to the extent of such repugnancy 'absolutely void and inoperative'. But was there not and had there not been always the possibility of conflict here? Canadian status was not fixed;

it was changing, it was developing fast. In Ottawa there was the Liberal Mackenzie King with his lifelong suspicions of imperialist machinations in Downing Street to see to that! Was it not the case that under the earlier provisions of the Treaty, Irish status should likewise develop and advance? But what if such advances were in conflict with other provisions of the Treaty? Was Irish status then to be regarded to that extent as frozen and immutable? English diehard opinion took this view and sought to except the Irish Free State from the Statute of Westminster on that ground. President Cosgrave objected; the Irish Free State was not excepted. President de Valera came to office. He announced his intention of removing the oath of allegiance from the Constitution. It was mandatory under the Treaty – though President de Valera voiced his doubts even about that. But was it mandatory under the statute of Westminster? President de Valera, it is true, did not pose this question; after all the statute was a British enactment. He deployed instead arguments grounded in national right. He told J. H. Thomas, the Secretary of State for the Dominions, on 22 March 1932, that the Constitution was the people's Constitution; that the government had an absolute right to modify it as the people desired. The people had declared their will. There was no ambiguity about their resolve to remove the oath. It was a relic of medievalism and an intolerable burden. It was the cause of all the dissension in Ireland since the Treaty. It made friendly relations with Britain impossible. It was a test unparalleled in treaty relationships between states, and it had been imposed under threat of immediate and terrible war.[3] It had to go and it was clear it was going, whatever the British government or the lawyers might say.

Was President de Valera in his assault upon the oath challenging the sanctity of the Treaty settlement as a whole? Mr Thomas, after some increasingly acrimonious exchanges, in which the area in dispute was widened both constitutionally and also economically by the Irish government's decision to retain Irish land annuity payments, was convinced that this was so. He maintained that the oath was mandatory under the Treaty, that it was an integral part of the 1921 settlement and that the Treaty as a whole was an agreement 'which can only be altered by consent'. In brief, he took his stand upon the twin foundations of constitutional law and contractual obligation. President de Valera, on the other hand, as was evidenced by his rejoinder to J. H. Thomas of 5 April 1932, continued to rest his case in the last resort upon indefeasible national sovereignty. 'Whether the Oath was', he said, 'or was not an integral part of the Treaty made ten years ago is not now the issue. The real issue is that the Oath is an intolerable

---

[3] The statement of 22 March 1932, here summarized, and the subsequent exchanges referred to below were reprinted in a British White Paper, Cmd 4056 and an Irish White Paper, P. No. 650.

burden to the people of this State and they have declared in the most formal manner that they desire its instant removal.' They desired the removal
of other things besides; and following the abolition of the oath in 1933,
there came a series of constitutional amendments culminating in the abolition of the office of the Governor-General, the keystone as it were of the
dominion constitutional arch, in 1936. The Constitution of 1922 in consequence became a thing of shreds and patches and whatever validity the
Treaty continued to possess, in contractual terms, it had lost in law since
the Removal of the Oath Act 1933 deleted the 'repugnancy clause' from
the Constitution. By 1936, therefore, the second policy, of which I spoke,
the revolutionary policy of breaking with the Commonwealth, neared its
climax. But the climax was delayed. Why?

The most important reason was concern for unity – an issue that was
part external, part domestic. Might it not be that further advances towards
republican sovereignty would impose a further barrier against national reunion? The question was debatable but at least its existence counselled
caution. Another reason is often overlooked. Parallel with the renewed up-
surge of Irish revolutionary nationalism there were, almost unnoticed in
Ireland, constitutional developments in the Commonwealth which, while
different in ultimate purpose, none the less in many respects kept pace with
Irish advances. Let me give two illustrations. First, a simple matter of fact
– it was not the Irish in November 1933 but the Canadians in May of that
same year who were the first to abolish appeals in criminal cases to the
Judicial Committee of the Privy Council. And secondly, the existence of
a curious legal paradox. The Irish courts, basing themselves on the Constitution of 1922 and the fundamental authority it gave to the provisions
of the Treaty, as late as 1934, maintained that the Irish government were
acting *ultra vires* in their constitutional reforms, because no power had
been conferred upon them by which they were entitled to repeal the
repugnancy clause in the Constitution. But what view was taken by the
Judicial Committee of the Privy Council, the highest appelate tribunal
in the Commonwealth, in London? They concluded, in a judgement
delivered in 1935, that the effect of the enactment of the Statute of
Westminster, the legal charter of dominion liberties, was to remove the fetter
that lay upon the Irish Free State legislature and that accordingly the
Oireachtas had become free to pass legislation repugnant to imperial legislation – in which the Treaty had also been embodied – and noted that they
had in fact done so. In other words, in British law, though not in Irish,
Mr de Valera's revolution was not in a narrow legal sense a revolution at
all. He had done in the constitutional field what under British law he was
entitled to do after 1931. It was J. H. Thomas who on this point had had
the ground cut away from under his feet. In general, the fact that the
overseas dominions were on the march towards independence within the

Commonwealth helped to defer the day of Irish departure to independence outside it.

This was more strikingly illustrated late in 1936. In December of that year, King Edward VIII, resolved to marry Mrs Simpson against the advice of his government, abdicated. Under the Statute of Westminster this required action on the part of all dominion governments. What action was Mr de Valera to take? He was at the time occupied in drafting a new Constitution. It would clearly have been at once more convenient and more logical to determine future relations with the Commonwealth after, and not before, the new Constitution was approved. But the Irish convenience and logic were minor casualties of royal impetuosity. The determination of external relations accordingly had to come before the Constitution. On 11 December 1936, Mr de Valera introduced two pieces of legislation: a Constitution amendment bill and an External Relations Bill. He assured Mr Cosgrave that they did not amount to a proposition to sever 'our connection with the states of the British Commonwealth'. But the first Act removed the King from the legislature, the executive and the Constitution generally; the second, the External Relations Act, proceeding from this elimination of the Crown in respect of internal government, allotted to it a narrowly defined place and limited functions in the external field. Diplomatic and consular representatives were to be appointed and every international agreement to be concluded on the authority of the Executive Council. But, so long as the Irish Free State was associated – and I quote because the precise wording is important – 'with the following nations, that is to say, Australia, Canada, Great Britain, New Zealand, and South Africa, and so long as the King recognized by those nations as the symbol of their cooperation continues to act on behalf of each of those nations (on the advice of the several governments thereof) for the purposes of the appointment of diplomatic and consular representatives and the conclusion of international agreements, the King so recognized may, and is hereby authorized to, act on behalf of Saorstát Éireann for the like purposes as and when advised by the Executive Council so to do'. It will be noticed that the Act was permissive and conditional. The procedure it outlined *might* be followed so long as the Commonwealth countries continued to cooperate and so long as they owed allegiance to the Crown. But permissive and conditional as it was, it acknowledged the rôle of the Crown in the Commonwealth without an explicit, or indeed implicit, recognition of Irish allegiance. The Constitution, when enacted in 1937, effected no change, but in a somewhat ponderously phrased article sanctioned the regulation of external affairs in this or other ways as national interest might demand. Relations with Britain and the Commonwealth had thus been taken out of the Constitution, where Mr de Valera felt that they had no place, and had become matters of external policy for the government of the day.

This was the most significant development in the whole period.

Taken together the External Relations Act and the new Constitution destroyed the dominion settlement of 1921. The oath had gone, appeals to the Judicial Committee of the Privy Council had gone, the Governor-General had gone, the Crown had been taken out of the Constitution, the Constitution itself had been replaced by a Constitution republican in all but name with an elected President as its head and all that remained on paper of dominion status was the permissive procedure sanctioned by the External Relations Act. What was the British and Commonwealth reaction to revolutionary changes which had substituted for a dominion relationship the external association relationship that had been for so long Mr de Valera's goal and which had been so vigorously repudiated by Lloyd George in 1921? The British government considered the matter; they consulted with dominion governments and in agreement with them they issued a statement. The statement said that the British Government was prepared to treat the new Constitution 'as not effecting a fundamental alteration in the position of the Irish Free State as a member of the British Commonwealth of Nations'. As a piece of understatement this has its place in histoiy. Well might one ask, well may Mr de Valera have asked at the time, what then could effect a fundamental alteration? And yet the British reaction was eminently wise and statesmanlike. Finality was well avoided at the price of inconsistency transparently papered over. And Mr de Valera for his part showed equal reluctance to burn his bridges behind him.

If indeed one looks at the situation in its widest context, here within a framework set by the details of past constitutional enactments was an attempt to experiment in a new form of external relationship, starting on the one side from a foundation in republican nationalism and on the other from dominion precedents broadening down to national independence within a Commonwealth of Nations. The experiment may have been premature, the External Relations Act may well have been, as its critics at home and overseas alleged, too much of an essay in political ingenuity to endure; but none the less many lessons were learned from it – not least by Jawaharlal Nehru, who concluded from it that it was in fact possible for an Indian republic to remain a full member of the Commonwealth.

If relations with Britain and the Commonwealth dominated Irish thinking in this period there was one sufficient reason for it. First, it had to be shown and recognized in principle that Ireland was a sovereign state able to pursue an independent foreign policy and then particular restraints upon her freedom of action had to be considered. The first, freedom in principle, was securely established between 1926 and 1936; the second was deemed conditional upon the abrogation of the articles of the Treaty which gave to Britain the right, in time of peace, to harbour and other facilities in the Treaty ports and in time of war, or strained relations with a foreign power, such harbour and other facilities as the British government might require for the defence of the British Isles. What would be the effect of the exercise of such rights by Britain in war time? Would a belligerent in such circumstances, to pose the crucial question, respect Irish neutrality? The question was one with which Mr de Valera, to judge by his speeches, was increasingly preoccupied. He had been President of the Council of the League of Nations in 1932 and he was convinced even then that the testing time of the League had come. When, following Japanese invasions into Manchuria, Mussolini decided to invade Abyssinia 'with Geneva, without Geneva, or against Geneva', Mr de Valera warned the League: 'Make no mistake, if on any pretext we were to permit the sovereignty of even the weakest state amongst us to be taken away, the whole foundation of the League would crumble into dust'. The Irish government supported sanctions. Opinion at home was troubled and divided. There were complaints moreover that Ireland was in this too closely associated with Britain – though as Mr de Valera observed 'if your worst enemy happens to be going to Heaven by the same road as you are, you don't for that reason turn around and go in the other direction'. The League failed, Abyssinia was followed by the Rhineland; all the portents were of approaching war. What was a small state to do? Mr de Valera, who was throughout his own Minister for External Affairs, was convinced, once collective security had broken down and the League had self-evidently failed, that for a small state there was only one course – neutrality. But was neutrality a possible policy with the Treaty ports in British hands? Mr de Valera, as his exchanges with J. H. Thomas in 1932 testify, was at the least doubtful. But would the British be prepared to cede control on the eve of another world war? The answer, and it was a surprising one, was in the affirmative.

The 1938 Anglo-Irish Agreement was in the nature of a package deal. It ended the economic war and it ceded British rights in the Treaty ports to Ireland. This was very largely the doing of the British Prime Minister, Neville Chamberlain. It is unfair to say, as his critics allege, that he was interested only in the appeasement of great and menacing totalitarian states. He was also interested in the appeasement of Ireland. He was concerned to conciliate, to end the bitterness of centuries. He felt that the return of the ports would further this broad political aim. He was assailed in the House of Commons by Winston Churchill. 'You are', he accused Chamberlain, 'casting away real and important means of security and survival for vain shadows and for ease.' But it would be nearer the truth to say that Chamberlain's action was prompted by faith and it is quite wrong to suppose that he disregarded altogether British strategic interests. On the contrary, he had, as we now know, a memorandum from the British Chiefs of Staff before him which did not on military grounds discourage the course which, for political reasons, he was resolved to pursue.

In the narrower context of Anglo-Irish relations it may be thought that the policy of appeasement bore lasting fruit. In the wider international context it ended in dismal failure. Hitler was not appeased. War came. Ireland adopted a policy of neutrality. She was enabled to do so in principle because the earlier redefining of dominion status coupled with the later vigorous reassertion of her national sovereignty, had freed her from all constitutional obligation or other commitment to go to war when Britain was at war. She was enabled to do so in practice because the Anglo-Irish Agreement of 1938, in restoring the Treaty ports to Irish sovereignty had freed her from the serious risk of involvement by contingent liability. Since a decision on peace or war is the supreme test of sovereignty, it may be concluded, therefore, that the period 1926–39 is marked out in external relations as that in which the dominion that was the Irish Free State at its outset had become the state that exercised unquestioningly the final attributes of sovereignty at its close.

9

SOME DIARY ENTRIES
1934–1939

Wednesday, January 24th, 1934 (Tipperary)

Lemass[1] advocated establishment of National Industrial Research Council in Ireland (see my book).[2] His last night's speech has had a mixed reception. The social democrats are apprehensive of a revival of capitalism. Having got rid of landlordism writes one, we are now being thrust under the tyranny of 'Oliver Cromwell & Co Ltd' . . .

Hear that E. Mansfield[3] and D. Browne[4] have been appointed judicial Commissioners under the New Land Act 1933. Have had several very interesting conversations with the former. His abilities were quite wasted as a Nat. School Teacher. Rather a terror to the more nervous landlords etc. He gave them a good stir up! Browne I have also met when he was Secretary

---

[1] Seán Lemass (1899–1971), in the Easter Rising 1916 and imprisoned several times; Minister for Industry and Commerce 1932–9 and subsequently; Tánaiste 1945 and twice subsequently; Taoiseach 1959–66.

[2] *The Irish Free State: Its Government and Politics* (London, 1934), p. 222.

[3] Eamonn Mansfield (1876–1954), National Teacher, Principal of Cullen National School 1913; President of First National Teachers Organisation 1910–11 and General Secretary 1913–16; Appeal Tribunal Lay Commissioner, Irish Land Commission 1934–50.

[4] Daniel Browne (1895–1959), born Listowel, solicitor, Secretary of the Department of Home Affairs 1920–2; organized Republican Courts; Secretary of the Department of Justice 1933; Appeal Tribunal Lay Commissioner, Irish Land Commission 1934–59.

to the Ministry of Justice. A pleasant man but terribly cautious. He carried it to ridiculous lengths. On the law he was good but about his own ministry a little shaky. Was and is an ardent republican and refused office – as did Mansfield from Cosgrave.

Saturday, May 5th, 1934 (Dublin)

A busy day. Saw Coffey[5] for a few moments. He and O'Sullivan,[6] the Clerk of Seanad, read over the Mss. Thought my opinions radical and made numerous suggestions which I could not see my way to adopting.

Saw Riordan.[7] He thought the Foreword a first class performance saying he would be a proud man had he written it. Was very encouraging saying that the book should prove of great importance and should influence even those in the highest places. A more helpful,[8] a more attractive, a more sincere patriot it has never been my privilege to meet. He is one of the men who has made the Ireland we know and if more of the farmers down the country had met civil servants like him there would be no antagonism between them.

Saw Mansfield at the Land Commission before lunch. He was in great spirits and wanted me to examine the whole of the annuity dispute. Introduced to S. Hayes[9] of the Co. Tipp deputies.

Sunday, May 13th, 1934

Went up to London and had an interesting conversation with R. B. Cunninghame Graham.[10] I tried to extract information from him of the detailed political application of his Home Rule Proposals. But he is concerned with the principle and the principle alone. As he said, good government was an issue very secondary to national government. He spoke with heat of the national disgrace of a depopulated Highlands and the possibility of small farming. But he is at his best when discursive. Memories of George

---

[5] D. Coffey, Assistant Clerk of Seanad Éireann.

[6] Donal Joseph O'Sullivan (1893–1973) scholar, Clerk of Seanad 1925–36; author of *The Irish Free State and Its Senate*, 1940; lecturer on international affairs at Trinity College, Dublin 1949–65.

[7] E. J. Riordan, Controller of Prices.

[8] Above is open to ironic reflections but quite (in this case only) unjust upon my vanity.

[9] Seán Hayes (1890–1968), farmer, last Officer Commanding 3rd Tipperary Brigade IRA; Fianna Fáil TD 1927–37; subsequently served two terms in the Senate; Chairman of Thurles Urban District Council.

[10] Robert Bontine Cunninghame Graham (1852–1936), traveller and prolific writer, journeys, essays, stories and sketches.

Moore, of E. Childers,[11] of Arthur Griffith, of Michael Collins whom he
did not like, of Cathal Brugha[12] who he thought a splendid fellow, of the
Countess Markievicz,[13] of the various writers Scottish and Irish and of
all people the O'Gorman Mahon.[14] His acquaintance with this polished
showman made me realise that I was talking to a man of another and long
distant generation. So two hours or more went by. I knew I was talking
to a master of language, to a great and adventurous figure and yet I went
away a little disappointed. How much substance was behind this polished
and aristocratic conversationalist? But his patronage of the Duke of Mon-
trose was priceless.

Saturday, September 22nd, 1934 (Tipperary)

Sensational news to the effect that General O'Duffy[15] has resigned the
leadership of the Fine Gael Party. It is possible that it was due to an adverse
vote on his policy of refusing to pay rates annuities etc. Cosgrave[16] has
taken his place. That was to be expected though some ill-informed persons believed him to have suffered a permanent eclipse. I noticed when
at the Party Headquarters with what deference the other ex-ministers treated
Cosgrave. If one must have a historical parallel I should compare him with

---

[11] Robert Erskine Childers (1870–1922), elected to Dáil Éireann in 1921 as Sinn Féin
deputy; Secretary to Irish delegation to Anglo-Irish Treaty Conference 1921; opposed
to Griffith and Collins in signing the Treaty; joined IRA; captured in the Civil War
by Free State forces and executed.

[12] Cathal Brugha (1874–1922), severely wounded in Easter Rising; leading part in War
of Independence; Chief of Staff IRA 1917–19; Minister for Defence until 1922; presided at first meeting of the Dáil, 21 January 1919; voted against Treaty; died from wounds
received in Civil War.

[13] Constance Georgina Markievicz (née Gore-Booth) 1868–1927, during the Easter Rising served at the College of Surgeons; sentenced to death, but reprieved 1917; first woman
ever elected to Parliament 1918; opposed the treaty; joined Fianna Fáil in 1926, when
it was founded by de Valera.

[14] Charles James Patrick Mahon (1800–1891), the O'Gorman Mahon, politician and
soldier helped Daniel O'Connell to win the Clare by-election in 1828; extensive traveller;
1871 joined Home Rule party; MP for Clare 1879–85, and for Carlow 1887–91.

[15] General Eoin O'Duffy (1892–1944) joined the IRA in 1917, active service in War
of Independence, imprisoned; supported Anglo-Irish Treaty of December 1921; appointed
Chief of Staff in 1922 and Commissioner of Police; dismissed by de Valera in 1933;
leader of the Blueshirts and elected first President of Fine Gael 1933, resigned 1934;
organised and led an Irish Brigade to fight for General Franco in the Spanish Civil War.

[16] William T. Cosgrave (1880–1965), first President of the Executive Council of the
Irish Free State 1922–32; in 1916 Rising and imprisoned several times; from 1932 led
the Opposition in the Dáil until retirement in 1945.

Liverpool[17] for though more energetic and more capable, he is greater as a party leader, as a master of men than as a statesman.

Tuesday, October 9th, 1934

Spent the day in Oxford. Called at All Souls. Adams[18] introduced me to André Siegfried.[19] As I have just started Guy (pupil) reading 'La Crise Britannique' I was able to say the right thing at any rate. His English is good and his appearance distinguished.

Adams thinks the book will have quietly successful career on account of its 'intrinsic merit'. He recommended it to Siegfried!

Thursday, October 11th, 1934 (Westwell)

I received a letter from Prof. M. Hayes.[20] He says, most encouragingly, of my book 'You have done an excellent piece of work . . . The book is fair and accurate and – what is more rare – sympathetic. I suppose the fact of being an Irishman with no political axe to grind gives you an advantage. I hope you will continue in the same field – it never remains quite the same for long'.

For a man who has done a great deal toward shaping the constitutional practice of the Free State, a letter of this kind is most welcome. Sir S.[21] who finds the chapter on political parties absorbing, so he says, thinks I have possibly been too favourable to the Administration.

---

[17] R. B. J. Liverpool (2nd Earl of), (1770–1828), Prime Minister 1812–27, brought the country successfully through the struggle against Napoleon.

[18] Professor William George Stewart Adams (1874–1966), Department of Agriculture for Ireland 1905–10; Gladstone Professor of Political Theory and Institutions, University of Oxford 1912–33; Secretary to the Prime Minister (Lloyd George) 1916–19; seconded to serve as adviser to the Prime Minister on Irish affairs 1917 and assisted in establishing the Irish Convention; Warden of All Souls College, Oxford 1933–45; he supervised the author and wrote the Foreword to his first book.

[19] André Siegfried (1875–1959), writer and professor, numerous publications including *La Crise Britannique au xx*[e] *Siècle*, 1931.

[20] Michael Hayes (1889–1976), politician and professor; fought in 1916 Rising; interned 1920; elected to Dáil for National University of Ireland, 1921; Ceann Comhairle (Speaker) of Free State Dáil 1922–32; Seanad 1938–65; Professor of Irish, University College, Dublin 1951.

[21] Sir (Reginald) Sothern Holland (1876–1948), born in Cape Province, wartime service in London, Director-General of Munitions Inspection 1915; Chairman of Central Mining and Investment Corporation Ltd, 1943–5 and earlier; his son, Guy, was a pupil of the author at Westwell Manor, near Burford, Oxon.

Friday, October 12th, 1934 (Westwell)

My book was well advertised today.[22] I came across the one in the Times and another fuller one in the New Statesman.

Monday, October 22nd, 1934 (Westwell)

Received a very cordial letter from W. T. Cosgrave. He pointed out that 'owing to a mild political sensation of which you may have heard' he had been as yet unable to read the book. The mild sensation is O'Duffy's resignation and subsequent activity. How the gallant General would appreciate the description! But that is Cosgrave's characteristic quality – a quiet sub-acid humour.

Tuesday, January 15th, 1935 (Dublin)

Went to see Hearne[23] at the M of ExA's [Ministry of External Affairs]. He was in his best form and widely discursive about his Geneva visit. Apparently after de V's Russian speech the Morning Post wired their correspondent that they desired full text of his speeches in future! Incidentally he tells me that President is reading my book and has reached p. 191. An impressive distance! Also developed his characteristic proposals with regard to Kingdom of Ireland instancing analogy of Norway and Sweden in 1901. Lent me a copy of Balfour's[24] Intr. to Bagehot.[25]

Riordan came round to lunch with me at the Hibernian. While waiting met B. [Browne] who tells me Hatch died before Xmas. R. [Riordan] in fine form and going off for a holiday at end of month. Tells me a lot of people borrowing vice buying my book. Expected Eng. sales to have been larger. Also Ed. I. P[26] very interested in book but for some political reason nervous

---

[22] Its publication was signalled in *The Observer*'s Diary of the Week, 'other chief books appearing this week . . . Tuesday'.

[23] John J. Hearne (1893–1969), constitutional lawyer and diplomat, legal adviser to Irish delegation to Imperial Conferences 1926, 1929 and 1930 and to Department of External Affairs 1929–37; 'architect-in-chief' and draftsman of the Constitution of Ireland, 1937; High Commissioner to Canada 1937–50; Ambassador to USA 1950–60.

[24] Arthur James Balfour (1st Earl) (1848–1930), Chief Secretary for Ireland 1887–91, Prime Minister 1902–5; Foreign Secretary 1916–19; 1926, the Balfour Report, which led to the Statute of Westminster 1931.

[25] Walter Bagehot (1826–1877), economist and influential journalist, author of *The English Constitution*, 1867.

[26] Frank Gallagher (1898–1962), journalist, took Republican side after the Treaty, imprisoned, hunger strike; first editor of *The Irish Press*, 1931; Radio Éireann, Director of Government Information Bureau 1939–48 and 1951–54; the National Library.

of reviewing. General impression that though impartial my leanings are to the left.

Wednesday, January 16th, 1935 (Dublin)

At one o'clock went round to see Prof. Hayes at National [University]. He was the complete party politician unable to restrain himself because of result, of election to Senate. He wished to introduce me to Father O'Keeffe who had reviewed my book so well in Studies. But latter out. Asked for some introductions in the North which he promised to give me. I said I should be glad to meet violent politicians of both parties up there but quite firmly he said no: 'There are people up there' he said 'whose politics are no more intelligent than the beating of an orange drum'. And he seemed to think I might be contaminated.

Saturday, February 23rd, 1935 (Westwell)

Worked in the morning and then into Oxford to lunch with Frank Hardie. The Oxford University Press have accepted his book[27] for publication and it should come out early in the summer. As regards his general outlook I was somewhat disappointed to note the rigidity both of his rationalism and his socialism. By which I do not mean to criticise the consistency of his outlook but the narrowness of premises. He builds, to my mind, too much upon too little.

Also suggested that I might care to write a pamphlet on the 'Irish Question' for the Fabian Society. I pointed out (i) that I was not English; (ii) I was not, in any party sense, a Socialist. The objections he considered trivial. The Question therefore is the usual one, Have I time.

Sunday, May 5th, 1935 (Belfast)

Went to the Cathedral for Service. Very *loyal* sermon and bored to extinction. The Cathedral is hideous, lacks proportion, style and beauty.

Went to see R. M. Henry[28] near the University. He is very interesting and obviously very intelligent. Went through all my questions and he is of the firm opinion that N. I. finances need very close investigation. Told

---

[27] *The Political Influence of Queen Victoria, 1861–1901* (London, 1935).

[28] Robert Mitchell Henry (1873–1950), brother of the artist Paul Henry; educated Methodist College; Professor of Latin, Queen's University, Belfast; Member of the Royal Irish Academy; author of *The Evolution of Sinn Féin*.

me that Horgan[29] had written the recent article in the 'Round Table'. Very interesting and apparently Craigavon[30] and Pollock[31] very upset by description 'loan'.[32] Saw O'Leary later. A nice old man and promised to give me an introduction to Campbell.[33]

Sunday, June 9th, 1935 (Tipperary)

Paul Flynn[34] came out to tea but his information on local archaeological remains was sound rather than brilliant. He did however verify the story of the old man – R. M. Mansergh[35] – with regard to Smith O'Brien's[36] rebellion in 1848. O'Brien and he were great friends but he thought rebellion ill advised. When O'Brien was arrested he was tried for high treason at Clonmel. R. M. was foreman of the Grand Jury and it fell to him to announce the verdict – Guilty. It is said that it was three years before he smiled again. Once more in 1865 there was a rising near Tipp. He judged it to be quite hopeless as indeed it proved. Knowing his tenants were involved he summoned them to a meeting a few hours before the appointed time. Once he got them inside the house he walked out and locked the door and so saved them from certain execution.

---

[29] John Joseph Horgan (1881–1967), solicitor, supporter of the Gaelic League and of the Irish Party under John Redmond; Member of Cork Harbour Commissioners 1912–61; publications included *Home Rule: a Critical Consideration* 1911 and *Parnell to Pearse* 1948.

[30] James Craig, first Viscount Craigavon (1871–1940), organised the Ulster Volunteers; 1921 succeeded Carson as leader of Northern Unionists; first Prime Minister of Northern Ireland.

[31] Hugh MacDowell Pollock (1852–1937), Belfast industrialist; Unionist MP at Stormont and Minister for Finance 1921–37.

[32] 'Ulster and the Irish Problem', 5 February 1935, *The Round Table*, Vol. 98, p. 263.

[33] Thomas Joseph Campbell, KC (1871–1946), Editor *Irish News* 1895–1906; Senator 1929–34; MP at Stormont for Central Belfast 1934–46, becoming leader of the Nationalist Party.

[34] Paul J. Flynn (1858–1937), local historian, author of *The Book of the Galtees and the Golden Vein: a border history of Tipperary, Limerick and Cork* (Dublin, 1926).

[35] Richard Martin Southcote Mansergh JP (1800–1876), great grandfather of the author. As foreman he said after delivering the verdict 'We earnestly recommend the prisoner to the merciful consideration of the Government, being unanimously of opinion that for many reasons his life should be spared. For self and fellow-Jurors'. *Report of the Trial of William Smith O'Brien for High Treason at the Special Commission for the Co. Tipperary held at Clonmel, September and October 1849* by John George Hodges, Government Short-Handwriter (Dublin, 1849), p. 887.

[36] William Smith O'Brien (1803–1864), led abortive rising at Ballingarry, County Tipperary, July 1848, arrested, found guilty of high treason, sentenced to death, commuted to transportation for life.

Saturday, June 15th, 1935 (Belfast)

Spent the morning in Ormeau Avenue trying to get hold of a map. When eventually I did get it they charged me 4/-. No doubt at all about the infusion of Scottish blood in Belfast! After lunch watched an Orange procession about 1500 strong march down from Donegal Square. They were carrying Orange banners with illuminated portraits of Dutch William and other persons of note in the Orange mythology. The music had the merit of a vulgar emotionalism. The parade was obviously determined on trouble if possible and was marching straight for Antrim road. It was not surprising to hear later that there were continuous riots throughout the evening.

Going down Belfast Lough at midnight was very impressed by the Harland & Wolff works. There was a full moon behind them and in that romantic light, represented more fully than Stormont or the rather provincial streets of the city, the strength of Belfast.

Sunday, November 24th, 1935 (Dublin)

Went to St. Patrick's Cathedral in the evening. Very empty as usual and I thought the preacher unduly complacent. I am not sure that that is not half the trouble with the Church of Ireland.

On my way to St. Patrick's I met a docker who was not I fancy quite himself. He had a look at me, stopped in the middle of the street and cried 'Glory be to God: sure it's himself'.[37]

Monday, November 25th, 1935 (Dublin)

At the meeting Prof. Edmund Curtis[38] presided. Prof. Liddell,[39] Dr. Dudley Edwards,[40] Miss Armstrong,[41] Willwood etc were present. I

---

[37] There was a physical resemblance between Mr de Valera and the author, which struck a number of people.

[38] Edmund Curtis (1881–1943), Professor of Modern History, University of Dublin; author of *A History of Ireland*, long a standard university textbook, going through many editions from 1936 to 1990.

[39] Maximilian Friedrich Liddell, appointed Lecturer in German, Trinity College, Dublin, December 1933; d. 1968.

[40] Robert Dudley Edwards (1909–88), author of *Church and State in Tudor Ireland*, 1935; DLitt National University of Ireland 1938; Professor of Modern History, University College, Dublin 1945.

[41] Olive Gertrude Armstrong, appointed Lecturer in Political Science, Trinity College, Dublin, May 1934; d. 1958.

thoroughly enjoyed myself, didn't feel a bit nervous reading the paper. It lasted 45–50 minutes. I could see that I had the undivided attention of my audience and the speeches of Lord Randolph and Mr. Asquith which I quoted went very well. The former's definition of Tory Democracy aroused a lot more amusement in this stronghold of Toryism than I expected. In fact the general tone of the discussion afterwards – which was lively – was more to the Left than I expected. The replies were all that the lecturer could wish – and I thought Prof. Curtis's opening remark 'We historians' very happy. Liddell challenged my description of P. [Parnell] as a Separatist. Curtis told me I had drawn the largest house since the society was formed. I learned afterwards that I was expected to be 'very controversial'. My book has been placed on T.C.D. Statutes.

Monday, January 11th, 1937 (Dublin)

At 7.40 I delivered the last of my three broadcasts on 'The Crisis of Democracy'. It was considerably less of a strain than the earlier ones and I must confess to enjoying it quite a good deal. As soon as I finished, the announcer (Hartnett)[42] came in and clasping me warmly by the hand remarked 'Brilliant just brilliant'. This of course was very pleasant and no doubt a large part of his enthusiasm was due to my decisive repudiation of Fascism as a possible system of government. The clerical party love being rather pro Fascist, everyone is inclined to hedge and H. remarked that few would have cared to be outspoken on the point.

Thursday, January 28th, 1937 (Oxford)

Guy warns me not to speak to Sir S. of the Duke of Windsor. During the crisis Sir S. so upset at Edward's behaviour that he went to bed off and on for ten days. Disgusted at Edward's farewell broadcast – thought it lowered the Crown to the lowest gutter of undignified sensationalism. Incidentally story going round that Edward used to make a practice of ringing Baldwin at 7 a.m. and asking 'Well; what are you going to do for South Wales today'.

I think Gallagher's story of the visit of the Archbishop of Canterbury[43] is better – and it appears to be true.

---

[42] Noel Hartnett (1909–1960), barrister and broadcaster; member of National Executive of Fianna Fáil 1933–7; co-founder of Clann na Poblachta 1947.

[43] The Most Rev. and Rt Hon. Cosmo Gordon Lang (1st Baron) (1864–1945), Archbishop of Canterbury 1928–42.

Archbishop of Canterbury (arriving at Fort Belvedere): Good morning.
Edward: Good morning. May I ask Archbishop in what capacity you have
come to see me today?

Archbishop: I have come as the head of the Church of England to speak
on. . .

Edward: (interrupting) Before you proceed may I remind you that I, as
Defender of the Faith, am head of the Church and you will please remember
the fact when speaking to me.

Thursday, June 24th, 1937 (Tipperary)

De Valera speaking at 11pm. P. J. M.[44] was a most flamboyant and
talkative Chairman but de Valera spoke with warmth but without rancour
for about 1¼ hours. It was a severe unadorned well reasoned account of
the Constitution and of the future policy of the party. I was impressed
even when not in entire agreement by his obvious sincerity and still more
by his firm refusal to descend to claptrap. Points from speech were:

(i) I would rather the Constitution were ratified than the F. F. party returned
to power.

(ii) We have tried to decentralise industrial development. It has been difficult and has not been as successful as I should have liked.

(iii) Mr. C. [Cosgrave] blames us for the catastrophic fall in cattle prices
in 1933–35. If it were true – which it is not – then he should give us credit
for the recent rise.

(iv) The Constitution is founded on a philosophy directly contrary to that
of Communism.

Monday, June 28th, 1937 (Tipperary)

Went in to hear Cosgrave after dinner. He was preceded by Col. Ryan,[45]
a soap box orator of some merit and Curran,[46] a former deputy from

---

[44] P. J. Moloney (c. 1868–1947), chemist in Tipperary; interned 1912; elected Sinn Féin
MP 1918; TD 1919–22; house and business burned by Black and Tans 1920; friend of
Eamon de Valera.

[45] Col. Jeremiah Ryan (1891–1960), Thurles, Vice-Commandant of Mid-Tipperary
Brigade of the IRA; took Treaty side in Civil War; resigned from national army in 1924;
leading figure in Blueshirt movement; defeated Cumann na nGaedheal candidate 1933;
Fine Gael TD 1937–44; made way for General Richard Mulcahy, leader of Fine Gael;
Senator 1948–54.

[46] Richard Curran (1879–1961), Carrick-on-Suir; member of Tipperary South Riding
County Council to advance farmers' interests; elected to Dáil for Centre Party January
1933; defeated as Fine Gael candidate July 1937, but TD again 1938–43.

Carrick. I thought Curran quite sound. Cosgrave got a magnificent reception and dealt effectively with interruptions. But the rest of his speech was not so good. He meandered on about some letter of his being opened in the Post Office to obvious boredom of the crowd. When he raised good points, it was only to play with them and then go off on some side issue. The speech was a disappointment to the most ardent Fine Gael supporters. Points he made:

(i) Vote against the Constitution. The President is an expensive office and menace of abuse of power.
(ii) Would make settlement with Britain.
(iii) Failure of F. F. regime shown in export of young boys and girls to find work in British market. (This aroused no little applause.)
(iv) Denunciation of calf-slaughter and advocacy of return to cattle farming. He recommended by implication maintenance of wheat scheme but farmers uneasy here.
(v) Rationalise new industries to lower cost of living. Industrialists (e.g. Bolton) uneasy here.

Tuesday, June 29th, 1937 (Tipperary)

The [M-Ms of B] came to lunch. He was pleasant. She was English and had in full measure that rather insolent contempt for all things Irish. The election campaign is quiet – therefore it is described as 'ominous'. If it were noisy she would say 'so Irish'. One would not mind this sort of thing if the people who said it could possibly be regarded as industrious, competent or of more than average intelligence; but with rare exceptions the products of the 'gentry' here seem to me the most incompetent, the most critical and in many instances the most idle people I have met. I am one of them myself.

Wednesday, January 26th, 1938 (Oxford)

I dined with Frank Pakenham[47] at the House[48] in the evening. Brogan[49] was there as well so had the lowdown on University politics. Lionel

---

[47] Francis Aungier Pakenham (b. 1905), later Earl of Longford; student in Politics, Christ Church, Oxford, 1934–46 and 1952–64; prospective Labour candidate for Oxford City 1938; various ministerial appointments and numerous publications including, *Peace by Ordeal* (the Anglo-Irish Treaty of 1921) and with T. P. O'Neill the biography of *Eamon de Valera* 1970.

[48] Christ Church, Oxford.

[49] Sir Denis (William) Brogan (1900–1974), Professor of Political Science, Cambridge University 1939–68; author of *The American Political System,* 1933, *The Development of Modern France 1870–1939,* 1940 and many other publications.

Curtis[50] and Sir Alfred Zimmern[51] mentioned as possibilities for head of Nuffield College. I should strongly support Zimmern. Had a very interesting time with Wheare[52] whose book is coming out shortly. Frank Pakenham expressed his views on Irish Politicals.

Sunday, February 13th, 1938 (Oxford)

I lunched with the Warden and Mrs Adams at All Souls and I enjoyed myself as I always do there. They are so naturally kind, so wise and so sincere that they create the perfect background for friendly intelligent conversation. L. S. Amery[53] was there, Mrs Amery and the son and a Miss Manson or Nanson of whom I felt I should know something but don't and Professor Radcliffe Brown.[54] Conversation turned onto the papers of Childers and Warden H. that had recently come to light and Miss M. urged the importance of keeping a completely unselfconscious diary. I think I was the only person who kept one at all and I doubt if it qualifies in that important respect. But even a record of incident and the externals of life may be of interest sometime. Though my own life may prove supremely dull to everyone except myself I am living at a time when men believe that the foundations of our civilisation are in danger of destruction. Even now when I am 27, I who was born in the last year of King Edward's reign, a citizen of the U.K. of G.B. and Ireland, can remember the troops leaving for the front in 1914, can remember stories of the Easter Rising of 1916, was fully conscious of the Anglo-Irish war and the civil war that followed as I was then all the time in Tipperary, where I greeted Republicans and Free Staters alike with equal enthusiasm; I became politically conscious in the last years of the Cosgrave régime, I lived through and suffered financially by the economic war and the world depression, as an Oxford

---

[50] Lionel Curtis (1872–1955), served in South African War; government work in the Transvaal; Beit Lecturer on Colonial History, Oxford; Secretary to the Irish Conference 1921; Adviser on Irish Affairs to the Colonial Office 1921–4; believed in World Federation; *Civitas Dei; World Revolution in the Cause of Peace* and numerous publications.

[51] Professor Sir Alfred Zimmern (1979–1952), Professor of International Relations, Oxford 1930–44; work in education and with UNESCO; ed. *Modern Political Doctrines* 1939; numerous publications.

[52] Sir Kenneth Clinton Wheare (1907–1979), Gladstone Professor of Political Theory and Institutions, Oxford University 1944–57; author of *The Statute of Westminster and Dominion Status*, 1938 and *Federal Government*, 1946; Rector, Exeter College, Oxford 1956–72.

[53] Rt Hon. Leopold Stennett Amery (1873–1955), from 1922 various Cabinet posts, Secretary of State for Dominion Affairs 1925–9, for India and Burma 1940–5; numerous publications.

[54] Professor Radcliffe Brown (1881–1935), leading British social anthropologist.

undergraduate I was an adherent of the League and sympathised with the wave of pacifism that swept over England in 1930–33, and felt strongly the justice of the demand for better social conditions, but today when I travel abroad I see a Europe dominated by dictators, watching Hitler in nervous apprehension. I see an England rearming and less sensitive to the horrors of war, whilst in my own country domain I hail the new year – the first year of the Consitution of Éire. What else shall I witness? I hope and believe the collapse of the dictators, the unification of Ireland, the birth of a new international order – but it may be just a Second World War.

Wednesday, May 11th, 1938 (Oxford)

Spoke in the evening at the meeting of the South Africa Society at Rhodes House. It was a sort of round table conference upon the consequences of recent British Foreign policy upon Dominions and Imperial sentiment and interests. Mostly Rhodes scholars speaking while I spoke for about 15–20 minutes upon Irish reactions to League and Imperial policy respectively. Quite a successful meeting. I took the line that the recent Anglo-Eire agreement had so far as Foreign policy was concerned merely papered over the cracks. So long as British policy was League policy and based on collective security then Irish policy would coincide but with the open return to power politics fostered by Chamberlain division would inevitably occur. I argued that a war, say on the issue of Czechoslovakia would probably find England and Ireland united in sympathy for defence of a small nation but that defence of imperial interests in Mediterranean would awaken antipathy in Ireland.

Tuesday, September 13th, 1938 (Tipperary)

Fair day but I had nothing to sell. Business almost at a standstill. Even in Tipperary we are dependent on the antics of a power-intoxicated Führer. It looks very like war today – though I cannot feel that the Western democracies have an entirely satisfactory casus belli in the refusal of a plebiscite in the Sudeten districts. But Hitler has been so utterly unreasonable in refusing to instruct H. [Henlein] to negotiate that he is quite likely to put himself still further in the wrong. Everything if it came to war will depend on the efficiency of the Russian army – an unknown quantity, on the decision of Poland and the little Entente. Italy one takes it will prefer neutrality and the U.S.A. would not become embroiled for some six months.

Saturday, September 17th, 1938 (Tipperary)

. . . Feeling depressed. The exhilaration of Chamberlain's dramatic flight to Berchtesgaden has worn off and looked at coldly the situation shows little improvement except that it is now possible that a settlement will be reached by granting Hitler's demands in substance, notably that for a plebiscite at the expense of Czechoslovakia. I was very interested to see that Sir Horace Wilson[55] who so kindly showed me over No. 10 Downing Street when I went to see him in July was one of Chamberlain's two companions in his flight.

. . . Feeling depressed because also Allen and Unwin are unwilling to publish my new book,[56] not on the ground of merit but because they can see little or no financial profit in it as so few people in Ireland read any serious books. This latter is obviously true. So that means looking around for another publisher – always a slow and thankless job even if successful.

Monday, September 26th, 1938 (Tipperary)

The international crisis is dominating everything. People are no longer hoping for peace but for a short war. But they will hardly get it. Opinion here in the working classes is very strongly anti-Hitler, only in Church circles is some favour shown him – surprisingly enough I had a conversation with Father O'Ryan this morning. He said Eden was a mischievous warmonger

(i) because Franco says so
(ii) because Eden's wife is a Jewess or has Jewish relations
(iii) that like all left wing pacifists of a few years ago he now urges war because it will be followed by a Red revolution in Germany or France, i.e. in whichever is defeated.

He also took the line that sanctions in Italy were ridiculous so long as England held India by force. This was a possible and arguable point – on the rest a wide gulf divides us.

Tuesday, September 27th, 1938 (Tipperary)

Prospects of peace seem hopeless now. No note of optimism was sounded in Chamberlain's speech in the evening. It was a sincere and impressive

---

[55] Sir Horace John Wilson (1882–1972), Chief Industrial Adviser to the Government 1930–9; became Chamberlain's closest adviser on almost everything, especially foreign affairs; Chamberlain's sole companion at Berchtesgaden meeting with Hitler.
[56] *Ireland in the Age of Reform and Revolution* (London, 1940), which Allen and Unwin did publish.

speech except for an apparent willingness to respond to aggression by neutrality. What precisely the Prime minister meant in saying that 'a great Empire – cannot be involved in war' in defence of a small state no matter how much its sympathies may be stirred unless wider issues are involved is incalculable. The A.R.P. [air-raid precautions] preparations in London are certainly in anticipation of the worst.

Friday, September 30th, 1938 (Tipperary)

The Four Power Agreement at Munich hailed with relief everywhere. Anti-German feeling very strong – though L. told me he liked working under a German foreman on the Shannon scheme[57] rather than under an Irish. But he said they were very excitable – when a truck slipped back on siding they shouted around 'like a lot of women'. But the relief is great in the middle-classes anyway because of a deeply-ingrained belief that the Communists would gain control in Germany and possibly in France which anyway is 'half-Red' already. For my own part, I distrust close collaboration between England and Germany such as Chamberlain would like and feel that Czechoslovakia was treated with unseemly discourtesy by her allies.

Monday, October 24th, 1938 (Oxford)

There was a meeting of the Bryce Club in the evening at which Mr Einstein for 10 years U.S.A. ambassador at Prague was the speaker. He said nothing very remarkable but it was noticeable afterwards in discussion that opinion here is alarmed to an extent that seems to me unwarranted. For example I suggested to the speaker that if Hitler was going to throw over-board the Bismarckian principle of limited liability and to antagonise both Russia in the N. East and England by colonial demands under threat of fleet building, then once again the penalty of overreaching ambition would have to be paid. But the suggestion was ridiculed and distinguished men as Ensor,[58] Keir[59] and the speaker insisted that Germany is probably in control of some 200,000,000 people by expansion in Europe, would be invulnerable by any combination of powers. Perhaps so – but I remain very

---

[57] The Shannon scheme, initiated in 1925 and in operation by 1929, was a vast hydro-electric undertaking, carried out with the assistance of German expertise. It became a showpiece of innovation and has been described as 'a potent symbol of nationhood'.

[58] Sir Robert Charles Kirkwood Ensor (1877–1958), Oxford historian and leader-writer; author 1936 of the *Oxford History of England 1870–1914*.

[59] Sir David Lindsay Keir (1895–1973), Master of Balliol College, Oxford 1949–65; author of *The Constitutional History of Modern Britain* 1938.

sceptical and think on the whole that German strength is now over-estimated.

Wednesday, December 14th, 1938 (Dublin)

Had an interesting conversation with MacNeice[60] – apparently the invitation to Dr. Gregg[61] to go to Armagh was *not* unanimous. MacNeice thought his refusal a great mistake chiefly because of impression that the Church of Ireland was divided between north and south. He wrote to Gregg strongly at the time. At the moment, the election takes place tomorrow, the issue is doubtful. Gregg would go to Armagh but not on a bare majority. In ignorance of this a great number of Bishops have pledged support to someone else. Can they withdraw or do they wish to? MacNeice himself of course would be admirable.

Tuesday, December 20th, 1938 (Dublin)

After dining at the Club I went to a meeting of the Irish Historical Society at the R.H.A. [Royal Hibernian Academy]. McDowell[62] was reading a paper on Russell of the United Irishman. Talking at his customary excessive speed, McDowell in the end proved extremely difficult to stop for when the Chairman rose to conclude the meeting with 'We must thank Dr. McD', McDowell interrupted with 'Well I don't know about that Mr. Chairman' and was off for another half-hour. But he is an extremely nice fellow and I think a very sensible one. Dudley Edwards was there and also George Ramsay.[63]

Saturday, January 28th 1939 (Oxford)

Went down to lunch with the Vernons[64] on Campden Hill. Mostly

---

[60] The Right Rev. John Frederick MacNeice (1866–1942), Bishop of Cashel and Waterford 1931–5; father of the poet Louis MacNeice.

[61] The Most Rev. John Allen Fitzgerald Gregg (1873–1961), Archbishop of Dublin 1920–38; Primate of All Ireland 1939–59.

[62] Professor Robert Brendan McDowell (b. 1913), Fellow of Trinity College, Dublin since 1951; historian, mainly of nineteenth century; author of *The Irish Administration 1801–1914* 1964, *The Irish Convention 1917–18* (London, 1970) and many other publications.

[63] George David Ramsay (1909–1992), born in Dublin, Fellow and Tutor in Modern History, St Edmund Hall, Oxford from 1937; author of *The Wiltshire Woollen Industry in the 16th and 17th centuries* 1943.

[64] Roland Venables Vernon (d. 1942), Colonial Office and extensive overseas assignments; joint editor with Nicholas Mansergh of *Advisory Bodies – A Study of their Uses in relation to Central Government 1919–1939* (London, 1940).

devoted to a consideration of editorial problems but he was also recalling his collaboration with Erskine Childers at the National Convention of 1917. Apparently he liked Childers very much but thought his outlook very rigid and doctrinaire. Childers drafted the Lord O'Donnell Memorandum and Vernon thought this improper for a civil servant. After he was presented with a gold watch, he asked Vernon whether he should accept it. Vernon replied 'You have done so much damage already you might just as well accept the watch'. Apparently Childers was taken aback. When Vernon told Churchill that he had been shot, Churchill said 'in this silly way', 'There is a fitting end to a dangerous revolutionary'.

I listened to the Prime Ministers's speech in the evening. Three things stood out.

(i) Appeal to peoples for peace against rulers.
(ii) Emphasis on England's future air strength which seemed a direct invitation to Hitler to strike *now*.
(iii) The comparison between his own career and that of the younger Pitt.

Saturday, February 25th, 1939 (Oxford)

The latter part of this week has been one continuous rush. Today I was most of the afternoon in Salter's rooms. Sir Horace Wilson turned up at 4.30. I was rather less impressed than when I met him at No. 10. For one thing he is not as tall as I imagined nor are his grey eyes quite so penetrating. There was a very large audience to meet him and I think I might well congratulate myself on the worthiness of the arrangements. Among the rather unexpected guests was Sir William Beveridge[65] who was a somewhat pertinacious enquirer on matters of detail. Sir Horace who was very discursive was impressive when challenged but was otherwise a little inclined to drift. He was surprisingly right in politics and spoke continually of Trade Unions almost as the enemy. He was informative but carried his mistrust of general principles to extreme length . . . One can well imagine his success as a negotiator in industrial disputes and he was always very careful not to say more than he meant to.

Sunday, April 30th, 1939 (Oxford)

The end of the first week of term, a week dominated by the prospect of war. On arrival I had a letter from Wolfers who is taking Finals this

---

[65] William Henry Beveridge (1st Baron) (1879–1963), Director of London School of Economics 1917–37; Master of University College, Oxford 1937–45; 1942 the Beveridge Report, which helped to shape welfare state policies and institutions.

summer saying that he found it almost impossible to concentrate on his work since it seemed likely war would come before June. I still hold to the opinion that the Germans will try and get their harvest in before embarking on so risky a venture. But anything may happen in so inflammable a situation. The introduction of conscription in the 20–21 age group has created a considerable stir but is on the whole approved. I attended a very crowded Union debate on Friday with Randolph Churchill the principal speaker on the conscription side. Could not but recall the high tide of pacifism only 7 years ago when R. C. was the villain of the King and Country debate. This time R. C. was brilliant and his devastating attack on Chamberlain 'that silly old man who is now on the run' was greatly applauded. He made the gloomy prognostication that within 5 months more than half the members of the Union would be dead and one's only consolation was that perhaps he has inherited Winston's notorious lack of judgment. I stayed up in the evening discussing the situation with the Dean.[66] Typically English in his innate arrogance he does not believe England could ever be defeated. Consequently he is, as most Englishmen, concerned only with how long the war will last and not with its result. On the whole too he considers it may yet be averted which seems to me an ill-founded hope, though one can still reflect that time is against the dictators. I had tea with Diana Keeton[67] yesterday and apparently the women undergraduates are being expected to stay in Oxford 'to keep the flame of culture lighting' – an unenviable task at such a time I should imagine. I have as yet received no reply to my offer of service – I wonder have Irish bombing activities made them mistrustful of every Irishman? Salter[68] takes a pessimistic view though he clearly thinks some months are still left for further preparations.

My article on Northern Ireland government in the March volume of 'Politica'[69] has had a great success here and even the notices in U.[Unionist] papers in Northern Ireland are quite appreciative and very detailed though indeed they describe me with remarkable unanimity as an 'English' writer.

---

[66] The Rev. Herbert S. Deighton, historian, fellow and Dean of Pembroke College, Oxford.

[67] Wife and Research Assistant of Nicholas Mansergh, December 1939–1991 and editor of this volume of papers.

[68] (James) Arthur Salter (1st Baron) (1881–1975), Gladstone Professor of Political Theory and Institutions, Oxford University 1934–44; Fellow of All Souls; MP for Oxford University 1937–50; important shipping appointments in both world wars.

[69] Vol. IV, No. 15, 'Local Self-Government in Northern Ireland – An Analysis of Cost and Achievement'.

Friday, May 5th, 1939 (Dublin)

Crossed over to Ireland last night to give a lecture to the T.C.D. History Society which was entitled – An Economic Interpretation of 19th Century Irish History, or in other words a critical examination of the views of Marx and Engels in this country. Quite a small meeting compared with my last one owing to exams, another lecture and the Spring Show but I thought a successful one. Miss Armstrong's summary was excellent especially on the philosophic implications. Young Hughes was indifferent but a scholar called Russell impressed me and Eoin O'Mahony[70] spoke at some length on a variety of subjects which had no relevance to the paper whatever but considerable interest none the less.

The subject of the day is whether Litvinov's[71] resignation means a Russo-German rapprochement. If it does, it will be viewed with genuine alarm. Russian isolation seems to me a more probable and only slightly more reassuring prospect.

Monday, May 15th, 1939 (Oxford)

Ensor was expressing the view that war was almost a certainty at the end of July. The German harvest would be reaped by Czechs and by women and the opportunity might well be considered favourable in view of the fact that Anglo-Franco-Russian relations would tend to become closer with the passage of time. The conclusion of an Anglo-Russian alliance would certainly mean war, but if as he thought, war was inevitable in any events, such an alliance was very much to be welcomed. He understood the delay to be due to now obviously unfounded hopes of detaching Italy from the axis and believed that such hopes were fostered in Chamberlain's mind by Lady Chamberlain who was acting as an unofficial go-between in Madrid and Rome and whose influence was most unfortunate. He also believed that Sir Horace Wilson was in favour of delay and preferred to conciliate Rome rather than ally this country with Moscow. The policy in Ensor's view was quite unsound and I agree that Rome is now clearly 'unappeasable' without a change in régime. Ensor believed the war would last about a year, that losses would be spread more evenly over the

---

[70] Eoin ('Pope') O'Mahony (1904–1970), barrister, genealogist, lecturer and raconteur; practised on the Munster circuit; joined Fianna Fáil in 1931, but unable to secure election to either Dáil or Seanad; many contributions to periodicals and author of *The Pathology of Democracy*.

[71] Maxim Litvinov (Wallach) (1876–1951), Soviet Deputy People's Commissar for Foreign Affairs 1921–30 and Commissar to 1939; important part in concluding the Franco-Soviet Pact of 1935; dismissed in May 1939 in preparation for the pact with Hitler.

population as regards age and sex than before and that it was more important than ever for young men to do well in schools – as great tasks will await them when the war is over. I own my view is even more pessimistic.

Part III

Post-War Ireland

10

POLITICAL PARTIES AT THE 1948 GENERAL ELECTION*

In the forthcoming general election in Éire a new party challenges the predominance of the old. Its name is the Clann na Poblachta, or new Republican Party. Its leader, Seán MacBride, a barrister by profession, is the son of Major MacBride, executed in 1916, and Madame Maud Gonne MacBride. A romantic and forceful personality, Mr MacBride appeals to republican-national sentiment, and challenges the social policy of Mr de Valera's government over a wide field. The time has come, he claims, for the old parties to make way. That they achieved much he does not deny, but now they are complacent, they are tired, their record is tarnished. Mr MacBride places his chief emphasis on the need for a new approach. Enthusiasm, integrity in public life, faith in positive political leadership must be restored. Characteristic is the listing among his party's aims of the need to end 'political corruption, quibbling, jobbery and graft'. And characteristic, too, is the party's decision not only that the recent increase in deputies' salaries should be rescinded, but also that party members should not accept salaries for themselves, but pay them into the party's funds. Like reforming and revolutionary parties before them, the new Republicans come forward as the 'sea-green incorruptibles'. However, it is against the broad background of Irish political life in recent years that their prospects must be judged.

---

* In *The Listener* this broadcast is headed 'Will Mr de Valera be beaten?'

While Britain and Ireland are at one in their respect for representative government, the pattern of their politics is very different. In Éire the dominant political force is nationalism. MacBride's party, whose successes in the October by-elections precipitated the general election, is a republican party, whose social aims are subordinate to its direct national appeal. And while post-war dislocation has focused attention on economic and social problems to a degree hitherto unknown, it is an illusion to suppose that this heralds the emergence of a political struggle between right and left, of the kind so familiar in western Europe. The Irish political scene is less simple just because nationalism cuts across the play of social forces. There is nothing illogical in holding at once extreme republican and conservative social views. There is no natural identity, that is to say, between the national left and social left. In the early days of the Irish Free State the Labour Party was a pro-Treaty party – that is to say in favour of the 1921 agreement with Britain – conservative on the national issue. Today when economic conditions throughout the world might suggest that organised labour would be a powerful factor in Irish politics, the two Labour parties, while putting forward fifty-six candidates in all in the election, had no more than twelve seats in the last Dáil.

Social and economic issues may be subordinate, but they are acquiring ever-increasing importance in the eyes of the electorate. After all, the national revolution is complete so far as the twenty-six counties are concerned. That has been the outstanding achievement of Mr de Valera. The programme on which he came to power in 1932 was a nationalist programme. Its economics were those of economic nationalism. The Constitution of 1937, republican in fact if not in name, marked the attainment of Mr de Valera's main objectives (with one exception). It is partition that remains. But as the years go by the problem seems no nearer solution, but Mr de Valera reaffirms his faith that somehow, some day, the boundary will go. 'I am certain Partition must be ended, will be ended . . .', he declared at the twenty-first anniversary of his party last year. But faith is one thing, a programme of immediate action another. In the early, exuberant days of Fianna Fáil it was a programme of action that carried the party from one electoral triumph to another.

The war and Éire's neutrality, on which there was no difference of opinion among the parties and which was regarded as the final vindication of Éire's sovereign independence, possibly prolonged Mr de Valera's period of power. His international experience at the League, his immense prestige at home, his steadying influence, all made him the obvious leader of a country undergoing the most exacting experience of its early nationhood. 'A friendly neutral', he described her after Pearl Harbour, and that policy guided the country till the end. It was an issue arising from neutrality. In 1944 the American note asking for the removal of the 'Axis' legations was presented which provided the background to the last general election. By his reply to the strongly worded note Mr de Valera was considered to have won a clear-cut dialectical victory which an appreciative electorate rewarded a few months later by returning him once again to power with his largest majority.

But Fianna Fáil cannot rest on the laurels of the past. A party so long in office is an easy target for attack; almost everything can be laid at its door, and pretty well everything is! After sixteen years both party and government are said to be showing signs of staleness. There has been an infusion of new blood in high office, but perhaps not enough. A long period of office is not merely a test of innate ability, it is even more a test of staying power. And in the meantime promotion is blocked and the young men of today on the look-out for political opportunities may not look as once they did to Fianna Fáil. The lustre of national achievement tends to be lost in a day-to-day concern with a rapidly rising cost of living; the reputation of the party has been 'smeared' by bitterly resented opposition charges of corruption; they claim that its vitality has been weighed down by the burden of responsibility.

Warning of the October By-elections

Against this background came the October by-elections, whose outcome precipitated the dissolution of the Dáil. Held in Dublin, Waterford and Tipperary, they were preceded by a warning from Mr de Valera that the defeat of the government candidates would be the signal for a dissolution. In both Dublin and Tipperary they were defeated by the new Republican Party, the Clann na Poblachta. More significant even than defeat was the way it was brought about. The elections were of proportional representation, which allows electors to indicate the order of their preferences if the candidate of their choice fails to secure election. The by-elections were made a vote of confidence in the government and the one thing that was clear was the electors, whether supporting parties to the right or to the left of Fianna Fáil, were united in a determination to defeat its candidates. The second preferences of voters both in Dublin and Tipperary made this clear beyond doubt. When candidates representing Fine Gael – Mr Cosgrave's old party – were eliminated, the great bulk of their second preferences went to the new Republican Party on the extreme left. Mr de Valera, already committed to a dissolution, probably welcomed the opportunity of testing opinion throughout the country before the opposition forces could consolidate their position. By-elections after all are a notoriously indifferent guide to the outcome of general elections.

Their results suggest that there has been a decline. But how far it goes remains uncertain. The party retains the great asset of Mr de Valera's personality. Long though he has dominated the Irish scene, he remains by general assent the outstanding figure in it. It is no exaggeration to say that most electors in the forthcoming election will vote pro- or anti-'Dev'. Austere, but not so aloof as is often supposed in this country, Mr de Valera combines intellectual ability with a shrewd political judgement. An Oxford tutor after meeting him for the first time said of their conversation, 'It was like one don talking to another'. This comment would, I think, be accepted by Mr de Valera, but not by many politicians, as a compliment. And yet if he is something of the professor among politicians, he is more than a little of the politician among professors. He is a man of inflexible will – ready to compromise when he has got what he wants.

Apart from its positive assets, Fianna Fáil, by far the strongest of the parties, benefits from the number of its opponents. At the dissolution of the old Dáil the strength of the parties was as follows: Fianna Fáil (Mr de Valera), 76; Fine Gael (General Mulcahy's party), 27; Farmers, 11; Labour parties, 12; Independents, 10; new Republicans, 2. All these parties have nominated candidates of whom there will be the record number of 408 for the 147 seats in the new Dáil. Fianna Fáil has nominated the most with 119. The chief opposition party, Fine Gael, though their representation has declined more or less consistently since Mr Cosgrave fell from power, have a fine record and they rely on the allegiance of a hard core of supporters. They have nominated more than eighty candidates. As the pro-Treaty party, they are to the right of Mr de Valera on the national issue and favour close cooperation with the British Commonwealth. Economically they place greater emphasis on livestock farming; greater dependence on cattle exports to Britain as in the days before compulsory tillage. The recent agreement with Britain has been criticised by them on the ground that it does not go far enough. Socially their outlook tends to be conservative, and among their supporters are to be found many of the larger farmers, the professional classes and former Unionists. The leader General Mulcahy favours a broad-based coalition government in which the experience of his party could be used to advantage. Over against the more dynamic appeal of other parties Fine Gael comes forward in favour of a realistic and moderate policy. But it is widely felt that the electorate may not be swinging once more in their favour and if there is a landslide to the left, they would be the first to suffer. Between Fine Gael and Fianna Fáil there lie the corroding memories of the Civil War. Were it not so, cooperation would no longer seem ruled out in principle. Against a background in which economic problems loom large, the Labour group might be expected to come into its own. It has put forward fifty-six candidates. The party remains divided, partly on the issue of affiliation of the Irish unions with our TUC and this internecine feud seems likely to prove a handicap. The appeal of the Farmers Party, the Clann na Talmhan, is also weakened by internal divisions and it is thought that they will do well if they can retain the eleven seats they now hold.

But it is not with the challenge of the Farmers, nor of Labour, nor even of his old Fine Gael opponents that Mr de Valera is principally preoccupied. It is with the new Republican Party whose successes in October first gave it representation in the Dáil. Like the Roman Consul at the battle of Lake Regillus, who from afar singled out among the Tuscan ranks the most dangerous of his foes

> and far before the rest
> I see the dark grey charger
> I see the purple vest.

so Mr de Valera has marked out Mr MacBride – all the more clearly, be it said, because the horse he rides and the colours he wears have a distinct resemblance to those Mr de Valera rode to battle against Mr Cosgrave long ago. Sensitive like Clemenceau before him and Pandit Nehru in India to-day to opposition from the left, Mr de Valera sees in Mr MacBride's new Republican Party, which has nominated no less than ninety candidates, the critical challenge to his régime.

While there is no national issue in the strict sense of the word in the electoral campaign, there is an all pervasive national background. While all parties are at one in their desire to end partition, it is Mr MacBride of the Republican left who has come forward with the suggestion, attacked by government spokesmen as 'simply childish', that members elected for Northern Ireland constituencies should take their seats in the Dáil. It is also the new Republican Party which has drawn attention to the number of large estates recently acquired by wealthy English settlers, thereby in its view artifically forcing up the price of land against the interest of the native Irish farmer. 'Away with the foreign landlords' is an election cry that has its appeal. On the other hand, while Mr de Valera campaigns with unabated zeal for the revival of Irish, the language is a question on which Mr MacBride favours a less rigid policy.

Attempt to Stabilise Cost of Living

To meet an inflationary economic situation, whose potential seriousness is generally acknowledged, the government introduced a supplementary budget last autumn. Its aim was to stabilise the cost of living by increasing the subsidies on essential foodstuffs. To meet the expenditure involved, income tax was increased by 6d to 7s in the pound and substantially increased duties imposed on many things including beer, spirits and tobacco.

These were remedies of the salutary rather than the popular kind. Moreover left-wing critics claimed that in relation to prices, wages and social services remained too low. Inevitable comparisons with rates prevailing in the United Kingdom reinforced the argument. The wide discrepancy, it was maintained, not only created hardship at home but was also responsible for the drain of emigration.

Mr de Valera and Mr Lemass, the Deputy Prime Minister, have devoted a good deal of attention to these criticisms. Mr de Valera argued, in his tour of County Clare, higher wages in Britain where they exist do not necessarily mean higher purchasing power. It is world shortages that have created underemployment at home. Labour and the new Republican Party are not satisfied. Social services must and can be raised, says Mr Mac-Bride, on the lines successfully followed in New Zealand. Emigration must be checked by a policy of full employment with a basic minimum wage.

Fianna Fáil is concerned to convince the electorate that while it may promise less it can do more for the workers than any of its rivals. The party is a workers' party, declared Mr Lemass, but not a class party because it does not believe in fundamental class antagonisms. According to an interesting analysis published in the *Irish Press*, of its 119 candidates, 45 are working farmers, 18 workers, 11 teachers, 45 professional and business men. The government maintain that living standards in Éire, in fact, compare favourably with any in western Europe, and they emphasise that steady progress towards recovery is dependent upon stable government. And that brings one to the great issue in the election – party government or coalition government.

In other words, can Mr de Valera possibly secure an overall majority – always difficult under proportional representation? Mr de Valera frankly recognises this time that the task is indeed a formidable one. If he does not succeed, what is the alternative? General Mulcahy declares that Fine Gael would welcome a broadly based coalition government. Mr de Valera asks who would compose it. Mr de Valera has categorically stated that for Fianna Fáil it is single party government or nothing. They will not take part in a coalition. If then, the other parties form one, what would be its common policy? Mr de Valera has challenged the opposition parties to declare it before the election.

So far, there has been no pre-election pact. If the results allowed of a predominantly left-wing coalition, there is a good deal of common ground between the Clann na Poblachta and Labour, but are they really moving in the same direction? Those are questions with which Mr de Valera has firmly confronted the electorate in the hope that by then the elements who favour stable government will be won over to his side. The fortunes of Fianna Fáil are generally judged to have risen since the low ebb of the by-elections, and for this the uncertainty about the nature of any alternative government may be mainly responsible. The prospect of government by coalition, likely to prove unreliable and unstable in Mr de Valera's view, has also led him to question once again the merits of proportional representation.

I have tried to give as fairly as I can an account of the parties and policies in the forthcoming election which is likely to mark the breakup of much that has become familiar in the Irish political scene. About its probable result you will not expect me to risk a forecast. Prophecy, as Dr. Johnson said, is the most gratuitous of all forms of human folly. And one last point, I have confined myself almost wholly to domestic politics. But from that no one should conclude that the Irish electorate is insensible or indifferent to the problems confronting the world today. These are not an issue in the election because opinion is agreed on the approach to them. If the ideal of one world is falling before the reality of two, it is quite clear in which world Éire lies. The Russian veto on her candidature for UNO and the offensive explanation given for its use made little impression on a country whose attitude has long since been defined for more fundamental reasons. In the consultations on the Marshall proposals the representatives from Éire have cooperated at all stages and Mr de Valera has displayed particular interest in the recovery of the west. Within this wider area of cooperation the trade agreement with Britain may be taken as the outward sign of the friendly relations between the two countries. Unless I am mistaken, there is growing up in Ireland a conviction that in a world which is becoming smaller as the dangers threatening it grow greater, the field of common interest between Britain, Ireland and the democracies of the west is ever widening.

11

THE IMPLICATIONS OF ÉIRE'S RELATIONSHIP WITH THE BRITISH COMMONWEALTH OF NATIONS*

It is not my intention to review the course of Anglo-Irish relations but to examine in some detail the implications of the political and constitutional relationship between Éire on the one hand and the United Kingdom and the British Commonwealth of Nations on the other in the years of Irish membership of or association with it. That these implications have been of far-reaching importance for Éire itself and for the development of the Commonwealth as a whole is evident and certain, but over and above that they have or have had a particular relevance in a wider field. In Asia, and in many parts of Africa, the British Commonwealth will be confronted with nationally self-conscious peoples balancing in their minds the relative advantages of equal partnership within the Commonwealth and independent existence outside it. Many factors will determine their choice and among them the psychological factor will be by no means least. However different in form, the problem that now confronts British statesmanship is the same in essentials as that which confronted it in Ireland a quarter of a century ago. The problem, broadly stated, is that of associating a people with a cultural tradition of its own and an intensely national outlook

* This lecture, which popularises Mr de Valera's pioneering concept of external association, was written after the author's return from the 1947 Asian Relations conference in Delhi. It was delivered in Chatham House to a large audience, including cabinet ministers, government officials and diplomats. Subsequently it was referred to the Prime Minister and to a committee, which was examining Commonwealth relations. India emerged as the first republic to be a full member state.

with a group of states whose existence depends upon the reconciliation of individual interests with those of the community as a whole. In 1921 the problem was solved by the grant of dominion status to the Irish Free State. Was this the right solution? Can dominions be made artificially as well as grow naturally? Has the wisdom of the solution been justified in the sequel? Did it display the right psychological approach? These are questions that seem to deserve critical examination. Like India, Ireland is a mother country with a cultural tradition that may be traced back to the earliest centuries of the Christian era, and for that reason, if for no other, recent experience of Anglo-Irish relations is likely to provide a source from which many lessons may be learnt. Of that, those who determine the destinies of India, of Pakistan, of Burma and of the other countries in south-east Asia, are well aware. The possibility of finding a solution to the Dutch–Indonesian problem in some form of 'external association' on the Irish model was examined in the past year and it was also considered, perhaps too casually, as a possible foundation for our future relations with Burma. In both instances, political tensions made progress difficult. But the lasting impression left from these somewhat desultory discussions is that there is a real need for some considered assessment of the concept of 'external association'; of its history in the general context of Anglo-Irish relations, and of the lessons to be drawn from it for application in other fields.

It was on 30 July 1921 that Mr Lloyd George invited Mr de Valera to come to a peace conference in order to 'ascertain how the association of Ireland with the community of nations known as the British Empire can best be reconciled with Irish nationalist aspirations'. That, concisely stated, was the problem on which the prolonged, tense Treaty negotiations turned. To Mr Lloyd George's question there were in fact two answers given. The first was that given by the Irish delegation briefed as they had been before leaving for London by the Dáil, the Cabinet and its President, Mr de Valera. It was external association. Opposed to it was the British answer, dominion status.

The phrase 'external association' was interpreted by the Irish delegates as meaning absolute sovereignty in all internal affairs for an Ireland associated with the British Commonwealth for purposes of common external concern. The significant points in the draft treaty which the Irish delegation took with them to London were: (i) that Ireland be recognized as a sovereign independent state; (ii) that Britain renounce all claim to govern or legislate for Ireland: (iii) that Ireland agree to become an external associate of the Commonwealth on the understanding that in this capacity her status should not be less than that of the 'sovereign partner States of the Commonwealth'. It followed logically from this concept of external association that while Irish citizens and citizens of the British

Commonwealth might and should enjoy reciprocal rights, the idea of a common citizenship had to be discarded. In broader terms, under the original tentative pre-Treaty drafts for external association and in the variant put forward by Mr de Valera and the dissident republicans in Document No. 2 after the Treaty had been signed, Ireland would have been a republic not within the Empire but associated with it. Throughout – and this is important – the emphasis was placed upon Ireland's internal sovereignty, upon which no restriction formal or informal was to be tolerated, to so great an extent that the Irish delegation to the conference were instructed, if compromise they must, to compromise on external affairs. After the issue had been decided Document No. 2, which constituted Mr de Valera's considered alternative to the Treaty settlement, explicitly recorded that the matters of common concern should include defence, peace and war and all matters considered as being of common concern among the members of the British Commonwealth. Throughout, one is left with the impression that agreement in the field of external affairs presented comparatively little difficulty in 1921 provided no concessions of substance or form were asked for the internal field.[1]

It was precisely on the question of the symbols of sovereignty in Ireland that the United Kingdom delegation were least prepared to compromise. Mindful of the problem of Northern Ireland and for more general reasons of policy and sentiment, they were insistent that the bond of unity represented by a common loyalty to the Crown should be recognized and that in conformity with existing practice in the dominions, the King be the head of the state, acting through a Governor-General appointed by him, and that an oath of allegiance to the King, in recognition of his position, be taken by the members of the Irish Parliament. Here the doctrinaire republicans remained adamant; it was an issue on which they were prepared to make no concession. To them as indeed to the United Kingdom delegates the form and symbols of the state were fundamental. The Irish delegation, led by Michael Collins and Arthur Griffith, influenced more by practical considerations than theoretical conceptions, decided on the other hand that dominion status offered a reasonable compromise solution and signed the Treaty. Civil war in Ireland was the sequel.

The Treaty which was signed in December 1921 gave dominion status to the Irish Free State which comprised twenty-six of the thirty-two counties of Ireland. The new state was to have the same constitutional status in the British Commonwealth as 'the Dominion of Canada, the Commonwealth of Australia, the Dominion of New Zealand and the Union

---

[1] See Frank Pakenham, *Peace by Ordeal* (London, 1935), Chapter IV, where a full and authoritative account of the Irish proposals is given. See also Miss D. Macardle, *The Irish Republic* (London, 1937), pp. 600–12, 653–64.

of South Africa'; more particularly the status of the Irish Free State was defined as being that of the Dominion of Canada, and 'the law, practice and constitutional usage governing the relationship of the Crown and of the Imperial Parliament to the Dominion of Canada shall govern their relationship to the Irish Free State'. This intimate association of the Irish Free State with the other dominions was intended to ensure that Ireland should evolve in status step by step with the oversea dominions; that she should feel her position guaranteed by the mere fact that it rested on the same constitutional foundation as theirs; and finally in this way the danger of defining dominion status, of which Lloyd George was so rightly conscious, was wholly avoided. Dominion status was therefore conferred on a country which had not evolved towards it but reached it in one revolutionary step. In 1921, Mr Latham wrote 'the quiet waters of the conventional Commonwealth' were disturbed 'by the immersion of a foreign body'.[2] What have been the consequences?

Between the British view of the Treaty and the Irish there has always been a gulf. The signature of the Treaty was regarded by Mr Churchill, in words which acquired a fuller meaning in 1940, 'as one of the most questionable and hazardous experiments upon which a great empire in the plenitude of its power has ever embarked'. If one may judge by the comments of the press on 7 December 1921, the popular welcome for the Treaty was cordial, all the more cordial because there was in it a sense of relief coupled with a satisfying sense of achievement. The *Daily Telegraph* on 7 December 1921 summed it up in saying 'this event is the greatest that has happened in the internal affairs of the country for generations'. The critics were on the right, the *Morning Post* denouncing the treaty as 'the most disastrous blunder ever committed by a British Government', and their intransigence explains many of the manoeuvres to which Mr Lloyd George felt bound to resort during the negotiations. Not to be overlooked either was the great body of opinion which regarded the whole affair as a tiresome intrusion in the brave, new postwar world. They found their voice in the *Daily Express* which commented: 'Now for business! The settlement of the Irish question throws wide open the door for the entry of the Boom in Trade'.

The Irish reaction is most faithfully reflected in the Dáil debate on the Treaty. There the settlement was endorsed only by a narrow margin of seven votes and even those who supported the Treaty took as their text Parnell's saying that 'no man can set a boundary to the march of a nation'. In other words the pro-Treaty party defended the Treaty as one step forward on the road to independence, while their opponents denounced it as a step sideways leading them on to a road along which they had neither the wish nor the

---

[2] *Survey of British Commonwealth Affairs*, Vol. 1 (London, 1937), p. 513.

right to travel. And to their denunciation was added the condemnation of the dead – of the martyrs of 1916. Nothing throws into clearer relief the width of the gulf that separated English and Irish opinion at that time than the fact that Document No. 2 was put forward by Mr de Valera as a compromise solution embodying every concession which republican opinion was prepared to make. The reaction to it in Britain is well known, but less well known is the fact that to this day doctrinaire republicans in Ireland taunt Mr de Valera with having gone too far and abandoned his principles in a vain search for compromise. No one on the Irish side, except perhaps Mr Arthur Griffith, regarded the treaty as an ideal settlement, though the majority believed it was to be preferred to any practicable alternative. In such circumstances its prospects of survival were clearly slight.

Looking back over the years one reflection can scarcely be avoided. Dominion status despite its flexibility was not the most obvious answer to Mr Lloyd George's question. What place was there for an inflamed self-assertive Irish nationalism in full and equal partnership with a British Commonwealth composed as it then was of states peopled for the most part by immigrants from the British Isles? Ireland herself was a mother country and for that reason, if for no other, felt she had little in common either psychologically or culturally with the oversea dominions. The very flexibility of dominion status, which was the pride of the statesmen of the Commonwealth, evoked only misgiving in Irish minds. They craved, whether wisely or not is beside the point, for precise, logical definitions. They thought not in terms of evolution but of revolution. While the majority were probably not convinced republicans, they certainly felt no natural, spontaneous loyalty to the Crown. Later Mr de Valera referred to the King as 'an alien king' because if given a free choice the people of Ireland would not 'elect him'. The Balfour Declaration of 1926 by its emphasis on the Crown as the symbol of the unity of the Commonwealth enhanced its importance as a factor in determining the attitude of Ireland to the Commonwealth.

The Treaty was a great step forward for the Irish Free State. There Griffith was right. Even Mr de Valera admitted, some ten years later, that progress under it had been rapid and substantial. But it must also be recognized that it was a step forward along a road different from that along which the Irish Nationalists had hoped to travel. The result of this incompatibility between status and ideology in fact on the one hand meant that Ireland never psychologically regarded herself as a dominion and on the other hand it introduced into the circle of the dominions a state which shared the ideals and the outlook of the oversea partners but remained unreconciled to the particular constitutional system which they had evolved. The sequel was very much as might have been expected. In the great period of the Commonwealth evolution between 1926 and 1931 Ireland played her full part. At the Imperial Conferences of 1926 and 1930 her representatives were in the forefront of every move to secure equality not only of status, but also of function. She strengthened greatly the fissiparous tendencies within the Commonwealth, though it is probable that the impact of the Irish Free State on the Commonwealth served for the most part to hasten a development which Canadian and South African opinion would in any event have demanded; this is a subject which deserves far more detailed study than it has so far received. One result of forcing the Irish Free State into the same pattern as the oversea dominions was to change the pattern. So long as it was a case of 'pulling asunder the old Colonial Empire', to use Mr McGilligan's phrase, there was a community of purpose with the oversea dominions, but when that task was completed it was inevitable that their evolution and that of the Free State should tend to diverge.

The divergence became apparent as soon as Mr de Valera assumed office in 1932. For the next six years in the constitutional field the symbols of Commonwealth unity were one by one removed. The first to go was the oath – that oath which Lord Birkenhead is reputed to have described as 'the greatest piece of prevarication in history', because there were embodied in it so many nice inflexions of meaning in a vain attempt to reconcile all parties to its adoption. It was denounced by Mr de Valera as 'an intolerable burden', 'a relic of medievalism imposed from outside under the threat of "immediate and terrible war" '. There followed the appeal to the Privy Council, the functions and then the office of Governor-General. In defence of this unilateral abrogation of the Treaty, Mr de Valera maintained that Commonwealth symbolism had been imposed under duress. That there was incompatibility between Mr Lloyd George's pressure, to use no stronger word, to secure the acceptance of dominion status in 1921 and the Balfour Declaration of five years later with its description of the members of the Commonwealth as autonomous communities 'freely associated as members of the British Commonwealth' is hardly to be denied. But whatever the merits of the dispute, by 1937 the wheel had come almost in full circle; Mr de Valera drafted a new Constitution, had it accepted by a plebiscite, and with the sanction of popular approval established a system of government in Ireland conforming in all essentials to the external association which had been rejected in 1921. Under this Constitution the Governor-General was replaced by an elected President, the oath of allegiance by an oath of loyalty to the state; its enactment was preceded by legislation which repudiated common citizenship and replaced it by the concept of reciprocal citizenship. Only one thing, however, the Constitution did not do. It did not declare that the state was a republic.

Why was Ireland (Éire) declared in the constitution of 1937 to be 'a sovereign, independent democratic State' without an explicit affirmation that it was a republic? The answer is threefold. Britain might have retaliated in the economic field at a time when Irish trade was still suffering from the economic war; more important, sentiment in Northern Ireland would have been further alienated with the result that the already slender prospects of bringing about the reunion of Ireland would have disappeared for generations; and finally, Mr de Valera's own predilections, which were not made known till 1946. For nine years the state remained without a name but in that year this regrettable lacuna was remedied when Mr de Valera rather casually, in answer to a question in the Dáil, stated that she was in fact a republic, and had been one since the Constitution of 1937 was enacted. To the question as to why no formal designation had then been made, Mr de Valera replied that while this state is 'a sovereign independent republic unfortunately it did not cover the whole of Ireland and for that reason I did not introduce into the Constitution the name of Poblacht na h'Éireann because that was a name which was sacred'.

What was the attitude of the republic to the Commonwealth and to the symbol of its unity, the Crown? In September 1947 Mr de Valera for his part defined the position. 'As a matter of our external policy', he said, 'we are associated with the States of the British Commonwealth of Nations. We are not members of it. We are associates of the States of the Commonwealth; but if they regard the existence of the King as a necessary link, if they consider that it is the bond they have, then we have not got that bond . . . We are externally associated with the States of the British Commonwealth'.

This view was at first accepted without substantial modification by the inter-party government which came to power the following year. Mr Mac-Bride, the Minister for External Affairs, stated categorically in August 1948 that Éire was not a member of the Commonwealth. The relationship was described by him and reaffirmed by the Taoiseach, Mr Costello, as being one of friendly association for purposes of common concern.

The Irish interpretation of her constitutional development has always conflicted with that of the United Kingdom government and of the other governments of the Commonwealth. In 1937 the United Kingdom government with the assent of the governments of the oversea dominions stated that they regarded the new Constitution 'as not effecting a fundamental alteration in the position of the Irish Free State'. This statement had unquestionable tactical merits. It averted a final severance; it left the next move to Mr de Valera and he did not make it for nine years. To maintain a bridge between the two countries was no mean achievement, and it was one evidently welcomed by Mr de Valera, for when asked to record his views about the United Kingdom government's statement he replied 'No comment'.

On a long-term view the wisdom of the policy of continuing to regard Éire as a dominion seems much more questionable. The statement of 1937 in the form in which it was made carried certain implications, the more far-reaching because the opinion then expressed is still understood to be the official view of His Majesty's government. It follows from it that Éire remains a dominion within the Commonwealth even though her Constitution is that of a republic, though the Crown has no place either in her executive or in her legislative organs of government, and, most important, even though in the view of her own government she owes no allegiance to the Crown, and is not a full partner in the Commonwealth but a sovereign state outside it associated with it for certain purposes. The statement introduced superficially a new element of flexibility into Commonwealth relations, but fundamentally did it not betray a disturbing rigidity of outlook? For if in fact Mr de Valera's sustained and unremitting efforts to uproot the Treaty settlement had effected no fundamental alteration in the position of the Irish Free State, then, after due allowance has been made for the changes in status embodied in the Statute of Westminster, the stand of the British negotiators against external association in 1921 was, at the least, short-sighted. Were not the United Kingdom government papering over political inconsistency by verbal consistency? Were they not saying, in effect, we will continue to recognize Éire as a dominion even though Éire herself does not consider she is a dominion and even though she does not pay allegiance to the Crown which was regarded by the Balfour Declaration as the symbol of the free association of the Commonwealth because it is tactically a good thing to do and because the admission of the existence of a new form of relationship within the Commonwealth might have all sorts of embarrassing repercussions? While the policy of maintaining a bridge was sound the method adopted seems in retrospect unfortunate.

It is true that it can be, and was, argued, for example by Professor K. C. Wheare, that Éire owed allegiance to the common Crown because the Constitution of 1937 provides that 'for the purpose of the exercise of any executive function of the State in or in connection with its external relations, the Government may . . . avail of or adopt any organ, instrument or method of procedure used or adopted for the like purpose by the members of any group or league of nations with which the State is or becomes associated for the purpose of international co-operation in matters of common concern'.[3] This skilfully drafted permissive clause sanctions the procedure already adopted in the External Relations Act of 1936, which authorizes the use of the Crown in the form of the King's signature for the purpose of appointing diplomatic and consular representatives to be accredited to foreign countries. The practical difficulties in war time were circumvented by the appointment of Chargés d'Affaires, and this use

---

[3] *The Statute of Westminster and Dominion Status* (Oxford, 1938), pp. 272–3.

of the King's signature remained thereafter as the one formal indication of the association between Éire and the Commonwealth. To say with Professor Wheare that it meant that Éire owes allegiance to the common Crown seems unwarranted except in a nice legalistic sense, and his view was not accepted by the Éire government. The link was one, as Mr de Valera emphasized time and again, that remained so long as it was useful and convenient. 'The day', he said in 1946, 'we find that inconvenient we can get rid of it very simply by arranging to have other methods in the accrediting of our representatives abroad.' The fall of his government two years later hastened its approach.

It is more profitable in trying to form some final opinion of the advantages and disadvantages of external association to leave on one side theoretic considerations and to examine its working in the field of foreign affairs both in peace and in war.

In the field of political realities, it may appear that external association proved a very negative concept. That was not and need not, in my opinion, be the case. One reason for it, so far as Ireland is concerned, may be that the imposition of dominion status provoked a greater self assertive desire for independent action in the foreign field than might otherwise have been the case. From 1921 to 1936 the place of the Crown in the Constitution was felt by the majority to be a symbol of subjection. Though it meant nothing of the kind in actual practice, the existence of the Crown in the Constitution carried, above all for the Fianna Fáil party, this implication. To offset it Mr Cosgrave and still more Mr de Valera were in turn at great pains to emphasize the importance of the League of Nations over against that of the Commonwealth. The Irish point of view has consistently been that intra-Commonwealth disputes are international disputes and, therefore, should not be reserved, but referred, to the international tribunal. In the broader fields of foreign policy, a distinctive line has been pursued so far as circumstances allowed, but the emphasis on the League resulted in the middle 1930s in a coincidence in outlook between British and Irish representatives at Geneva. To take the outstanding example, despite the very close links between Ireland and Italy, Mr de Valera advocated a strong League policy and supported sanctions in the Abyssinian dispute as he had done in the earlier Sino-Japanese dispute. He felt profoundly that here the League had its last chance of effective self-assertion. But he had to face considerable opposition at home particularly when the policy of sanctions against Italy brought him face to face with Catholic sentiment and with an anti-British sentiment to which the thought of such intimate cooperation with Britain in the international field was anathema. To a protagonist of this school of thought, Mr de Valera retorted in the Dáil, 'if your worst enemy happens to be going to heaven by the same road as you are, you do not for that reason turn around and go in the opposite direction'. But once the League had failed to save Abyssinia, Mr de Valera made no secret of the fact that he believed, also, that the experiment in international government, which it had embodied, had broken down and must be abandoned. From then onward he was convinced that another European war was coming and publicly stated that the only course to be adopted by Éire was neutrality.

To Mr de Valera, and indeed to the great majority of Irishmen, neutrality appeared as a final vindication of sovereign status. It was final, convincing evidence of freedom and in that sense it was a psychological necessity. But there are two things to be noted about the policy of neutrality. The first is that it was a policy not deriving exclusively from the concept of external association. As the debate in the South African House of Commons in September 1939 made so abundantly clear, the decision between peace and war rested with each dominion Parliament. If Éire be regarded as a dominion, there was no difference in principle between a South African Parliament deciding by a small majority against neutrality and the Dáil deciding virtually unanimously in favour of it. However important the consequences in practice, the neutrality of Éire did not mark a final break with dominion status. Here again there is something in the argument that because Éire remained a dominion in name, her determination to pursue her own course was thereby reinforced. But this is not to be pressed too far. Neutrality was not so much the product of external considerations as of internal conditions. Mr de Valera gave the most convincing summary of them immediately after the American entry into the war, a moment when the foundations of Irish policy were challenged. After describing Ireland's position as that of a 'friendly neutral', he added, 'from the moment that the war began there was for us only one policy possible – neutrality. Our circumstances, our history, the incompleteness of our national territory from the partition of our country made any other policy impracticable. Any other policy would have divided our people, and for a divided nation to fling itself into war would be to commit suicide'.

By this policy of neutrality Éire's detachment from the other nations of the Commonwealth during one of the most critical periods in their history was underlined, but the character of her association with it was not fundamentally altered, though the normal and elaborate machinery of intra-Commonwealth consultation was presumably suspended so far as she was concerned and her policy made inevitable her exclusion from the Commonwealth Prime Ministers' Conferences of 1944 and 1946, and she was not invited in 1948.

About Éire's neutrality there was an element of misunderstanding on both sides – and by misunderstanding I mean a genuine failure to understand. In Britain it was recognized that Éire had a right to exercise a free choice on the vital issue of peace and war, but it was felt by some that in the case of war against aggression, naked and unashamed, there was a certain moral obligation for all members of the Commonwealth to act in concert. It was felt in such circumstances that the unity of the Commonwealth should transcend individual or sectional interests. Membership of the Commonwealth carries with it obligations as well as benefits, and in a war for survival the obligations could not be lightly overlooked. These feelings though they received expression from persons in official positions were given no official endorsement. To this wise restraint Mr de Valera inserted a diplomatic tribute in his reply to the American note of 1944 requesting the removal of the Axis legations from Dublin. He observed then, 'It is perhaps not known to the American Government that the feelings of the Irish people towards Britain have undergone a considerable change, precisely because Britain has not attempted to violate our neutrality'. Britain, he remarked on another occasion, had behaved 'not unworthily'. All is well that ends well, but undoubtedly Éire's confused constitutional relations with the Commonwealth were responsible for a good deal of the misunderstarding that existed in both Britain and Ireland; an influential section of opinion approached neutrality from different points of view because each started from different premises. The United Kingdom government had stated that Éire remained a dominion; Éire maintained that she was not a Dominion but a sovereign state externally associated with the Commonwealth. Because she was externally associated, her moral obligations – she had no Treaty obligations after the return of the ports in 1938 – were, so it was argued, comparable, not with those of the oversea dominions, but with those of Holland or Belgium, Norway or Sweden, or Portugal or indeed the United States. None of these countries had in fact entered the war unless and until they had been attacked. Therefore, why should Éire enter the war unless she were attacked? The Commonwealth, it was concluded, had no justifiable cause for complaint. This line of argument implied that association unlike dominion status carried no obligations in a war against aggression, without its exponents fully realizing that they were, by implication, fixing upon external association so negative an interpretation. Was there then no difference between a foreign state and an associated state?

To condemn neutrality as unrealistic was an altogether different matter. The Irish correspondent of the *Round Table*, writing after the Munich crisis, remarked, 'One has only to look at the map to realize that Ireland could not remain neutral in a major war in which Great Britain was engaged'. But Mr de Valera calculated otherwise and partly by diplomatic skill and, still more, thanks primarily to Ireland's position on the map, was enabled to pursue his chosen policy, without deviation and not without dignity, until the end of the war.

Now that the tensions – let us admit them – and the growing cooperation

– let us not overlook it – of the war years are a matter of the past, it is well to consider what lessons are to be drawn in the field of Commonwealth relations. One lesson, I think, is that calling a country a dominion, which does not aspire to be a dominion, is liable at critical moments to promote not understanding, but misunderstanding. Another is that external association on the lines originally contemplated by the Irish delegates in 1921 is likely to provide a more satisfactory basis for common action in external affairs between two countries, who share a wide community of interest but different political concepts, than dominion status, based as it is on unwritten conventions. External association came into being as an alternative to dominion status because it allowed of a form of government more acceptable to Irish opinion, but, at the same time, envisaged cooperation between Ireland and the Commonwealth in matters of common concern. This cooperation might well have been based on certain minimal common obligations freely undertaken by both parties. Its foundation would, therefore, have been more rigid, because defined, than the unwritten conventional basis of Commonwealth cooperation. Definition incurs some risks, but I submit they are not so great as the risk of conventions, which may be misunderstood or which may prove unacceptable. In the case of Éire, so intimate in many respects is the association with Britain and the Commonwealth, both socially and economically, that cooperation is a necessity, but in other places where these non-political bonds are less strong, the soundness and the suitability of the constitutional foundation may well prove of the most vital importance.

In thinking of external association it is easy, in the light of Irish experience, to put too much emphasis on the adjective, too little on the noun. But the essential foundation for this concept is the desire on the part of two or more countries to be associated. If one turns one's eyes away from the frigid, constitutional field, one finds indeed that relations between Britain and Ireland are in many respects more intimate than between any other of the partners of the Commonwealth. In the economic field the trade figures over the past twenty years bear the most striking testimony to the mutual interdependence of the two countries and, more recently, no one will have missed the significance of Éire's cooperation in the Marshall Plan. There is a profound truth in Mr Lemass's remark on his visit to Paris to the effect that 'We have an interest in preserving the exchange value of British money', though he added characteristically and reasonably that any plan which emerged from the Paris Conference must be designed to benefit all countries equally, and concluded that provided that was done 'Éire was ready to cooperate in any measures to protect sterling and to develop the resources of the sterling area'. Behind Mr Lemass's statement lies the fact that the Irish sterling balance totals now some £400,000,000, while on the other hand her balance of trade with the dollar area is exceedingly unfavourable. In the first five months of 1947, Éire's imports from North America are calculated to have amounted to some £8,500,000 and her exports to only £117,000 and only a small part of this gap will be bridged by invisible exports.[4] Éire's interest, therefore, in reducing dollar expenditure and increasing trade within the sterling area is almost as great as Britain's. It is in this context that the recent trade agreement between Britain and Ireland should be viewed. Its conclusion will strengthen the balance of payments position of the sterling area as a whole, particularly by effecting substantial reductions in dollar requirements. More important still, the machinery which has been set up in the form of a standing committee of officials to keep trade relations between Britain and Ireland under review will enable all proposals for increasing trade to be considered sympathetically and practically 'within the limits of the economic policy of each country'. The possibilities of developing trade to mutual advantage have been underestimated in recent years, and the agreement affords welcome evidence that they are no longer to be neglected even if not yet to be fully exploited. The export of coal, agricultural machinery and fertilizers from Britain, coupled with the proposed upward revision of prices for Irish agricultural products, should lead to a substantial increase in the exports of Éire's products to Britain. Certainly that has been the consistent policy of Mr Costello's inter-party government since its accession to office. Close and continuing economic cooperation between the two countries at home and in the broader field of the European recovery plan is likely to have far-reaching and beneficial consequences.

But while the economic interdependence between Britain and Ireland must be duly underlined, more fundamental still is the scale of social intercourse between the two countries. Even during the war years there was a continuing flow of Irishmen into the United Kingdom. The number of volunteers from Éire serving in the forces was certainly not less than 50,000 and the number of workers in war factories somewhere between 120,000 and 150,000. These are almost all men and women of the younger generation; and the fact of their having lived in England, in many cases having settled here permanently or married English wives, should have a lasting and beneficial effect on Anglo-Irish relations. Of the reactions to some of the recent English settlers in Ireland it is difficult to feel so confident. If in the political field the area of cooperation between Britain and Ireland is narrower than between Britain and the other dominions and, in Mr de Valera's view is likely to remain so, so long as partition exists, the field of common interest is at least as wide. This is a point to be borne in mind because, if my line of thought is justified, the more important conclusions

---

[4] *The Economist*, 4 October 1947.

to be drawn from this review of Éire's relationship with the Commonwealth apply with most force not to Anglo-Irish relations, but to future relations with former non-self-governing territories in the East. The smaller the area of common interest in the social and economic field, the greater the importance of establishing a right relationship in external policy, in which I am including the all-important and related fields of foreign affairs and defence.

External association is in a sense a *via media* between dominion status and treaty relationship, but it is a mistake to think of it as a colourless compromise. Rightly regarded, it is the positive answer to a certain set of circumstances. Its foundation should be the desire of two or more independent countries to form a close and lasting association. In that, it is similar to dominion status, but distinct from a treaty relationship which is normally founded on a short-term coincidence of interest in a limited and particular field. On the other hand, as distinct from dominion status, it rests, not upon a sense of underlying unity in history, development and tradition, symbolized by allegiance to a common Crown, but upon a sense of partnership between two peoples with different histories and different loyalties but sharing common interests, common aims in world politics and, above all, a common sense of values. Viewed in this context it is at once apparent that the lessons to be drawn from Éire's relationship with the Commonwealth are instructive but limited. External association has never been put into practice because the United Kingdom and the oversea dominions have never recognized that it exists. To them Éire remains a dominion. And external association is naturally dependent for its proper working upon all parties to it recognizing it as the foundation of their relationship. Equally on the other side, the value of Irish experience is limited by the isolationist policy pursued for many years though not recently by the Éire government. External association, rightly viewed, is an instrument for cooperation between independent states, not a means of bringing about an ever greater degree of detachment.

From this survey of Ireland's relationship with the Commonwealth certain conclusions emerge which suggest that the wisdom of British policy in the strictly political field was not matched by an equal understanding in the constitutional field. Politically the resolute determination of the United Kingdom to treat each question on its merits as it arose, to avert a final breach in the face of considerable provocation, to escape from formulae, and to eschew finalities seems in retrospect to have been more than justified. For that policy the war provided the supreme test and it is greatly to the credit of the United Kingdom government that it refused to be deflected from its chosen path during those critical years. The marked improvement in Anglo-Irish relations which we see today is the fruit of this policy of wise restraint. It represents a considerable political achievement towards which in recent years Lord Rugby, the first United Kingdom Representative to Ireland, has made no small contribution.

On the constitutional side, the conclusions are more negative. The initial mistake was made in 1921; it was persisted in in 1937, and only today are Anglo-Irish relations escaping from its consequences. That mistake was the application of dominion status to the Irish Free State. Because of it the constitutional ties with the Commonwealth acted as an irritant in relations with the United Kingdom and more and more, as years went by, were a barrier to the partnership which community of interest demanded. The removal of the symbols of this status by Mr de Valera was – it is paradoxical but true – an essential preliminary to full and cordial cooperation with the countries of the Commonwealth. From that point of view it is open to question, particularly in the light of recent debates in the Dáil, whether the one remaining constitutional link embodied in the External Relations Act any longer possesses practical advantages outweighing its psychological disadvantages.

Unfortunate also in some respects have been the consequences of the initial constitutional mistake for the Commonwealth as a whole. Irish policy in the past twenty-five years has been directed not deliberately but inevitably towards a loosening of the fabric of Commonwealth cooperation. Every step she has taken to emphasize her national as against her dominion status has stimulated one or more of the oversea dominions to follow in the same path. The emphasis she has placed on the theoretic conception of absolute national sovereignty has deflected the thought of the Commonwealth away from its natural line of development. By making the Irish Free State conform to a constitutional relationship inappropriate to her circumstances and outlook, the character of the relationship itself has been modified. Many Irishmen, profoundly concerned to maintain the strength and unity of a Commonwealth in the postwar world, acknowledge that almost every step towards the fulfilment of their national aspirations has incidentally involved some weakening of this community of nations. But they maintain they were placed in a position in which no alternative course was open to them just because in 1921 the Irish Free State was forced into a pattern in which she had no natural place. From the point of view of the Commonwealth the lesson to be drawn is the supreme importance of reconciling constitutional forms with political and psychological realities.

It is because external association was the constitutional relationship contemplated by Irish republicans in 1921 that it provides so good a starting point for an examination of what may be the most satisfactory relationship with the newly established nation-states of the East. Today indeed the new relationship between the United Kingdom and Burma in certain essentials corresponds more closely to external association than that with Éire, but possibly it was not so designated because the political background of the governing group of parties in Burma, the Anti-Fascist Peoples Freedom League, made any association with the Commonwealth difficult. Burma, it is stated in the Burma Independence Bill, shall become on 6 January 1948, 'an independent country neither forming part of His Majesty's Dominions nor entitled to His Majesty's protection'. By that decision, Burma is likely in the long run to lose considerably, for while the material foundation remains the same, the sense of intimate and growing partnership may well be lost. No one would wish to question the very real measure of goodwill that exists towards Britain in Burma today, but goodwill tends to be transient. Under the Treaty of Relationship which has now been established, it will find little scope for expression in day-to-day relations over a period of years. Whatever may be the intentions and hopes of the signatories, treaties are usually interpreted in a literal and restrictive sense. They are not a stepping-stone to a closer and more intimate relationship, just because they provide no machinery for making relations more intimate. It is here that the concept of association could have made a valuable and distinctive contribution. Even had it been based upon a treaty whose essentials corresponded in almost every particular to the details of the treaty just signed, association with the Commonwealth would have allowed for a continuing and expanding consultation and cooperation in all matters of common concern. As a direct consequence, the area of common interest might have widened as the years went by and the friendship deepened. Therein lies the supreme merit of association as against treaty relationship. It allows, it is designed to allow, for growth.

In 1921 Mr Lloyd George asked the question how best can Ireland's national aspirations be reconciled with the community of nations known as the British Empire. The question to be asked today is, can the interests of India, of Pakistan, and in a rather different context of Ceylon be reconciled with those of the community of nations known as the British Commonwealth and if so, how can this best be done? Tomorrow the same question will be asked in Africa and in the West Indies, and they will be profoundly influenced by the Asian precedents, whatever they may be. It is quite certain that in answering this question Irish experience has a significance all its own. So far as India and Pakistan are concerned, the question is answered by dominion status, for Ceylon it is answered by 'fully responsible status within the British Commonwealth of Nations'.[5] For India and Pakistan this is acknowledged to be a temporary expedient. What is the long-term solution? It goes without saying that there will be no lasting relationship unless the peoples of Asia desire it. Whether they will desire it depends now to no small extent on what is offered to them. The statesmen

---

[5] *Proposals for conferring on Ceylon fully responsible status within the British Commonwealth of Nations*, Cmd 7257 (London, HMSO 1947).

of the British Commonwealth have always maintained that its greatest virtue is flexibility and adaptability to changing circumstances. The boast is justified, but recently – is it since the 1926 declaration? – there has crept in an element of standardization. Dominion status is the goal whatever the background.

A few months ago in New Delhi a distinguished Indian statesman remarked to me that dominion status could not in the long run work in countries like Ireland or like India which were themselves mother countries. In that there is much truth. But an even graver objection exists when in addition there is no common historical background. That a final solution will be found to Anglo-Irish relations may be regarded as a reasonable expectation, just because over and above the wide area of common interest there is a common background. Both Britain and Ireland and the oversea dominions are peopled by men of European stock who are the heirs of the Christian civilization of the West. A much more formidable problem arises when one contemplates transplanting a political concept peculiar to this Western civilization to the East. It is perfectly true that one of the results, and I believe one of the most beneficial results, of British rule in India has been the spread of ideas of democracy and constitutional government. At the Inter-Asian Conference in New Delhi in the spring of 1947 English was the official language and the delegates from almost all countries, other than the Soviet Asian republics, tacitly assumed in this dawning of liberated and triumphant nationalism that a parliamentary social democracy was the form of government at which all should aim. During its deliberations I thought more than once of Macaulay's words: 'The sceptre may pass from us. Victory may be inconstant to our arms. But there are triumphs which are followed by no reverse. There is an Empire exempt from all natural causes of decay. Those triumphs are the pacific triumphs of reason; that Empire is the imperishable Empire of our arts and our morals, our literature and our laws'. Of our language and our laws that still seems true today. Politically it is very important and it encourages the hope of close and lasting cooperation in the future. What form should it take?

Dominion status depends for its working upon a whole set of ideas, a whole range of common associations, containing nice implications only to be readily understood by people whose background and whose training have been very similar. But how can the peoples of the East attach precisely the right weight to all these unwritten conventions and think instinctively along the lines on which we have been accustomed to think in Commonwealth affairs? What is dangerous is not a difference of view within the Commonwealth – that in many respects is healthy – but misunderstanding. The appeal of the Pakistan government to the other Commonwealth governments at the height of the communal warfare in the Punjab is a portent and a warning. It may be, and in many cases will be, that representatives of the Eastern states will have difficulty in recognizing precisely what are the obligations or what, for that matter, are the benefits of Commonwealth membership. Even a paper so well informed as the *Manchester Guardian* recently remarked that 'as long as India and Pakistan remain Dominions they have the automatic guarantee of the British Alliance'.[6] What does that mean? We know that there is no alliance in any formal sense binding the partners of the Commonwealth. But do the great mass of the Indian people? We know from past experience that in the event of aggression, the member states of the Commonwealth of their own choice will freely unite to resist it, but we know equally that this common action derives from a common outlook and common sense of values and rests on no formal obligation arising automatically when war begins. But it is doubtful if public opinion in an Asian country, or for that matter any country with a different historical background, would rightly understand anything so flexible and so conventional. They might well tend to assume that at the least there existed an overwhelming moral obligation which, in certain not inconceivable circumstances, not all the partners in the Commonwealth would be prepared to admit.

Mr Peter Fraser said recently in a message to the Indian people that dominion status means 'independence plus'. But Indians wondering whether or not their country should continue to have dominion status will want to know plus what? The advantages are solid and substantial, but I think that the Indian mind which, in common with the Irish and French, inclines towards precision, would welcome them more if at least the foundations on which this new relationship may be built could be more closely defined. It was, for example, my impression both in New Delhi and in Karachi that informed public opinion was not favourably impressed by the fact that Commonwealth flexibility today was so great that it allowed the neutrality of one partner in a major war. The prevailing view seemed to be that the right to remain neutral in such circumstances might well be regarded as an asset for countries in a sheltered geographical position, but for India and Pakistan it was not an asset, but a liability. It subtracted from the strength of the Commonwealth and introduced a disturbing degree of uncertainty. The Irish precedent in effect reinforced the demand for greater definition. Now definition is wholly alien to dominion status: Mr Lloyd George said in 1921 it would be extremely dangerous to attempt to define it and that is equally true today. There is left one expedient, external association, or association as I would prefer to call it, which would diminish the dangers of definition and which, at the same time, would maintain partnership. It is here that the most valuable lesson of Anglo-Irish

---

[6] 11 October 1947.

relations is to be found. It is not in external association as it has evolved, but rather in external association as it was originally conceived. In other words it should have a foundation of common purpose and mutual obligation stated and clearly understood by both parties. On that foundation the association could grow without fear of any fundamental misunderstanding and little by little conventions could be added which would enrich and deepen the association. As against a treaty, such as that recently signed with Burma, it would, as I have already emphasized, have the great advantages of allowing for growth. We would not have to treat one another as foreign countries. That in itself would be an immeasurable gain. As against dominion status, external association, by defining the foundations to the extent that seems desirable in each individual case, removes many potential causes of misunderstanding and, incidentally, the slightest suggestion of subordination. Otherwise thorny questions of allegiance and of the place of the Crown would be settled on their merits by mutual agreement and it must be frankly recognized that the concept of a common Crown as a symbol of unity might or might not prove acceptable. 'If no place can be found in a British Commonwealth for republics', wrote the late Professor Berriedale Keith in 1938, 'then the enduring character of the Commonwealth may well be doubted.'[7] The new constitution of India is a republican constitution. If the Union of India is to remain within the Commonwealth it will remain so as a republic.

Here the decision of Burma to leave the Commonwealth must be considered again from a different point of view. The choice which she made is not one which the members of the Commonwealth can, or should, regard with any complacency. It suggests at the least that a new approach is required. The problem is perhaps as much psychological as political. It is believed in Burma, as it is believed in every Asian country, that dominion status means subordination. No amount of explanation will remove the conviction that somehow or other, whatever its material advantages, dominion status implies something less than full sovereignty. It is perfectly understandable how this conviction became implanted in the Asian mind. It is only within the last two decades that dominion status has, in fact, carried with it full sovereign status, and many of the political leaders and intellectuals, to whom these things are a matter of direct concern and who influence public opinion, first learned of dominion status in the years when it meant something less than it means today. The very fact that the years that elapsed between the Imperial Conference of 1926 and the outbreak of the Second World War witnessed an intense preoccupation within the Commonwealth with questions of status, of the right to neutrality, of secession, inevitably suggested that the dominions doubted whether they

---

[7] *The Dominions as Sovereign States* (London, 1938), p. ix.

were fully masters of their own destinies. If they were certain, why were they so concerned with these things? The impression then received has not been eradicated and it is my firm conviction that no amount of discussion will eradicate it. The stigma, if that is the right word, is one that cannot be removed by lucid exposition of the facts, or at any rate cannot be removed in this way in time. If, therefore, the only possibility that lies before the Asian peoples contemplating partnership within the Commonwealth is dominion status, the misapprehensions and the psychology that lies behind them may well lead to a decision to go outside the Commonwealth. The emotional background in this way reinforces the political and constitutional considerations, which lead one to suggest that some new form of association, call it external association or any other name you will, is needed. One advantage of external association is that no one in Asia, or in any other continent, has ever supposed that the actions of Mr de Valera are in any way controlled by the British government, or that any subordinate status would ever be acceptable to him. The integrity of his nationalism is above suspicion. By broadening the basis of the Commonwealth in this way, the associated states including Éire need not, unless they so desire, feel outside it, but a natural element within it.

At this stage one important question arises. In a Commonwealth composed of autonomous and sovereign states there can be no distinction in status, but there would be difference in relationship between the states that are dominions and the states that are more formally associated. Both would be full and equal partners, but the origin from which their partnership derived would be different. What would be the relation between them? If the experiment were tried, I believe that in practice this problem would be solved satisfactorily by regarding all partners in the Commonwealth as having equal privileges and equal obligations and using the defined relationship of the associate states as a statement of first principles to which appeal is made only on those rare and critical occasions for which it was designed to provide. In saying this I do not wish to dismiss this difficulty lightly, but I believe it is certainly not insurmountable. An element of constitutional untidiness is a small price to pay for a flexibility in Commonwealth relations which enables peoples of many races and different traditions to cooperate wholeheartedly in the common purposes which the Commonwealth serves in the world.

The implications of Éire's relationship with the Commonwealth have led us, therefore, into new fields. They suggest a Commonwealth of the future in which there are both member states and associate states, the distinction between them being one, not of status, but of history, tradition and cultural background. By such a development the Commonwealth could only be strengthened, for it would mean that political and constitutional realities would once again be brought into harmony. In this great community there would be a natural place for nations peopled by many races and speaking many tongues but all, from their vast store of varied experience, contributing to the common good of the whole and thereby to the peace of the world.

12

IRELAND:
The Republic Outside the Commonwealth

In the last thirty years there have been three distinct experiments in the ordering of Anglo-Irish relations. Two of them have failed. The first was the experiment of Commonwealth membership embodied in the Anglo-Irish Treaty of 1921 in which the status of the Irish Free State was specifically associated with that of the senior dominion Canada, and generally with those of the oversea dominions. That experiment may be said to have come to an end in 1936–7 when the External Relations Act was passed and the new Irish Constitution enacted with the sanction of popular approval in a plebiscite. Then from 1936 to 1949 there was the experiment, not in a full but in an improvised form, of external association. During that period Éire owed no allegiance to the Crown and was not, in the Irish view, a member of the British Commonwealth of Nations, but a state whose association with it from without was symbolized by the King's signature to the letters of appointment of Irish representatives to foreign countries. With the decision to repeal the External Relations Act in the autumn of 1948 this experiment too was brought to a close and Éire, or the Republic of Ireland as she was now described, formally seceded from the British Commonwealth. She did not, however, become a foreign country, as did Burma which also seceded, and, while her citizens are no longer to be regarded as British subjects or Commonwealth citizens, they retain a special non-foreign status.

The three successive experiments in the ordering of Anglo-Irish relations are recorded in three different names which have been given or are commonly attributed to the sovereign state which comprises twenty-six of the thirty-two counties of Ireland. Between 1921 and 1937 she was known as the Irish Free State. In the Constitution of 1937 the name of the state was declared to be Éire, or in the English language, Ireland. Since the jurisdiction of her government extended only to twenty-six of the thirty-two counties this created some confusion, and outside the twenty-six counties the name Éire was commonly, if incorrectly, used as though it were a synonymous successor title to Irish Free State. Within the twenty-six counties explanatory comments were inserted in legislation and in government orders. Thus at the head of the notices of assessment income-tax payers were told, with that elegance of language for which tax gatherers are famous the world over, that the 'word Éire throughout this form is to be interpreted . . . as referable to the area to which the laws of Éire have application'. In 1948, contrary to general belief, the name of the state was not changed by the Republic of Ireland Act.[1] Any such change would have necessitated an amendment of the Constitution. The Act merely declared that the description of the state should be the Republic of Ireland. Evidently this refinement was too much for British draftsmen, for the Ireland Act 1949 speaks wrongly of 'the Republic of Ireland' as the name 'attributed thereto by the law thereof'.[2]

It is not, however, with technicalities but with the reality behind them that I wish to deal here. The two questions to which I shall try to find some tentative and provisional answers are these. To what extent did the secession of the Republic of Ireland from the Commonwealth mark a break in the pattern of relations that had existed previously, and particularly in the preceding twelve years when Éire had been a state associated with the British Commonwealth, and, secondly, what have been the more important practical consequences of secession? The two questions are of course closely interrelated. With regard to the first, Mr Churchill failed to detect any radical transformation in Anglo-Irish relations in 1949. Before then, he remarked, Éire so far as the Commonwealth was concerned was 'in and out'; thereafter it was 'out and in'. If generally Mr Churchill's comments on Irish affairs are to be regarded as remarkable for pungency rather than for precision, yet on this point legislation enacted in the United Kingdom and in the dominions goes quite a long way toward endorsing his view. The Ireland Act of 1949 states that though Éire ceased from 18 April 1949 to be a part of His Majesty's dominions yet 'notwithstanding that the Republic of Ireland is not part of His Majesty's dominions' she is not a foreign country. Parallel legislation was enacted by other members of the

---

[1] No. 22 of 1948.

[2] 12 & 13 Geo. VI c. 6, s. I, ss. (3).

Commonwealth. The New Zealand Republic of Ireland Act 1950 goes so far as to say that: 'All existing law . . . shall, until provision to the contrary is made by the authority having power to alter that law, have the same operation in relation to the Republic of Ireland, and to persons and things in any way belonging to or connected with the Republic of Ireland, as it would have had if the Republic of Ireland had remained part of His Majesty's dominions'.[3] Is such language really in accord with the facts? Can the formal act of secession have made as little difference as that?

In seeking for an answer the first thing to keep in mind was that Éire was not a full member ol the Commonwealth before she seceded – she was in her own view an externally associated member and in any view her membership was diluted. It was not, therefore, as though a full membership had ended. The second is to recall for a moment what external association represented in theory and meant in practice. External association was the product of a logical and coherent line of thought. It had been first advanced in 1921 by the Sinn Féin leaders as their alternative to dominion status. Ireland, they argued, being a mother country long subject to foreign rule was not and never could be a dominion in spirit. That was a status appropriate to countries of settlement such as Canada and Australia, not to countries with long and cherished traditions of their own. So it was that the Crown, which to British peoples whether at home or settled overseas symbolized their conception of law and constitutional government, remained for the Irish no more than the symbol of alien rule. At the same time the Irish freely acknowledged the interdependence of Britain and Ireland and, in 1921, they went so far as to suggest that defence and foreign policy should be matters of common concern, while the very special relationship that existed between Ireland and the Commonwealth countries should be recognized by Irish acknowledgement of the King as head of the Commonwealth association. In the summer of 1921 a solution on these lines would seem to have had the support of most of the principal Irish leaders. In his Document No. 2, which constituted Mr de Valera's republican alternative to dominion status and was drafted after the Treaty, Article 2 proposed that for 'purposes of common concern Ireland shall be associated with the States of the British Commonwealth' and (Article 6) 'that for the purposes of association Ireland recognized his Britannic Majesty as Head of the association'. But in Britain in 1921 such an idea was considered almost fantastic. Even eleven years later when Mr de Valera returned to office and elaborated once again this conception of the appropriate relationship between an Ireland external to but associated with the Commonwealth he found in Mr J. H. Thomas, the Dominions Secretary, a singularly unappreciative audience. Yet despite discouragement

---

[3] No. 13, Art. 3.

both within and without Mr de Valera was not to be deflected from his chosen course and by the passage of the External Relations Act[4] and of the Constitution the following year he partially achieved his purpose. It was not, however, arranged as neatly as might have been wished. For this the abdication was responsible, for it meant that the order of the legislation had to be reversed, the External Relations Act preceding the Constitution to which it was meant to be the sequel. More generally it demanded improvisation where deliberation was greatly needed. Yet whatever its defects the External Relations Act fulfilled for a time the purpose its author had in mind. It made possible the continuing association of a country which after 1937 was a republic in all but name with a Commonwealth of Nations owing common allegiance to the Crown. It may be that the solution was too subtle; certainly it had about it the air of a temporary expedient. But then time was needed not only for emotions to calm but also for the pattern of Commonwealth relations to evolve. And by this ingenious arrangement which, in the view of the United Kingdom government and the governments of the oversea dominions, effected no fundamental alteration in the position of the Irish Free State as a member of the Commonwealth, Mr de Valera felt that he attained the goal of an independent republic associated as a matter of external policy with the states of the British Commonwealth. When he was pressed to define exactly Éire's relationship with the Commonwealth he replied that was something which he alone could not do and, when urged by Mr Dillon to declare whether Éire was a republic or not, he referred him to the Constitution and to the *Oxford Dictionary*. The solution, however, had one quality of statesmanship. It closed no doors. But it was too subtle to last – and in fact it did not last quite long enough.

And now we come to one of the ironies of Commonwealth history. In 1949 a republic – how inconceivable it had seemed a quarter of a century earlier – was accepted in accordance with its own expressed wishes as a full member of the Commonwealth. Irish experiments had encouraged Indians to think that after all a republic might be associated with the Commonwealth; and in the event the actual phrase by which the membership of India as a republic was reconciled with the Crown as the symbol of Commonwealth association had its Irish origin. The Irish, it is true, had never imagined that a republic could be a full member of the Commonwealth and the phrase they had contemplated in 1921 recognized the King as the 'Head of the association', not as 'Head of the Commonwealth' which was the formula adopted in the London Declaration of 1949. Yet the intention of that earlier phrase, which embodied the essence of Mr de Valera's thought, was intended to resolve the very problem which was

---

[4] Executive Authority (External Relations) Act 1936.

resolved by the Commonwealth Prime Ministers in April 1949.[5] And at the very moment when it was so resolved Mr de Valera was out of office for the only two years since 1931. It is not for me to speculate what would have happened had things been otherwise; but is it not inconceivable that he could have done other than welcome the fulfilment in so large a measure of his own ideas and feel that thereby the door at last was opened for an agreed solution of Éire's relations with the Ccmmonwealth? After all, while it is true that India remains a full member of the Commonwealth and not an associate, she owes no allegiance to the Crown however oblique, and her ambassadors are accredited in the name of the Indian President, and not of the King, as was the case in Éire before the repeal of the External Relations Act.

It was an inter-party government under Mr Costello which contained Republican, Labour, and Fine Gael members which decided that while India was to become a republic within, Ireland was to be a republic without the Commonwealth. Though the members of the government had differed profoundly in the past about Éire's relations with the Commonwealth they were united in opposition to Mr de Valera and to his solution of them. Of particular importance were the views of Fine Gael, the principal party in the government. They were the party who in 1922 had fought to establish the Irish Free State as a dominion and though in recent years their support of dominion status had cooled, none the less their leader, General Mulcahy, had openly advocated full Commonwealth membership in the general election of 1944. In the following year Mr Dillon, who though not a member of the party was closely associated with it, declared in the most emphatic terms that Commonwealth membership was the condition of Irish unity. If, therefore, Fine Gael attacked Mr de Valera's exercises in academic formulae they had done so hitherto from the standpoint of a party that championed full Commonwealth membership. It is for that reason that, while in 1948 it was recognized on all sides that the External Relations Act could not much longer survive, it was a matter of surprise that the inter-party government in which the predominant partner was the Fine Gael party should actually bring about its repeal in such a way as to sever all ties with the Commonwealth. Yet for their dramatic change of front there were reasons not to be lightly discounted. Mr Costello himself laid most emphasis upon two of them; upon the imperative need for unity at home, for taking the gun out of politics, and secondly for opening the way to frank friendship with Britain and the Commonwealth by removing the psychological barrier of the Crown and all ambiguity and source of friction in constitutional relationships. By a repeal of the External Relations Act friendship would henceforward, he argued, be easy and natural, not

---

[5] *The Times*, 28 April 1949.

artificial and constricted; and it would be closer, for to use his own words it would be unthinkable for the Republic of Ireland to draw further away from the countries of the Commonwealth.

Some have found these reasons for secession convincing; some have not. There is just one point that I would like to make. And that is that one reason for the failure of the external association experiment, as indeed for the experiment of dominion status which preceded it, was that neither fulfilled the principal purpose of their respective supporters. In the 1920s Mr Cosgrave's government believed that by being a loyal member of the Commonwealth they would bring closer the day when Ireland would be reunited; Mr de Valera believed in 1937 and later that by refraining from the open declaration of a republic and by continuing Éire's association with the Commonwealth he, too, would at least leave the door open for reunion. But both felt that they had been mistaken. All parties had convinced themselves by 1949 that neither full dominion status nor still less external association would contribute towards the removal of the border. In the North the majority wished to remain part of the United Kingdom irrespective of whether the twenty-six counties became a dominion, an associated state or an independent republic. And that prompts the further reflection that British policy was mistaken in so far as it ever conceived that partition and dominion status could form parts of one consistent whole. Experience suggests that either there was a partitioned Ireland or there was an Irish dominion. There could not be both. There could not for the simple reason that within the twenty-six counties there was no solid basis of support, as the Fine Gael party learned to their cost, for Commonwealth policies. There was nationalist sentiment to be wooed, there were no Commonwealth votes to be won. The Commonwealth votes were on the other side of the border.

The repeal of the External Relations Act was regarded both in London and in Dublin as tantamount to secession. I am not myself certain whether in constitutional law this was a necessary conclusion since the London Declaration of April 1949 made it clear that allegiance to the Crown was no longer to be regarded as an essential condition of Commonwealth membership. In any event the real difference in the history of the relations of the Indian and Irish republics with the Commonwealth is to be found not in the field of constitutional theory but in the realm of political intention. India expressed an explicit desire to remain a full member of the Commonwealth after she had become a republic, Éire did not.

It was largely because the Indian question had still to be resolved that Irish secession provoked anxiety and a spate of lugubrious comment. Yet the suggestion of catastrophic consequences involving the ending of trade preference and the conversion of citizens of Éire in the United Kingdom overnight into aliens at least made clear the resolve of the Irish government to go ahead whatever happened. At the same time they had considerable, and as it proved well-founded, confidence that there would be no very drastic repercussions. One reason for it I have already suggested. Éire was not a dominion when she seceded. Under the 1948 British Nationality Act her citizens were not regarded as British subjects or Commonwealth citizens but as falling into a special category. In the field of citizenship, and also in trading relations, it was not therefore necessary to devise new arrangements but more simply to decide whether the old should or should not be continued. In the making of that decision the oversea Commonwealth countries, more especially those with a considerable Irish element in their populations, Canada, Australia, New Zealand, played a notable part. The Lord Chancellor in the House of Lords answering criticisms implying that more drastic action should have been taken consequent upon Irish secession replied that no such action could have been taken with the agreement of the oversea dominions. On the contrary, he said, had any such steps been contemplated the United Kingdom government would have had to act 'in the teeth of advice' from the Commonwealth countries overseas. Fundamental, however, was the very special relationship which exists between Britain and Ireland. It has existed since the beginning of time and presumably will exist until the end. The relationship is parallel to the relationship between Norway and Sweden, Portugal and Spain, Canada and the United States. For this reason the Republic of Ireland might secede from the Commonwealth without profoundly affecting her relations at least with Britain. These relations had existed long before the Commonwealth came into being and they would in all probability exist after it had disappeared. All this deserves much emphasis because it means that the secession of Ireland from the Commonwealth and its consequences are really no guide at all to the consequences of secession by an oversea dominion. In their relations with Britain the Commonwealth tie is fundamental; for Ireland it was never more than a superstructure.

This, however, is not to suggest that secession has had no significant consequences. On the contrary, some are already apparent, though at this early stage it is only in relations between governments that they may be at all clearly discerned. When Ireland seceded the Lord Chancellor forecast that Ireland would not retain all the advantages of Commonwealth membership and, in particular, that she would be excluded from Commonwealth consultation and not be considered as a partner in Commonwealth defence matters. This, of course, has happened. At the Commonwealth Finance Ministers' Conference held in London on 15–21 January 1952, for example, the Republic of Ireland was not represented. Instead the Ministers for Finance and for Industry and Commerce came over a few weeks after the conclusion of the Conference to have bilateral consultations with the Chancellor of the Exchequer. Now it is perfectly clear that however useful such bilateral conversations may be they do preclude contact between Irish ministers and ministers in the oversea Commonwealth countries. This same thing is also to be noted in the course of day to day business. The Irish Ambassador in London does not attend the meetings of the Secretary of State for Commonwealth Relations with dominion high commissioners. Likewise in Dublin there is no ground for the Taoiseach, the Prime Minister, to have specially close contact with the representatives of Canada, Australia, or India. Indeed, were he to do so, representatives of other countries would have legitimate ground for complaint. In these ways, therefore, personal contact with the Commonwealth overseas is declining and must inevitably decline still further in the future. The same is true in the equally important field of written communications. There the Republic of Ireland no longer comes within the Commonwealth system. As a result the Irish government loses valuable sources of information particularly about events in countries where they are not themselves diplomatically represented, for example the Soviet Union. More generally this both precludes the Commonwealth from exercising an influence on Irish policy and deprives the Irish of opportunities of making their views heard in world affairs through one of the great groupings of states. All this seems to me to be to the disadvantage of both parties and a clear loss.

Having said so much, however, it must be added that the loss is potential rather than actual. In fact Commonwealth consultation with Éire ceased in the early months of the war, at the request of the Irish government. It was not thereafter resumed. The Irish were in fact represented at no Commonwealth Ministerial Conference since 1932, though their officials did attend conferences of experts, particularly that on nationality, in the postwar years. In general, relations since the economic war (1932–38) were not normal, but I do not think that the force of the conclusion which I have drawn is thereby much diminished, even though it was the prospect, not the actual existence, of intimate consultation between the Republic of Ireland and the Commonwealth countries overseas that virtually disappeared with secession. At a time when western Europe is declining in influence and power and some of the Commonwealth countries overseas at least seem to be treading the path to greatness that is something not to be lightly disregarded.

If, however, the secession of the Republic of Ireland would seem to preclude more intimate relations with the oversea Commonwealth countries no such easy verdict can be pronounced in respect of relations with Britain. There Mr Costello's hope that secession would remove misunderstanding has not been unfulfilled. Even in the realm of practical affairs it may well be, to go back to the example I have already given, an advantage to the Republic that her ministers should discuss the financial problems of the sterling area and trading relations with Britain on a reciprocal basis, for they are quite exceptional in character. In a wider field there would seem, too, to be a perceptible improvement in relations. It so happens that I was in Dublin at the time of the King's [George VI] death. There could be no doubt that the general and sincere expression of sympathy reflected a feeling which for the first time was uninhibited by political or constitutional reservations. Here the contrast with sentiment at the time of the death of George V was marked and there seems little doubt that the disappearance of ambiguities in Anglo-Irish relations have contributed to the changed atmosphere. I found even among ex-Unionists, who had been greatly shocked by the somersault of Fine Gael, some who commented on the easier relations and allowed, albeit a trifle sadly, that perhaps Mr Costello had been right after all. Nor indeed should one fail to note that the Fine Gael party which had hitherto stood, or had been regarded as standing, for the Commonwealth connexion, alone of the parties comprising the inter-party government greatly strengthened its position at the 1951 general election.

I have already alluded to the reciprocal arrangements about citizenship made possible, so far as the United Kingdom is concerned, by the continuing application of the provisions of the British Nationality Act under circumstances different in respect of Éire to those contemplated when the Act was drafted. In general terms the effects of those provisions is that in the United Kingdom while citizens of Éire are no longer British subjects they are not regarded as foreigners and in practice they enjoy the rights and obligations of citizenship. In the Republic citizens of the United Kingdom enjoy reciprocal rights. In the relevant Irish citizenship order issued in 1949 it is stated that citizens of the United Kingdom and colonies 'shall, subject to law, enjoy in Ireland similar rights and privileges to those enjoyed by Irish citizens in the United Kingdom and Colonies by virtue of the British Nationality Act, 1948'.[6] Similar orders have been made in respect of all Commonwealth members other than Pakistan which included no special provision for citizens of the Republic in her Nationality Act.

It must be recorded that these citizenship arrangements, practical and sensible though they are, have not escaped criticism. English people, many of whom are apt to regard Irish insistence on a distinct and wholly separate nationality as an example of Irish contrariness, complain that by means of these reciprocal arrangements the Irish are getting the advantages without assuming the responsibilities of Commonwealth membership. Nor indeed is it only Englishmen who have questioned the appropriateness of these arrangements. In the Oireachtas, the legislature, one voice, that of Senator Margaret Pearse, sister of Patrick Pearse, the leader of the 1916 Easter

---

[6] Statutory Instrument No. 1 of 1949.

Rising, protested that in Britain she felt herself to be an alien as much as she did in France and would prefer to be so regarded.[7] Her father, as has been the case so often with extreme nationalists that it can hardly be mere coincidence, was English. Mr George Bernard Shaw, too, after living in Britain for nearly half a century, though starting from a different premise reached the same conclusion. 'I shall always be a foreigner here', he said, 'whether I have to register as an alien or not, because I am one of the few people here who thinks objectively. Englishmen are incapable of doing this.' (One can only hope that his impressions were in no way derived from his long membership of this Institute! [Royal Institute of International Affairs])

Too much should not be made of these criticisms, for the reciprocal citizenship arrangements command general approval on both sides of the Irish Sea. But it may be worth while saying something about one or two points connected with them. Some of the difficulties of English people in recognizing the existence of a separate Irish nationality have been due to the fact that most English people, at least of a certain class, tend – or until recently, have tended – to meet as many Anglo-Irish as Irish in the strict sense of the word and to confuse the two. Now the Anglo-Irish in the sense in which the term is generally accepted are for the most part descendants of Elizabethan, Stuart, Cromwellian, or Williamite settlers. Unlike the earlier Norman settlers they have not much intermarried with the native Irish because of the religious barrier that has existed since the Reformation. Many, therefore, are the descendants of English settlers in Ireland and have little or no Irish blood. They are mostly Episcopalians, members of the Church of Ireland, and to be distinguished from the Scottish Presbyterians who are settled in the north-eastern counties as well as from the Catholics who comprise more than 90 per cent of the population of the Republic of Ireland. For them the border is historically meaningless for they are on both sides of it. They have, however, acquired distinctive characteristics from their history and environment. Friedrich Engels noted some of these without enthusiasm when he visited Ireland almost a hundred years ago and he described them for the edification of Karl Marx who was then greatly interested in the Irish question. The Anglo-Irish landowners, wrote Engels, were 'mostly tall, handsome men with enormous moustaches under colossal Roman noses', who gave themselves 'the sham military airs of retired colonels' and were 'laden with debts'. They should all, he said, be shot. His description might almost pass today though the allusion to sham military airs is out of place in reference to a small community from whom almost all the successful British generals of the last war were drawn. I asked an Irish economist in Dublin a little while ago

---

[7] Senate Debates, Vol. 36, Col. 339.

how it was that people of almost wholly British descent should have acquired the marked characteristics which impressed Engels so unfavourably. He replied without hesitation, 'Everything in Ireland including the stature and features of Englishmen goes to extravagance'. Now the purpose of this digression is to point out that the Anglo-Irish comprise only some 6 per cent of the population of the Republic, are politically uninfluential and, however loyal to their country of settlement, are unrepresentative particularly in their psychological reaction to the problems of Commonwealth citizenship and Crown. This is something which English visitors should keep in mind if they wish to form a true impression of the innermost impulses of Irish political life.

On the more general question my view is that on balance the reciprocal citizenship arrangements work to the advantage of both parties. It is true that the Irish are the more obvious beneficiaries in that the number of Irishmen coming to work in the United Kingdom exceeds the number of Englishmen seeking refuge from austerity in the Republic. But then the principal reason why Irishmen come in such large numbers to the United Kingdom is because they are needed to undertake heavy and mostly unskilled work for which there is no sufficient alternative supply of labour. Nor must one think of men alone. In the last five years, 1945–51, women emigrants exceeded men by nearly 40 per cent. Most of them find their way into domestic work, factories, and hospitals. I understand that more than half the nurses in English hospitals are now Irish. Is it not in fact much to the advantage of Britain that there should be this labour reserve so conveniently at hand and that those drawn from it should not have to be regarded as aliens? Indeed the fantastic administrative problem involved in any alternative precludes its adoption.

Finally, in the event of a war in which Britain is involved and the Republic is neutral, alien status would certainly place difficulties in the way of Irishmen wishing to volunteer in the British forces. Is this wise or even just? However one may write down some estimates of the number of Irish volunteers in the 1939–45 war it it quite certain that the total was no fewer than 70,000–80,000. Their quality was high perhaps because they were volunteers and the list of their distinctions semi-officially published by the United Kingdom government was indeed impressive. As coming from Tipperary I may perhaps mention that the number of VCs awarded to Tipperary servicemen was four, which is believed to be as high as the number won by any individual county in the British Isles. Few things elicited warmer response than the late King's tribute to these wartime volunteers in his message of goodwill on the proclamation of the Republic. Clearly in such dangerous times as these it would be folly to place any possible obstacle in the way of wartime contribution of this kind.

In the economic field the secession of Ireland made no difference to trading relations with the Commonwealth countries. It was suggested that there was some risk that the continuance of preferential duties in trade with a country which had left the Commonwealth would be challenged as conflicting with the most favoured nation clause in commercial treaties with foreign countries and the General Agreement on Tariffs and Trade made at Geneva in 1947. Here, however, the Irish were always, and it seems rightly, confident. They argued that the very close and long-standing trading relationships between the two countries warranted exceptional treatment, and more particularly they pointed to the fact that the schedule to the Geneva Agreement listed the Commonwealth countries by name and individually without any general heading implying that the preferences they exchanged were dependent upon Commonwealth membership.[8] In 1950 the Irish government reached formal agreement with the United States government in a Treaty of Friendship, Commerce, and Navigation ensuring that the continuance of the existing trade preferences would not be questioned by Washington. The advantage to both Britain and the Republic of Ireland of this close trading relationship is not in question.

In the financial field the Republic of Ireland, though not a member of the Commonwealth, is, like Iceland and Iraq, a member of the sterling area. No country, other than Britain herself, has a greater interest in the maintenance of the strength of sterling as an international currency. That is partly because of Ireland's large oversea investments, mostly in the sterling area, which were estimated in 1947 to amount to £150 per head of the population, and probably larger than for any other country in the world;[9] and partly because of her sterling balances. These balances, which at the conclusion of the war amounted to some £400 million and are now estimated to stand at about £160 million, are not – this is a point on which the Irish are insistent – to be compared with the Egyptian or Indian sterling balances since they were not built up for services rendered but for food supplied at low prices during the war years when it was impossible to buy consumer or capital goods on any comparable scale from Britain. Their existence has the effect of knitting the Irish economy yet more closely to that of the United Kingdom. At the present rate of spending these balances would, however, not last more than three years at most and the government, concerned at the heavy drain on dwindling sterling reserves and of an overspending of dollars, have in recent months struck a note of alarm. The reaction to their solemn warnings was, however, a trifle disconcerting. The economists expressed doubt about the exactitude of the figures, the opposition insisted that the crisis was being greatly

---

[8] *Report on the Geneva Tariff Negotiations*, Cmd 7258, Article 1 and Annex A, 1947.

[9] R. C. Geary, 'Irish Economic Development since the Treaty', *Studies*, Vol. 40, No. 160, December 1951.

exaggerated for political purposes, and Mr Warnock, the Northern Ireland Attorney General, intervened in the ensuing inter-party dispute to say that the language used by ministers clearly indicated that the Republic was far along a road to economic and financial ruin. In fact, while there has undoubtedly been overspending on luxury or quasi-luxury imports the country's economic position would seem to be tolerably sound. The terms of world trade have turned in favour of primary producing countries and the Republic is benefiting and seems likely to continue to benefit in consequence. One small but interesting illustration of this is the export for the first time of chilled beef from Cork to the United States, a development which is satisfying for economists thinking in terms of increased dollar earnings for the sterling area but not so satisfying for those who still hope for good red meat in Britain.

In respect of the essentials of foreign policy secession would seem to have made little difference. The Irish attitude to the Atlantic Pact as defined in 1949 remains unchanged. In an exchange of notes with the United States government that year Mr Sean MacBride, Minister for External Affairs, stated that while partition continued no Irish government whatever their political views could participate with Britain in a military alliance without running counter to the national sentiments of the people and thereby incurring the risk, in the event of a crisis, of civil war within their own jurisdiction.[10] That is the view that continues to prevail. In respect of the United Nations the Irish application for membership still stands, but the presumption is that the Soviet veto will continue to operate and that the Republic will therefore not be admitted to membership. Were some compromise to be reached at the United Nations on the basis perhaps of pairing off applications sponsored by the Soviet Union and by the Western powers the resulting election of the Republic to membership might be somewhat embarrassing to the Irish government. This is partly because of prevailing disillusion with the United Nations and still more because membership in certain circumstances would be inconsistent with neutrality.

The long-standing and deep-seated hostility of the majority of the Irish people to the Soviet Union has not, so far as one can judge, sensibly modified their conviction that neutrality is the only possible policy. It is true that there has been some anxiety in political circles about the possible influence of what are described as 'professional Catholics' in persuading the people that neutrality is not a justifiable policy when atheistic communism is the enemy, but no competent observer suggests that a policy other than neutrality would be followed on the outbreak of war. This does not, however, alter the fact that opinion is anti-Soviet in a sense in which it was not anti-Nazi in 1939. Moreover, however insistent on neutrality,

---

[10] No. 9934.

the Irish government are anxious that their country should not be a weak link in the Western defensive zone. It seems that the requests for arms recently made to the United States government have not been official but there is no doubt about the desire of the Irish government to secure the equipment essential to effective self-defence.

Continuing insistence on the part of political leaders on the risk of internal division, even of civil war, in the event of Irish participation in a world war, deserves some attention. It will be remembered that Mr de Valera in 1939, and particularly in 1941 when the United States came into the war, laid much emphasis on this point saying that for a divided country to throw itself into war would be tantamount to committing suicide. It would be unwise to discount the risk altogether. In the last war any challenge to the authority of the government was effectively forestalled by the internment in 1940 of all suspected of subversive activities. These suspects included communist as well as Nazi sympathisers, and after Hitler had attacked Russia in 1941 life in the Curragh internment camp evidently became so intolerable that both parties are said to have petitioned the Minister for Justice to be separately interned. To these petitions the Minister is said to have replied 'in this war the government is neutral', and to have left them interned together.

At the present time all the evidence available suggests that the number of communist sympathizers in the republic is negligible. Irish nationalism is in fact extremely conservative in its outlook. When the Home Rule party was founded some eighty years ago one important reason for its demand for self-government was, as its manifesto stated, to secure Ireland from the dangers of English revolutionary violence. The predominant opinion in Ireland today is how right they were. In such circumstances it is not surprising that the correspondent sent by the *Daily Worker* to survey the political scene in 1950 should have reported it 'required a considerable amount of courage to be a Socialist in Ireland' and saw no 'hope of improvement' except perhaps through the ending of partition. On the other hand the systematic thought which Engels, Marx and, later, Lenin devoted to the Irish question may well have prompted a Soviet analysis of the possible rôle of Ireland in the class war in its contemporary context. The conclusions drawn from any such analysis might be negative – or they might not.

Partition remains the overriding consideration in all Irish external policies. The extreme tension which followed the insertion in the Ireland Act of the provision stating that in no event should Northern Ireland or any part thereof cease to be part of His Majesty's dominions and of the United Kingdom without the consent of its own Parliament[11] has relaxed. Mr de Valera's statement on his accession to office was notably moderate

---

[11] 12 & 13 Geo. VI c. 41, Art. 1 (2).

in tone and in recent months there has been joint action in respect of hydro-electric schemes, fisheries, and transport involving ministerial conferences in Belfast and Dublin. Such functional cooperation may not be without importance for the future. The fast through train that is now running experimentally from Cork to Belfast – appropriately named the 'Enterprise' – may perhaps be the herald of cooperation in a widening area of common interest.

It has been felt outside the Republic that the late [inter-party government] government overplayed their hand in declining to subscribe to the North Atlantic Treaty and almost simultaneously seceding from the Commonwealth. They could afford to do one or the other but not both without incurring some risk of weakening their position. With that criticism I agree. At the same time the Irish reaction to United States policies should not be disregarded. One of the most striking developments of the last decade has been the decline of American influence in Ireland. It is still very great, particularly in country areas where they have long memories of the many emigrants who in dark days travelled to the United States and who found wealth and welcome there, but it is no longer something to conjure with.

In the past, *Whitaker's Almanack* used to divide the world into the British Empire, the United States, and foreign countries. Today the Republic of Ireland has rightly been added to the intermediate category and the Commonwealth Parliamentary Association is adopting a similar course in inviting the United States and the Republic of Ireland to form associate groups in their respective countries. But if the Republic of Ireland is neither a foreign country nor a member of the Commonwealth there is still considerable latitude permissible in the emphasis which one places on her relation to those two categories. Looking at the position first from the point of view of Britain herself I believe it to be a mistake to go on regarding the Republic of Ireland as a Commonwealth country which has strayed from the fold. One cannot go back on history and it is the duty of statesmanship to make the best of an existing situation. Looking to the future Britain might be well advised therefore to forget a good deal of the past. Though every fair-minded person will recognize that dominion status was imposed on the Irish Free State, none the less the fact remains that, taken as a whole, she was an unsatisfactory dominion. From the first she worked for the dilution of dominion status, for the removal of the Crown from her Constitution, for the abolition of Privy Council appeals, though here Canada took the first step; she was the first dominion to replace the concept of common citizenship with that of reciprocal citizenship; she was the first, too, to set the lamentable example of neutrality in a major war; and finally the first to secede.[12] All this makes a depressing and

---

[12] Burma who seceded a year earlier had never been a dominion.

discouraging record. On the other hand, if the Republic of Ireland is regarded as a foreign country how very different is the impression that emerges. How fortunate indeed is Britain to have as her nearest neighbour a country remarkable amongst the countries of western Europe for her devotion to and effective working of the British parliamentary system, for her exceptional stability of government, for her comparatively strong financial position; a country moreover which is a reservoir of labour, whose principal export is food, of which more than 90 per cent comes to the United Kingdom, and who above all can be relied upon, whatever the policy of her own government, to send material reinforcement in the form of volunteers to serve in the British forces in wartime. In short, is Britain not much to be envied in her Atlantic neighbour?

Now I have deliberately heightened the contrast but does it not suggest that psychologically at least it is of importance that the United Kingdom should regard the Republic of Ireland more as a foreign country than as an ex-member of the Commonwealth with all that implies? Has not the time come, to take a practical example, when the possibility of securing greater supplies of food from our food-exporting neighbour should be more thoroughly explored than they have been in the past and without any political reservation? Indeed the desirability of regarding Irish affairs in a new context is such that I have come to the reluctant conclusion that responsibility for them might with advantage be transferred from the Commonwealth Relations Office to the Foreign Office.

But if all this is the right approach from the British point of view I would have thought it would be quite the wrong approach from the Irish point of view. The major objective of Irish policy is the ending of partition and that can be done only by agreement. There, to my mind, the possible contribution of the Commonwealth has been consistently underestimated largely because it has been viewed in too narrow a context. Nowhere has the Republic better friends than in the oversea dominions. For that reason alone it is important that the possibilities implicit in association in one form or another with the Commonwealth should always be kept to the forefront in Ireland. Is the reunion of Ireland in the foreseeable future conceivable except within some wider framework which must include the countries of the Commonwealth? May it not indeed be that in the fullness of time India, who learned so much in the past from Ireland about the ways in which republicanism might be reconciled with Commonwealth membership, will, in her turn, suggest to Irishmen how their differences may be reconciled through a Commonwealth whose guiding principle is national self-government and which now embraces within its fold both republics and monarchies?

13

NOTES ON CONVERSATIONS

Conversation with Eamon de Valera, February 1952
(first interview)

(i)   If in office, Eire happy to accept Indian solution – would have
        striven for it.

(ii)   In 1936–7 idea Const. [Constitution] first – Ex. Rel. [External Rela-
        tions] Act second.

(iii)   Ex. A. [External Association] Act not satisfactory but moving
        forward. Powers to An T. [Taoiseach] for accreditation.

(iv)   Secession in 1949 because C. [Costello] regarded Republic as in
        existence since 1936 – but no need to express view.

(v)   Dict. Rep. [Dictionary Republic] (a charming smile) a mistake –
        he saw it now but afraid of definition.

(vi)   In war – satisfaction 1939–40. Pressure for Germany, later reversed
        – v. difficult position.

(vii)   UN [United Nations]? accept membership if came. Favoured
        smaller but united organisation.

(viii) No gap in defence if supplied with arms for which asked.

(ix)   Noticeable less close to Commonwealth since 1949: often held H.
        C. [High Commissioner] Meetings before that.

Conversation with Eamon de Valera, February 1952 (second interview)

(i)   Citizenship – reciprocal since 1921. In practice perhaps not over much difference but avoided suggestion of organic union. Revision of [External Relations] Act contemplated when he left office. Perhaps necessary. But arrangement seemed satisfactory – If dual citizenship, that concerned other countries. Only if war between them serious problem.

(ii)   Ext. A. [external association] 'The idea that failed'. In 1920 draft suggested to colleagues (some 25) referred to association. They were dissatisfied. While tying bootlace on the side of his bed thought of 'external' to qualify. Knew at once it was right. Colleagues accepted, only question later from pro-Treaty man, 'Would it be only external'. 'It would'. Supreme importance of words – of the right word in politics.

(iii)   Dictionary republic speech – Chuckled over it himself. Mistake. But intended to make clear that if allegiance waived Eire would remain associated with Commonwealth. It was for U.K. to decide if that was possible. For his part favoured that solution. It was as far as majority would or should go to secure unity. It was a compromise and like all compromises attacked from every side. One shouldn't propose compromise until assured of its acceptance.

(iv)   Position now – not external association or association. Best regarded as foreign country with Treaty arrangements, extensive but still best angle of approach.

(v)   Redmond & Carson – Laughed outright at suggestions of offering more – never persuade Unionists to accept – whole of Ulster in 1914 had political appeal to Carson's followers.

(vi)   Never kept diary or papers. Not fair or safe in civil war. But had notes and a lot of unsorted correspondence including exchange of letters with Smuts. He had 'the most able and penetrating political mind that I have met'. Far superior to Lloyd George because he was concerned to solve problems. Angry because he published letter to him (de V.) simultaneously with despatch.

(vii)   V. pleased at suggestion that he should write autobiography.

Conversation with J. A. Costello, February 1952

Repeal of External Relations Act

Not occasioned by slights from Lord A. [Alexander] G. G. [Governor-General] of Canada.[1] True embarrassment first with St. Laurent and later at banquet about National Anthem. Agreement reached that at banquet C. [Costello] should propose 'God Save the King' and G. G. reply, 'The President'. Mr. C. proposed but G. G. did not respond. He had on menu card 'Roaring Meg' Londonderry Cannon, a further cause of offence.[2] But none of this reason for repeal.

On Sunday before announcement, Sunday Independent published forecast of repeal. Press enquiry to C. who put receiver down. On reflection and suspecting deliberate leak (MacBride) and clearly influenced by incidents above decided at Press Conference next day to say Yes. This was in accordance with general Cabinet view as recorded in minutes but evidently not in point of time.

Did Repeal mean Secession?

This would not seem to have been carefully considered. Antipathy to formula pronounced. Mackenzie King[3] – to whom many tributes – understood and would not appear to have thought so. (? speech) Nor did Irish Times. Everything depended on U.K. U.K. attitude stiffened (? because of India). At Chequers Conference however attitude mollified in face of strong pressure from New Zealand, Australia and above all Canada. Agreement to make no statement till Irish returned. But 6 o'clock news made full and grave pronouncement. Bitterly resented as breach of faith. Attributed to D. O. [Dominions Office] spokesman? Gordon Walker.[4] Also broadcast earlier (? by Wheare[5]) indicated allegiance essential. Then on secession pressed. But in any event Indian solution unacceptable because of reference to King as Head of the Commonwealth.

Consultation

Discontinued – Irish request some months after war – fear of commitment, not resumed. At Conferences – e.g. finance – advantage of reciprocal talks, but loss of contact with overseas dominions (confirmed by Australian Ambassador).

---

[1] Field-Marshal Harold R. L. G. Alexander, 1st Earl Alexander of Tunis (1891–1969), several wartime Commands; Governor-General of Canada 1946–52.

[2] Roaring Meg, a cannon famed in Ulster for its role in the defence of Derry against the Catholic forces of James II.

[3] William Lyon Mackenzie King (1874–1950), Leader of Canadian Liberal Party 1919–48; Prime Minister 1921–6, 1926–30, 1935–48.

[4] Patrick Christien Gordon Walker (Life Peer) (1907–80), Commonwealth Relations Office, Parliamentary Under-Secretary of State 1947–50; Secretary of State 1950–1.

[5] Sir Kenneth Clinton Wheare, see above p. 129.

Conversation with Seán Lemass, February 1952

(i) Consultation possibly better on reciprocal basis – certainly full information.

(ii) Closely tied to sterling area – more closely than most – 90% of exports.

(iii) Sterling balance – largely accumulated during war – low prices (probably mistaken pigs and butter) but all for goods supplied.

(iv) Diversification of agriculture. Many reasons – strategic one – balance in agriculture another. Export of fat cattle to U.S. Dollar earner and change system of store export.

(v) Crisis? difficulties of calculating exactly – exports through customs and border Agreement of 1948 – renewal of 1938 – criticized at time – but probably right. Imp. pref. [imperial preference] of mutual advantage.

Conversation with Frederick Boland,[6] 1952

Mr de Valera before his fall from power in 1948 had it in mind to introduce legislation to give the President powers to appoint Ambassadors and Ministers on his own authority, but he felt that there was no need to repeal the External Relations Act at the same time. It was only remissive in intention and it would fall into practical disuse.

The coalition Government had not very clear views about the repeal of the External Relations Act until the summer of 1948. The question was brought to the fore by an enquiry from the C. R. O. [Commonwealth Relations Office] asking whether the Irish Government would like to be represented at the October meeting of the Commonwealth Prime Ministers and suggesting that if they expressed such a desire a formal invitation would probably be forthcoming. This was discussed in the Irish Cabinet. It was felt there that Irish representation would be all to the good but that before the Irish went they would have to clarify their position. Accordingly the balance of opinion came down in favour of informing the U.K. Government through Lord Rugby[7] that if the Irish came they would feel (1) that the question of partition must be raised and (2) that they would take the opportunity of discussing in the Conference the position created by the

---

[6] Frederick Henry Boland (1904–1985). Secretary, Department of External Affairs 1946; Irish Ambassador to Britain 1950–6; Irish Permanent Representative at the United Nations, 1956 (President 1960).

[7] John Loader Maffey, 1st Baron of Rugby (1877–1969), distinguished interwar service in India and the Sudan, UK Representative to Éire 1939–49.

External Relations Act and their desire to repeal it. Lord Rugby without expressing any clear view did not seem disturbed by these proposals but pressed Mr MacBride for an answer to the main question, that is to say, whether the Irish Government welcomed an invitation? Mr MacBride explained that the Cabinet had as yet taken no clear decision but suggested that he thought that they might favour representation.

The Cabinet itself while it had discussed the desirability of repealing the External Relations Act had reached no conclusions when Mr Costello went to Canada. His announcement there of the Irish intention to repeal the External Relations Act came as a 'bomb shell' to his colleagues. Mr MacBride had had his conversation with Lord Rugby either the day before or that morning and it was only about an hour before he was due to dine with the Secretary of State for Commonwealth Relations, Mr Noel-Baker, that the news of Costello's pronouncement was brought to him. As External Affairs Minister he was highly indignant and felt he had been placed in a very difficult position. One of his first actions was to send a note to Lord Rugby saying that his conversation with him had in fact been entirely in good faith.

These decisions were taken entirely without relation to developments in India. The Indian delegation had come to see de Valera in 1947 and he had impressed upon them the desirability of some sort of external association, probably on the lines of Document A of 1921. They were duly impressed and in fact the Indian policy coincided almost exactly with the policy advocated in Document A (see Appendix 16, D. Macardle, *The Irish Republic*). His feeling was that once external association had been more formally established the Irish mission in the Commonwealth would be much strengthened, particularly in respect of partition. Throughout he believed strongly in Irish cooperation with the Commonwealth overseas. The great difference of emphasis between him and MacBride was that the latter believed in Western European cooperation, de Valera in Commonwealth cooperation.

Boland was himself present at the November 1948 meeting in Paris. The Irish Government intended to go ahead with secession whatever the consequences but in the Paris discussions the influence of the overseas dominions was strongly in favour of compromise. Fraser[8] took the lead in advocating a reciprocal citizenship arrangement and the maintenance of their provinces. Evatt[9] supported him but it was the intervention of Lester Pearson[10] made with great weight which was decisive with the U.K. In fact

---

[8] Peter Fraser (1884–1950), Labour Prime Minister of New Zealand 1940–9.

[9] Rt Hon. Herbert Vere Evatt (1894–1965), Australian Attorney-General and Minister for External Affairs 1941–9; Deputy Prime Minister of Australia 1946–9; President of the UN Assembly 1949.

[10] Rt Hon. Lester Bowles Pearson OM (1897–1972), Canadian Secretary of State for External Affairs, 1948–57; Prime Minister of Canada 1963–8.

the preference seemed to be safeguarded both by the Burmese precedent which had been carefully studied in Dublin and by the wording of the special provisions of the Irish schedule. Originally the list of countries between whom preferences were excepted and which include both Eire and Burma had been Commonwealth countries. Boland himself proposed in 1947 that there should in fact be no heading to the list. This weighed decisively in later discussions with Washington. In fact through the negotiation of the Irish American treaty, the Irish Government ensured that the preferential differences would not be questioned by Washington.

   With his return to Office, de Valera made no secret in that he thought secession had been a mistake. He could not, however, go back and he now placed emphasis on the reference in the Paris Communiqué to their special relations with Commonwealth countries. He favoured provisions for citizenship and felt that if partition were ever to be resolved, something of the kind was essential. For the rest he was inclined to feel that direct conversations and direct contact with Belfast on administrative matters was the right approach to the problem. At the same time what had been done could not be undone and for example Irish representation at Finance Ministers Conferences which they were deeply interested in was now not possible. But all the time de Valera had his eye on the possibility of working in more closely.

Conversation with President De Valera, 21 September 1965[11]

The President recalled his meetings with General Smuts on the latter's visit to Dublin before the truce in 1921. Smuts, he said, set out the argument for the Commonwealth most persuasively – more persuasively than he had heard before or read since. Smuts's greatest emphasis was on the value of free association always developing as against a fixed and limited treaty relationship outside the Commonwealth. De Valera said he would have found the arguments irresistible, had his mind not already been otherwise made up. 'If I could have been persuaded, Smuts would have persuaded me' and again 'I have never heard the case so well put'. Smuts, he thought a man of finer intellect and of greater depth than Lloyd George. But Smuts was 'slim'. He knew from his own experience this was so. Smuts published private correspondence, which he must have known was private, in an attempt to appeal to the Irish people over or behind de Valera who was their leader. De Valera never forgave him and never trusted him again.

---

[11] Conversation held at Áras an Uachtaráin; the President's biographer, T. P. O'Neill joined them for lunch.

When reminded that he had admitted that he had never expected such advances as took place under Dominion status the President laughed and said he must have been 'in a generous mood'. He added he probably had another – 'a British audience' – in mind.

He had some contact with Canadian and South African statesmen in the thirties, but it was clearly limited and he said expressly he was not interested in them as representatives of dominions. He was interested and concerned with the Statute of Westminster only in so far as it might undermine the British position. He did not use it as a weapon because if he did so he 'might have got too far drawn into the Commonwealth by so doing'.

He had no knowledge of any favourable Commonwealth influences on Anglo-Irish relations either at the 1921 or 1937 Imperial Conferences. He thought Chamberlain's 1938 initiatives were his own. He had many conversations with Malcolm MacDonald preparing the way for the 1938 Agreement, as well as talks in the concluding stages with Neville Chamberlain. He was convinced that Chamberlain was under no illusions about the imminence of war. Chamberlain had remarked to him 'It may come at any moment – before we are ready'. Why did Chamberlain return the Treaty Ports? Chamberlain said that with regard to submarines 'we have the answer'. De Valera realised that meant the answer without the Treaty Ports. He did not ask why. He later assumed the answer was radar. Once Chamberlain had made that remark he knew he would get the Treaty Ports back. He spoke of Chamberlain throughout with warm affection. His opinion had not been qualified in any way by subsequent criticisms. He had thought of Hitler for long as a nationalist and conceded that also for long he thought that many of the things said about Hitler were propaganda. He knew Beneš well and he thought he had weakened his position by not standing firmly on principle in 1938. He referred admiringly several times to de Gaulle. That was where he stood.

At lunch the President gave an account of his court-martial in 1916 in a schoolroom (or in a room like a schoolroom). Appropriately enough he recalled the court-martial as being like an examination. The verdict was 'Guilty'. He was taken to a cell. The death sentence was read out to him. There was what seemed to him a long pause. Then it was added that the death sentence had been commuted to life imprisonment. He assumed it meant literally this. A fellow prisoner said to him he would be out in a year. The thought surprised him.

In 1921, negotiations with Lloyd George were deliberately prolonged throughout the summer so that the war would not in any circumstances be resumed during the long evenings. The idea of external association came to him one morning as he was tying his bootlaces, sitting on his bed, and he conceived of it first in mathematical terms with a large circle, including five small circles (Britain and the four dominions) with another small circle outside touching the large circle and representing Ireland.

The President was evidently much more interested in recalling events of the period 1916–21 than those of the thirties, in which on this occasion I was especially interested. He said to me at one moment, with a smile, that I would have to act as chairman of the meeting on this account.

The President asked me about my address to Chatham House on *The Implications of Eire's Relations with the British Commonwealth of Nations* and which of the Labour Ministers (and others) had been present. He had evidently known or been briefed about its contribution to the Indian settlement.

Part IV

Reappraisals

14

IRELAND:
From British Commonwealth Towards
European Community

I

In the first volume of Professor Sir Keith Hancock's *Survey of British Commonwealth Affairs* two chapters are devoted exclusively to Irish relations with the Commonwealth. The first is entitled 'Saorstát Éireann' and the second 'Ireland Unappeased'.[1] The titles are themselves virtually self-explanatory – the earlier chapter dealing with the coming into existence of the dominion of the Irish Free State and the later with the second wave of the revolutionary movement under de Valera's leadership in the thirties. The chapters are distinctive in style and content and, most of all, in the nature of their analysis. No Irishman, it may be thought, could have written with so much detachment and no Englishman in such perspective. The achievement is the more remarkable in as much as the topic was in part peripheral to the theme of the *Survey*. Anglo-Irish relations had their own past, they had developed their own momentum and, divorced from Commonwealth, they have now moved towards new conclusions. But even though the Irish relationship with the Commonwealth proved brief and transient, the issues raised by it at a particular juncture in time had great significance, not least in terms of a complex case-study in the relevance of the concept of Commonwealth to the resolution of problems of imperial–national relations.

---

[1] *Survey of British Commonwealth Affairs,* Vol. 1, *Problems of Nationality* (Oxford, 1937), Chs. 3 and 6.

In the Irish, as in the more general chapters of the *Survey*, Professor Hancock worked upon a broad canvas, but his focus was sharp. He examined the circumstances that were relevant to his theme, he entered into the thought and action of 'the Troubles' (it is in the plural that they are more often spoken of in the east and south, as against the singular, 'the Trouble' in the north and west, and as 'the Bad Times' among the Anglo-Irish for whom, indeed, they were so) but his viewpoint, as indeed he reminded his readers more than once, was external. He was engaged by interest not by origin; he was a historian neither of Ireland, nor of Anglo-Irish relations, but of the Commonwealth.

It was the meeting point between the two that provided him with his theme. In the aftermath of the fiftieth anniversary of the 1916 Easter Rebellion, signalized in Ireland by nationwide celebrations – in respect of commemoration revolutionaries are the great traditionalists – and a flow of books, many of considerable interest,[2] and within a few years of the fiftieth anniversary of a Treaty, not likely to be the occasion of such united national acclaim, Professor Hancock's pages have still their own original contribution to offer. The two surprising things about them are, first, how comparatively little later evidence, even where it adds to knowledge, modifies the essentials of the analysis, and second, the freshly minted ring even now of the commentary.

After remarking that throughout the nineteenth century the Irish question had been in form a domestic problem of the United Kingdom, Professor Hancock proceeded (in the first of his two Irish chapters) to say that in fact it was

> an Empire matter also for Irish brain and brawn were playing more than their proportional part in building up the new British communities beyond the seas. In more than one of these communities men of Irish name predominated in the opinion making professions of the publican, the policeman, the poet, and the politician.[3]

He noted also and more generally that Ireland's influence upon the Empire, though indirect, had been considerable before 1921 and that in 1923, when representatives of the Irish Free State attended their first Imperial Conference, it became direct.

With the passage of the years interest in the broad theme of the interrelation between Ireland and Empire has been enhanced rather than diminished. Two aspects of it in particular would seem now deserving of

---

[2] Among them may be noted *Leaders and Men of the Easter Rising: Dublin 1916*, edited by F. X. Martin (London, 1967); *1916: The Easter Rising*, edited by Owen D. Edwards and Fergus Pyle (London, 1968); and *The Irish Struggle 1916–1922*, edited by T. Desmond Williams (London, 1966).

[3] *op. cit.*, p. 92.

inquiry in the light of recent disclosures and reappraisals. Those aspects can best be formulated as questions: what was the place of Ireland in British thinking about Empire, and of Empire in the shaping of British attitudes to Ireland in the period that preceded Irish membership of the Commonwealth?

II

The interest that attaches nowadays to these questions derives largely from reconsideration of the significance of the events of 1886. In the past historians of Commonwealth, most of whom belonged to the liberal tradition, thought principally in terms of the defeat of Home Rule for Ireland. Their premise, whether stated or unstated, was apt to be that an opportunity had been missed which, if it had been seized, would have enabled Ireland to travel peacefully with the overseas colonies of settlement along the broad highway that led to dominion status.

The resulting concentration on what did not happen may seem now to have led to an underestimate of the significance of what did, i.e. of the actual consequences of the defeat of Home Rule. Principal among them at this distance in time would seem to have been the emergence of an English party, the Unionist party, which, while priding itself on the pragmatism of its approach to domestic and imperial affairs, was in one particular tied to dogma. That particular was Anglo-Irish relations and that dogma was the sanctity of the Union. Even though it would now appear that the Unionist party, out of office from December 1905 till the formation of the first wartime coalition in 1915, moved less rapidly and more reluctantly than was formerly supposed towards political extremes, it could be argued that from 1886 onwards Unionist insistence upon the Union, and nothing but the Union, was in itself the extreme, fundamentalist position.

In a pamphlet published in 1913[4] A. J. Balfour, by then superseded in the leadership of the Unionist party, argued not merely that Home Rule was financially, administratively and constitutionally unworkable (as Balfour indeed believed it to be) but furthermore that it was in logic indefensible. That was so because, in Balfour's view, there was and there could be no middle ground between Union and separation. Those who concluded, as Balfour himself did not, that 'Irish patriotism in its exclusive and more hostile form, is destined to be eternal' ought, he argued, to be thinking of separation rather than introducing one more Home Rule bill, in the mistaken Gladstonian belief that Union might be strengthened by

---

[4] A. J. Balfour, *Nationality and Home Rule* (London, 1913).

timely concession to indigenous local sentiment. Either Union stood intact as a part of the constitution or the political entity that was the United Kingdom disintegrated. While historically, therefore, the issue dividing Unionists from Home Rulers narrowed down before the First World War to Ulster, it was not, on Balfour's line of argument, from Ulster that it derived. It was rather from a concept, common to Unionists and to Sinn Féiners, of the nature of Anglo-Irish relations that excluded a half-way house – a Home Rule Ireland and by necessary inference an Irish dominion – between Union and separation.

The domestic argument against Home Rule was reinforced by an imperial one. In 1886 Salisbury was persuaded that the concession of Home Rule to Ireland would lead inexorably to the disintegration (a favourite word of his) not only of the polity of the United Kingdom but also, and as a result, to the disintegration of Britain's imperial position. By his party, by most members of his class and by eminent imperial administrators, this seemingly highly debatable proposition came to be accepted *in toto* almost as an article of faith, and because of this the Union had to be upheld not only in the interests of the United Kingdom but also of the whole Empire.

This explains how it was that by 1914 the cause of Ulster had become the cause of the Union and the cause of Union the cause of Empire. Ulster was a means to an end; the end was the preservation of the Union and thereby the integrity of the Empire. And it was this imperial interest that moved imperial administrators, soldiers and even statesmen not otherwise interested in Irish affairs, to action. Many of them had a qualified faith in democratic processes, Lord Milner providing the outstanding example. Milner felt 'only loathing for the way things were done in England in the political sphere' and he disdained the whims 'of a rotten public opinion'. Before 1914 he used his remarkable administrative gifts for the organization of opposition in Great Britain, chiefly through the Union Defence League, to Home Rule, securing by 1914 close on two million signatures for the British Covenant. He also sought and apparently obtained substantial financial backing for measures which he was ready to contemplate, but from which even Craig and Carson shrank. Compared with all the other leaders, writes his most recent biographer, A. M. Gollin, Milner 'was the least anxious to seek a solution to the Ulster problem'.[5] Later Milner became a member of Lloyd George's War Cabinet and he was Colonial Secretary (1919–21) in Lloyd George's post-war Coalition. And it was Bonar Law, a statesman also with an imperial background, though of a different kind, who was to the last among the strongest opponents of a dominion settlement.

---

[5] A. M. Gollin, *Proconsul in Politics* (London, 1964), pp. 45–6 and 187–8. See generally, Chap. 8.

Professor Hancock observed with justice that after 1916 Irish leaders who found themselves negotiating with English statesmen carried not only a heavy burden of responsibility towards the living, but upon their shoulders they also carried 'a dreadful tyranny of the dead'. But what of the position of those English statesmen, or at least of the Unionists and imperialists among them? Did they not also have a burden, the burden of a dogma and was not this also a major factor in determining the timing and the nature of the Irish settlement? Lloyd George sometimes described himself as the prisoner of the coalition with its large inbuilt Unionist majority, and in the light of Unionist tradition it becomes *inter alia* as pertinent to ask how it was that Lloyd George contrived a dominion status settlement, as it is to explore the devious means he employed to reach that goal.

III

If it be suggested that some reappraisal of the nature of Unionism in its English and imperial manifestations and its bearing on British policy from 1916 (when there is reason to suppose Lloyd George and members of his Cabinet first seriously inclined towards partition) to 1921 might be put side by side with Sir Keith Hancock's analysis of the Ulster Unionist position[6] and of Irish republicanism, in assessing the forces that went to the making of the dominion settlement and the political balance which it represented, Professor Hancock himself has recently added some important particulars to our knowledge of how the negotiations for that settlement first began.

They are set forth in the second volume of his biography of Smuts where there is an exciting account[7] of the South African Prime Minister's mediatory role, hitherto known in outline and chiefly from the point of view of King George V, as described in Sir Harold Nicolson's *Life*.[8] The King believed that Smuts 'of all men will be able to induce Mr de Valera to be reasonable and to agree to a settlement'. In one sense he was right; in another mistaken. Smuts expounded the virtues of dominion status to de Valera and de Valera subsequently acknowledged that no man – and most certainly not Lloyd George – then or subsequently recommended it to him with such force and logic. But while Smuts, in some remarkable phrases reproduced by Professor Hancock, discounted republicanism and indeed much of his own brief Transvaal past – it was as a Transvaaler by adoption that he served in Kruger's government – he was speaking to one who was not to be convinced. 'As a friend', Smuts concluded, 'I cannot

---

[6] See especially *op. cit.*, pp. 95–7.

[7] W. K. Hancock, *Smuts: The Fields of Force* (Cambridge, 1968), pp. 49–61.

[8] H. Nicolson, *Life of King George V* (London, 1952), pp. 346–9.

advise you too strongly against a Republic. Ask what you want, but not a Republic.'

De Valera followed this advice in the sense of not asking for a republic by name, but he disregarded it in the sense of remaining an uncompromised champion of the republic. Not many men indeed were so adaptable in such matters as Smuts and, given his republican past, he appears strangely uncomprehending of the Irish psychological commitment to the republic. But much more important, the episode serves to illustrate in a personal context, and from a fresh angle, the continuing interrelation in a changing context of Anglo-Irish and imperial affairs. 'I need not', wrote Smuts to Lloyd George, 'enlarge to you on the importance of the Irish question for the Empire as a whole.'[9]

This brings one to the grand theme lying at the heart of de Valera's correspondence with Lloyd George in the summer of 1921 and preliminary to the Treaty negotiations, which formed the focal point of Professor Hancock's analysis of the issues underlying the Treaty settlement. Writing in the thirties with the anti-Treaty republicans firmly entrenched in office, Professor Hancock showed himself preoccupied most of all with the meaning and nature of Irish republican concepts. His critique remains as readable and as relevant as the day it was written. But all the same the balance has somewhat shifted. The Irish desire for a republic, even in the context of Commonwealth, no longer appears exceptional, but rather as normal. The great majority of peoples of non-British extraction, when given a free choice, has opted not for monarchy but for republicanism.

In the longer perspective, therefore, one might be disposed to probe more closely into British attitudes. Why was Lloyd George so insistent throughout his correspondence with de Valera, and so uncompromising in negotiation, upon allegiance to the Crown as the essential condition of settlement? Was he moved by his own convictions, or by the composition of the Coalition over which he presided, or by an appraisal of British or imperial interests? Or, as may be nearer the mark, was the thought of a relationship not conditional upon allegiance (though Neville Chamberlain was apparently not averse to weighing its possibilities) so novel as by that alone to be precluded from serious consideration? After all it remains the case that the Irish leaders were prepared to make substantial concessions in respect of defence and trade in return for recognition of a republic externally associated with the Empire and acknowledging the King as head of the association. Lloyd George, however, was at one with de Valera on the importance he attached to political symbols, and today the position of each would seem equally demanding of examination.

---

[9] Quoted in Hancock, *Smuts*, p. 53.

IV

Professor Hancock remarked, not without approbation, upon the policies both domestic and external of the pro-Treaty party under President Cosgrave, who for the first ten years of the existence of the new state presided with quiet distinction. 'In domestic affairs', Professor Hancock wrote, 'as in its relations with fellow-members of the Commonwealth and of the League, the Irish Free State under Mr Cosgrave's guidance sought to demonstrate the capacity of the Irish to pass the most stringent tests of political capacity and respectability.' They pursued the political and economic orthodoxies of the day 'with a proud resolution'. And he sums it all up in these words:

> The Irish Free State under Mr Cosgrave was the objective, the unemotional, scientific, intellectual State. Throughout Europe, and not least in Ireland, people were beginning to tire of this kind of state. They wanted more emotion and more drama. The political artists were pushing aside the political scientists. The party state was challenging the neutral state. In Ireland people were getting weary of their Government's very virtues. They were tired of hearing Mr Cosgrave called the just.[10]

Perhaps one might enter a modest caveat here. Yeats, briefly and improbably ensconced in the Irish Senate for one, and the young Frank O'Connor for another, would surely have sharply repudiated the adjective 'intellectual', while, whatever may have been the position in the capital, few in the southern counties at least would have had much occasion to grow weary of Cosgrave for the reason the Greeks grew tired of Aristides. But more important, did this impressionistic sketch in one respect imply a clearer sense of direction on the part of the Cosgrave government than in fact it possessed?

In external, as in domestic affairs, Professor Hancock wrote of the pro-Treaty administration as being logical in its thinking, straightforward in its purpose. That certainly was the impression the party leaders wished to leave in the early thirties. They had accepted the Treaty; they had fought for it. In the Treaty debate they had argued in the words of Michael Collins that the Treaty 'gave freedom to achieve freedom' and they had contended, in the words of Kevin O'Higgins, that even though Ireland had been forced into membership, the Commonwealth was in fact a 'league of free nations'. The purpose of their government subsequently was to enlarge the area of freedom and to give detailed practical effect to the conception of dominion equality with Britain. They had been concerned, recalled Patrick McGilligan speaking in the Dáil on the passage of the Statute of Westminster, to pull 'the old Colonial Empire asunder'. They believed,

---

[10] *Survey*, Vol. 1, pp. 322–4.

and rightly, that they had played an important part in so doing.

But, and here a certain ambivalence creeps in, what was their ultimate purpose? Were they concerned to remodel the Commonwealth in accord with prevailing dominion national 'orthodoxies' so as to make it at once more acceptable to Irish opinion and more suited to further Irish interests? Or were they rather concerned to weaken the ties of Commonwealth so as to make easier Ireland's ultimate secession? Or were they themselves uncertain of their goal and was this one contributory factor in their downfall?

These are questions, not susceptible of an explicit answer, but inviting further consideration in the light of a wider range both of experience and of evidence than was available thirty years ago. On the first, namely experience, most relevant at this stage is the fact that it was an inter-party government, in which Fine Gael, the lineal successor of the pro-Treaty party of the twenties, and including most of its prominent surviving personalities, were the principal partners, that was responsible for Irish secession from the Commonwealth. Did this represent an inner consistency of purpose throughout the whole period 1921–48 as members of the party subsequently contended, or did it represent a 'somersault fit to make a skeleton merry' as their critics alleged? Recently opened British official records, coupled with some Irish commentaries, while not at this stage providing material for an answer, serve to lend added interest to the enquiry.

The Irish would appear to have played little active part at the Imperial Conference of 1923 and for them 1926 provided a first full-dress occasion for the formulation of attitudes. The records of the meetings of the Committee on Inter-Imperial relations confirm conclusively that the initiative in respect of a formal declaration of dominion rights and a comprehensive definition of dominion status was South African. There is no evidence in the papers of any Irish draft for the Balfour Report, though it is to be noted the record is not complete, since by agreement minutes were not taken of discussions upon drafts of the italicized formula in the report. In the opening discussion on South African proposals the observations of Kevin O'Higgins suggested that the Irish Free State government set, at least by comparison with the South African, little store by a general declaration and much by action on points of particular concern to them. In comparing the situation in the Irish Free State to that of the Union of South Africa, Kevin O'Higgins noted that there was in both countries an intense and sensitive nationalism, but he is reported to have proceeded:

> A declaration such as has been suggested [by General Hertzog] would be of little value if contradicted by the facts. There are certain anomalies and anachronisms which appear to be a denial of equal status and which should be removed. . . . All these matters should be adjusted and insofar

as they can be met, every sacrifice of form will be more than compensated by increase of satisfaction.[11]

The Irish Free State delegation further developed this theme in a full-length paper on 'Existing Anomalies in the British Commonwealth of Nations'[12] which, in itself, sufficiently indicated their principal purpose. It was to identify inequalities in status and to establish equality with Britain on the basis of their elimination. The memorandum opened as follows:

> The principle of the absolute equality of status and the legislative, judicial and constitutional independence of the British Commonwealth of Nations is now admitted beyond controversy. It is accordingly thought that it would be opportune to direct attention to some of the more outstanding anomalies and anachronisms which appear to detract from that principle with the object of abrogating anything which in form or substance interferes with its complete application in practice.

The memorandum proceeded to urge the approval in principle and the recognition in practice of the fundamental right of the government of each dominion to advise the King in all matters whatsoever relating to its own affairs. There followed proposals to delimit the functions of the Governor-General; to establish equal rights in territorial legislation; to ensure the repeal of the Colonial Laws Validity Act (the very title of which was said to imply subjection and its substance, subversion of the principles of autonomy and constitutional co-equality); to amend the royal titles so as to place the Irish Free State in due dominion order after South Africa and before India (this was not precisely achieved); to ensure that appeals might lie to the Judicial Committee of the Privy Council only at the wish of the dominion concerned (on which a separate memorandum was submitted);[13] to remove restrictions on extraterritorial legislation by the dominions; and to ensure direct correspondence between dominion Ministries of External Affairs and foreign countries.

All these points, and most of them were by no means peculiar to the Irish Free State, demonstrated, as did the recorded Irish contributions to the general discussions upon them at meetings of the Inter-Imperial Relations Committee, the Irish resolve to remove all elements of subordination. This tactical approach did not, however, necessarily disclose their broader strategy.

It has long been known, one important source being T. de V. White's biography of Kevin O'Higgins, that the Irish delegation remained attracted

---

[11] Cab. 32/56 E (I.R./26) 1st Meeting, p. 10.

[12] Cab. 32/56 E (I.R./26), p. 3.

[13] E 115.

by Arthur Griffith's notion of a dual monarchy.[14] But it was uncertain how far this was a personal or an official view. The conclusion to the memorandum on 'Anomalies' also leaves the question unresolved. It read as follows:

> If the British Cornmonwealth of Nations is to endure as the greatest fac-
> tor for the establishment of peace and prosperity throughout the world,
> its cohesive force must be real and permanent, whether viewed from within
> or without. It cannot be held together by a mere collective expression,
> which serves only to create doubt in the minds of Foreign Statesmen and
> discontent among the diverse nationalities of which it is made up.
>
> The King is the real bond, and forms used in international treaties will
> be devoid of all meaning so long as they do not give complete expression
> to that reality.
>
> The co-operation resulting from the bond of a common King will be
> effective only because it is free co-operation and to the extent to which
> it is free. Antiquated forms dating from a period when common action
> resulted from the over-riding control of one central government are liable
> to make co-operation less efficacious, because they make it seem less free.

It would be possible but unwise to draw a broad political inference from this conclusion to a highly technical legal-constitutional submission, but it may be assumed that the Irish Free State delegation, in thus underlining the significance of the King as 'the real bond', at the least did not wish to question the appropriateness of the monarch for this purpose. The memorandum, it will be noted moreover, used the phrase, 'the bond of a common King'. It was the basis of Mr Costello's argument in 1948 – and he was Attorney General in Cosgrave's government and legal adviser to the Irish Free State delegation at the Imperial Conferences both of 1926 and 1930 – that it was the Crown that was the major cause of friction between Ireland and Britain from 1921 onwards. Why then did the Irish memorandum in 1926 allude in such terms to the rôle of a common King – a phrase the implication of which would hardly have been acceptable in Budapest after 1867 and which was seemingly inconsistent with the concept of a dual monarchy? Does this suggest that pro-Treaty Irish attitudes changed significantly with the intervening years or that their approach in 1926 was essentially tactical?

Pending further evidence and detailed analysis the presumption remains that the former was the case and, as Professor Hancock inferred, the Cosgrave administration, while much preoccupied with the ending of all elements of continuing subordination, continued to think of Irish fulfilment within the Commonwealth and that their conviction in this respect departed, no doubt progressively, only during the long years of de Valera's

---

[14] T. de V. White, *Kevin O'Higgins* (London, 1948), pp. 220–2.

administration, 1932–48. If so, this is a fact of historical importance, for it meant that an Irish party, deeply committed to Commonwealth membership, came as the result of experience to the conclusion that its continuance was not in their country's interests.

V

The development of Anglo-Irish relations modified established attitudes, on the British at least as much as on the Irish side. The Dominions Secretary, Malcolm MacDonald, at the 1937 Imperial Conference – and here we pass beyond the period covered in Professor Hancock's *Survey* – submitted a paper on Irish affairs to the assembled Dominion Prime Ministers.[15] It gave a resumé of developments particularly since 1932 in respect both of the constitutional and of the economic disputes and the consequent economic war. Malcolm MacDonald accepted the fact that the new Irish Constitution, shortly to be submitted to the people in a referendum, was a republican constitution. He also underlined the fact that common allegiance to the Crown had been an essential part of the 1926 declaration and added 'we regard the position of the Crown as one of the things that must be maintained'.

There was a discussion on the paper, one notable feature of which was the continuing British and dominion insistence on the unique and indispensable position of the Crown, with General Hertzog alone seeing no reason why even a republican dominion was not a possibility, so long as the symbolic position of the Crown in the Commonwealth was still acknowledged. The other feature of note was the marked reluctance on every side to push Anglo-Irish estrangement to further extremes. 'What the British government does now as regards Ireland', observed Hertzog, 'is most important for the future of the Commonwealth.' Chamberlain explained that to the Irish mind there was nothing illogical in having a republic within a Commonwealth owing allegiance to the Crown and, in his concluding summary, he stressed in particular the disadvantages of taking any decision which would have the effect of pushing Ireland out when she wished to remain in. They were so obvious that such steps could only be justified if they were clearly necessary to save the Commonwealth 'from a worse fate'. Accordingly 'we do not propose to lay down any conditions, which if the Irish Free State were to trespass, she would put herself out of the Commonwealth'.

This conclusion, in which all the dominion prime ministers concurred, makes clear the response of the British and dominion governments to the

---

[15] Cab. 32/130 (1937).

Irish constitutional changes which culminated in the External Relations Act 1936 and the 1937 Constitution. They were determined to find technical evidence for adducing allegiance in the former (and duly found it) and firm in their resolve to disregard the republican character of the latter. Yet, it will be noted, the *modus vivendi* was reached without conceding that a republic could be a member of the Commonwealth or even, apart from Hertzog's passing allusion, considering the possibility. This meant, and was probably bound to mean, despite the ingenuities of the External Relations Act, a postponement rather than a resolution of the problems of Irish–Commonwealth relations.

In Mr de Valera's view Éire remained between 1937 and 1948 a republic externally associated with the British Commonwealth of Nations. While expressly repudiating allegiance he did not, during this period, explicitly challenge the British view that Éire was still a member, though clearly he did not subscribe to it. On a visit to London early in 1948 de Valera's successor, J. A. Costello, noted without satisfaction that at an official occasion at No. 10 Downing Street, Attlee proposed the toast of 'The King' as appropriate for the country of his guests, thereby indicating that in the British view Éire continued to owe allegiance to the Crown and remained a member of the British Commonwealth of Nations.[16] Costello was not prepared to acquiesce in opinions he thought incorrect and nationally unacceptable. From the first he had been an outspoken critic of the anomalies and prevarications of the External Relations Act and, given furthermore the composition of the inter-party government over which he presided, he caused surprise more by the place (Ottawa) and the timing of his announcement of its impending repeal than by his actual decision to effect it.[17]

VI

In introducing the Republic of Ireland Bill 1948 in the Dáil Mr Costello made two points that are worth recalling. The first was that the bill would:

> end, and end forever, in a simple, clear and unequivocal way this country's long and tragic association with the institution of the British Crown and will make it manifest beyond equivocation or subtlety the national and international status of this country is that of an independent Republic.

---

[16] M. McInerney, 'Mr Costello Remembers', *The Irish Times*, 4 September 1967.

[17] The argument that follows is more fully developed in the author's forthcoming *The Commonwealth Experience*.

The other was retrospective. Mr Costello said that for ten long years,

> those people who undertook the duty and the task of honouring the
> signatures to the Treaty walked the *Via Dolorosa* of those bitter years,
> but at the end of those ten years, when the efforts of the representatives
> of this country at Imperial Conferences and at international gatherings
> had borne their fruit, those developments had brought us to the point
> where we had achieved for this country international recognition as one
> of the sovereign countries of the world, and we had swept away all the
> old dead wood of British constitutional theory that lay or appeared to
> lie in the path of constitutional progress.

The result, he argued, had been better relations between Britain and Ireland
and he conceded further that the different policies of de Valera's successor
government had also in their own way to some considerable extent achieved
the purpose of bringing still more closely together the relationships between Great Britain and Ireland 'and the peoples of these two neighbour-
ing islands'.[18]

Whatever may have been fortuitous about the timing of Irish secession,
there is no doubt that the issue was deliberately settled apart from the Commonwealth so as to avoid possible Commonwealth, or more precisely British
pressures. Yet despite this the Commonwealth did play a rôle, presumably
for the last time, in Irish affairs. That rôle had two aspects. The first was
negative. The British government considered the possibilities of a sharper
reaction, notably in respect of citizenship and trade, to Irish secession than
the one they in fact adopted. So much was made clear by the Lord
Chancellor who explained that, if the British government had taken a different line from that which they decided to take, 'we should have acted
in the teeth of the advice of the representatives of Canada, Australia and
New Zealand'.[19]

What lay behind his words? At the time of the Commonwealth Prime
Ministers' Meeting in October 1948, there were separate discussions, first
at Chequers and then at Paris, between representatives of the Irish government and those of the British, Canadian, Australian and New Zealand
governments. It was at these discussions that there emerged, as Costello
himself subsequently confirmed,[20] something liked a united 'old
dominion' view to the effect that Irish secession should not be allowed
to impair relations between Ireland and the other countries of the Commonwealth or even, as Chifley later emphasized, that the way should

---

[18] Dáil Debates, Vol. 113, Cols. 347–87, reprinted in *Documents and Speeches on
British Commonwealth Affairs 1931–1952,* edited by N. Mansergh (Oxford, 1954), Vol.
II, pp. 802–9.
[19] *H. of L. Deb.,* 15 Dec. 1948, Vol. 159, Cols. 1087–93, reprinted, *ibid.,* p. 809.
[20] M. McInerney, *loc. cit.,* 8 September 1967.

be left open for Ireland's return. Peter Fraser, when asked what difference secession would make to New Zealand's attitude to Ireland, replied 'What difference could there be? There has been friendliness always'. In the New Zealand Republic of Ireland Act it was expressly stated that New Zealand law should have operation in relation to the Republic of Ireland 'as it would have had if the Republic of Ireland had remained part of His Majesty's Dominions'.

But on Easter Day 1949 the Republic was proclaimed and Ireland on any interpretation ceased to be a part of His Majesty's dominions. 'The pirouetting on the point of a pin', remarked Costello with satisfaction, 'was over.' Professor J. D. B. Miller has noted that:

> the 1948 arrangements put paid to the whole score, with goodwill on all sides. Except for some mild scuffling between Mr Menzies' government in Australia and the Irish government about how the Australian Ambassador to Eire should be designated, later relations between Eire and the Old Dominions had little to offer the historian.[21]

For one thing Irish representatives no longer attended the Prime Ministers' Meetings. What they might have had to contribute about some of the issues of succeeding years – African membership, the Suez affair, South Africa's secession, immigration, and Southern Rhodesia – are matters only for speculation.

Two things alone are certain. One is that the distinctive voice, that of a European nationalism (to be heard henceforward only at the UN), was lost, with the result that racial and national reactions came to be too closely identified, or indeed often confused, almost as if nationalism were an original African vice or virtue. The other is that twenty years after secession Ireland as a republic would have been constitutionally in a comfortable majority within the Commonwealth. By 1968, the trend was still that way, even it might prove to be in the oldest of the dominions.

The breach, of course, was effected not by Ireland but by India and in the year of Irish secession. The apparent paradox might be explained in terms of changes in British opinion, or more generally in terms of Commonwealth development in the intervening twenty-eight years as a whole, or again of differences between Indian and Irish attitudes, in as much as in India it was the independence movement that mattered with the republic incidental to it, whereas in Ireland it was the republic that was the symbol of independence. But behind the forms were interests, which it would be a serious error to discount. What signified was that at the moment of decision the Republic of India acceded to and the Republic of Ireland seceded from the Commonwealth because of their respective governments'

---

[21] J. D. B. Miller, *Britain and the Old Dominions* (London, 1966), p. 147.

interpretation of their respective state interests.

Professor Hancock in the first of his two Irish chapters dwelt upon the continental sources of inspiration for Irish concepts of nationhood. In his second Irish chapter, he underlined and documented Anglo-Irish economic interdependence in terms of trade. With the advantage of a longer time span it seems reasonable to draw even more far-reaching inferences. On the negative side Irish economic and social ties with members of the Commonwealth other than Britain were in no way exceptional. Nor did they in most instances seem likely to become so. It is true, for example, Irish emigrants went to Australia, but this was evidently less conditional upon any Commonwealth connection than upon Australia's desire for immigrants of European origin. Trade between the two countries was small and there seemed no serious possibility of development of it, except on highly specialized lines. Despite recent economic advances, Ireland remains an underdeveloped country. Apart from British investment on a fairly substantial scale and Canadian mining enterprises at Tynagh, Gortdrum, the Tara mines and elsewhere, there is incoming German, Belgian, Dutch and, at Shannon, Japanese capital behind the two hundred and fifty or so new international companies, mostly on quite a small scale, set up in the Republic, but little or no signs of interest on the part of the rest of the Commonwealth.

The future in economic-financial terms, it seems, therefore lies not with the Commonwealth but with Britain, in her European rôle, Western Europe and North America. The counterpart to Irish secession, apt to be ignored by Commonwealth commentators, was Irish association after the Second World War with the European recovery programme, her foundation membership of the Council of Europe, of EFTA, followed in the sixties by the negotiation of the Anglo-Irish Free Trade Agreement with the prospect of a free trade area in existence by the early seventies and the contemporary Irish application, without reservation or qualification, to subscribe to the Treaty of Rome.

In the broadest sense all of these developments may be taken to reflect a return of Irish interests from countries overseas, where in times of famine or distress many emigrants settled in the past, to the geographical area of which Ireland was a part. Not for the first, nor for the last time, may this be represented, at least when the 'offshore islands' of the Gaullist phraseology become a part of the Common Market (and with certain transatlantic qualifications), as a triumph of geography over recent history.

VII

Professor Hancock concluded his analysis of Irish relations with the Commonwealth in these words:

Looking back upon these years of dispute between Great Britain and the Irish Free State, the writer feels that their experience reveals the strength of the objective facts working for the interdependence, the co-operation, and in the end for the reconciliation of the two countries. Economically and politically each of them had so much power to harm the other; yet neither could inflict this harm without doing extreme damage to itself. The two countries would remain inseparably bound, even if they were bound in a mutually inflicted ruin. Given a newly created friendship between them all things were possible. A friendship which would extinguish forever all fear of conflict between them could not fail to bring with it the fruits of appeasement between north and south. Yet would Great Britain and Ireland discover the secret of friendship? Or would they discover it in time?

These were wise words and would still command general assent today. If one were to probe further and ask in the light of later experience what have been the conditions of such greater friendship as has developed since Professor Hancock wrote, three things suggest themselves. The first is the partial fulfilment of Irish political aspirations symbolized by the concept of an all-Ireland republic. The second, and probably as important, has been Britain's retreat from Empire. On that a younger Irish poet, John Montague, has said all, or more, that needs to be said in a poem entitled 'At Long Last':

> At long last
> We are free to be friendly with England
> As she sinks back towards herself
> Shorn and exhausted of empire, . . .[22]

And thirdly, deriving from these two and from improved standards of living and yet having a lineage of its own, is the qualified withdrawal on the part of the younger generation, in Ireland as in England, from politics in the sense their fathers still think of them. There, too, the new 'realists' are taking over.

Professor Hancock wrote of Ireland in a revolutionary period when the intensities of politics cast their reflections on the pattern of living. Political zeal demanded austerity in social life. That atmosphere is passing. To quote an earlier poem of John Montague:

> Puritan Ireland's dead and gone
> A myth of O'Connor and O'Faolain.

In the Ireland of the revolutionary and post-revolutionary years, it was no myth, but even so there were always evidences of other scales of values

---

[22] *The Irish Times*, 6 April 1968.

and of other kinds of preoccupation. Conor Cruise O'Brien remarked of one of them that there was some reason to believe that on Easter Monday 1916 the main focus of the interests of the middle class in Dublin was not the GPO but the Fairyhouse racecourse. 'It can do us no harm to remember', he continued, 'that what we might call the "Fairyhouse tradition" is not less pertinent, [than the revolutionary tradition] although it does not cut such a figure in the history books.'[23]

In the Ireland of today non-political traditions are no longer overshadowed by the consuming demands of an all-pervasive, militant nationalism. This relaxation in the temper of nationalism, itself the product of the achievement of substantial national aims, was also a precondition of a friendship founded, as Professor Hancock recognized it must be, on a solid basis of common interest. How far Irish membership of the Commonwealth, already regarded by the younger generation as a remote and somewhat intangible episode in national experience, contributed to, or delayed the measure of understanding that has been achieved, is susceptible of no easy judgement. But at least it can be said with assurance that anyone who wishes to formulate such a judgement can do no better than begin by studying the perceptive and telling analysis offered by an Australian historian thirty years ago.

---

[23] *The Shaping of Modern Ireland*, edited by C. C. O'Brien (London, 1960), pp. 14–15. In a footnote (p. 124, n. 2) in the *Survey* Professor Hancock has given cause for dismay to the followers of that tradition by placing the Black and Tan Hunt, associated for generations with the Ryans of Scarteen, Co. Limerick, in the country of the Galway Blazers – though perhaps he can find some reassurance in the thought that they are not among the more likely readers of *Surveys of British Commonwealth Affairs*!

15

EOIN MACNEILL –
A REAPPRAISAL

Some few men – very few – may justly be said to create revolutionary situations; more seize advantage from them to promote causes they cherish; more still find themselves in a less enviable position partly of directing, partly of promoting and finally of being swept along, or aside, by forces over which they have little control and perhaps indeed do not fully comprehend. One of the hazards of biographical writing on a revolutionary period is the elevation of the person above the situation; the individual above the cumulative revolutionary pressures which he serves, or happens to release.

When, therefore, one reads on the wrapper of this commemorative volume[1] – perhaps it is unreasonable of reviewers to read wrappers? – that Eoin MacNeill had the unique distinction of being the only man in modern Irish history who successfully launched three revolutions – that ushered in with the foundation of the Gaelic League in 1893; that in Irish historical studies with his lectures in 1904 and that which began with the founding of the Irish Volunteers in 1913 – one is tempted to inquire, what in this context is meant by launching? If the implication is that these revolutions – and perhaps that is becoming a term which scholars should handle with increasing care – would not have taken place without the impetus given

---

[1] *The Scholar Revolutionary: Eoin MacNeill 1867–1945 and the Making of a New Ireland*, edited by F. X. Martin and F. J. Byrne (Shannon, Ireland 1973).

by MacNeill, that is a large claim in itself and one which might be taken to imply that in each case a revolutionary situation was not already in existence seeking resolution. If, on the other hand, the phrases that are used are intended to indicate no more than the uniqueness – and that is a good deal – of MacNeill's contribution in respect of the timing of that unleashing of revolutionary forces already in being, that is a contention which prima facie has in two of the three instances much to recommend it. But if this indeed were so, the proper tribute to MacNeill is not assertion of his place in history divorced from the succession of situations in which he played his part but close assessment of his rôle within these historical situations. Of this most of the contributors to this volume generally show themselves very much aware – that is one of its many merits – and two in particular, Professor F. X. Martin and Professor Geoffrey Hand, provide just that detailed analysis of the man in his situation in the two most controversial episodes of his career, the Volunteers and the Boundary Commission. The fact, indeed, that it is vital to get those equations right suffices in itself to indicate the continuing importance of assessing aright MacNeill's place in modern Irish history.

By temperament and training MacNeill was not a revolutionary at all. He was a scholar in the older tradition, independent and without, so Professor Dudley Edwards reminds us, formal professional training as a historian, idiosyncratic, exact, until his later years when apparently a certain carelessness in transcription entered in, and of the highest integrity. There was a Johnsonian opening to his scholarly career for where Johnson had declined to pay a fine of two pence for absenting himself from his tutor's lectures which he declared to be not worth a penny, MacNeill when caught reading during his master's lesson refused to be punished, asserting the principle that it was better to read a good book than listen to a bad teacher! It was his integrity, allied to his independence, and coupled with indispensable mastery of linguistic sources, that, in the words of the late Professor Francis Shaw, enabled MacNeill to achieve 'his great triumph as a scholar', namely the bringing of accepted accounts of the earlier history of Ireland up against the hard test of scholarly proof. Much did not survive. Father Shaw writes of the transformation in the concepts of early Irish history which MacNeill thus effected; Professor Francis Byrne, in a candid appreciation of MacNeill's seminal contribution to medieval studies, writes of him as the only scholar of his time of the first rank to be interested primarily in Irish history. The impact of MacNeill's writings is said to have been iconoclastic: cherished anecdotes had to be discarded, traditional assumptions were undermined. In that sense, therefore, or so a modernist, taking this on trust, must conclude, MacNeill, the historian of pre-Norman Ireland, is to be accepted as a revolutionary influence – in the restricted sense of the phrase a scholar-revolutionary. And perhaps it may be added, though a modern historian is generally well advised to refrain from pronouncements on medieval historiography, that despite MacNeill's innovatory rôle a strong impression remains of his underlying conservatism. 'So far am I', he wrote, 'from despising tradition, that my main effort is to find tradition and establish its authority.' That is precisely what MacNeill would seem to have essayed – and with great initial impact. Yet it was, perhaps, symptomatic of his cast of mind that he thought in terms of establishing the 'authority' of a historical tradition where today we think in terms of questioning all such.

However, the historical transformation effected by MacNeill was not confined to historical reinterpretation. It was directed perhaps even more importantly in the longer run to provision and preservation of source material. From the establishment of the Irish Historical Manuscripts Commission to the launching of *Irish Historical Studies* MacNeill was and remained the prime mover, or the focus, for new departures in historical research. There his reputation rests secure and no chapter in this book conveys more successfully, and indeed at times movingly, the stature of the scholar in the age immediately antecedent to contemporary historical professionalism than that of Professor Dudley Edwards.

There was a self-evident link between the scholar seeking to reconstruct a distant past on the basis of tested evidence and the revivalist of a wellnigh discarded language. Yet the nature of it is important for an understanding of the man. Nowadays academics are apt to drift in and out of public affairs: in MacNeill's day, or even more in his case, there was no element of drift. 'He loved Ireland', writes Professor Dudley Edwards, 'and he liked people. But his Ireland was linked to traditional learning, and his patriotism came before his devotion to history. That is why he put the Gaelic revival before scholarship, why Volunteering came before academic work . . .' He had his order of priorities and the first manifestation of them was appropriate on what mattered to him most – the language.

Professor Edwards accepts the view that MacNeill was the man who first conceived the idea of founding the Gaelic League, while Father Shaw regarded him as the prime mover though he concedes in effect the existence of a revolutionary linguistic situation by writing that, as in the later founding of the Volunteers, 'it was a case of putting the match to a fire ready for kindling'. Dr McCartney in effect agrees, adducing as evidence MacNeill's calling of the meeting for the purpose of establishing a popular language movement and thus, in the Bismarckian phrase, seizing 'the psychological moment'. And yet, as set out, despite this impressive coincidence of view, the evidence of a decisive initiative that is adduced seems to fall a little short of the conclusive. What does not is the depth of conviction. Here the linguistic scholar and Irish patriotic impulse were, as perhaps never again, at one.

An American political scientist has recently applied statistical techniques to the assessment of organizational commitments of the revolutionary élite in this phase of Irish history and from his analysis there has emerged, first, that sixty-nine per cent of that élite were members of the League; secondly, and despite disavowal of political aims, that Gaelic League membership, statistically analysed, to an astonishing extent preceded revolutionary activity; and thirdly, deriving from both, 'that the most important by-product of the League may well have been the production of a generation of nationalists willing to fight for Ireland's independence'.[2] This provides some quantitative reinforcement, if such is needed, for impressions generally accepted. The restatement, however, serves to underline MacNeill's potential place in the Irish national revolution. If indeed he be accepted as the founder of the Gaelic League; if, as seems established statistically and otherwise, the League produced a generation ready to fight for independence, then MacNeill's revolutionary historical position is established, irrespective of his Volunteer rôle.

The thesis has a tempting simplicity. But, before we can be carried away by it, there is Professor Martin to remind us obliquely of its possible inadequacy. Professor Martin is well aware of the importance of establishing the precise sequence of events and their interrelationship before making any assessment of MacNeill's rôle in the founding of the Volunteers. Indeed he has attempted, and most valuably, to unravel it in some detail. But there is no doubt about the general theme he develops. It is not that MacNeill, or for that matter any Nationalist, whether in the constitutional or even in the physical force tradition, was primarily responsible for their founding: it was the Ulstermen by virtue of example. MacNeill, to judge by one quotation, went far towards accepting such an explanation. Like Pearse, he was a supporter, though a conditional one, of Redmond and, unlike Pearse, he remained so down to 1914. The constitutionalism inherited from O'Connell, Butt and Parnell was put in jeopardy by Carson and his Orange-Unionist supporters and ultimately abandoned only because their challenge had placed the fair working of the democratic process in doubt. 'It was the Ulster Unionists', writes Professor Martin, 'who set the pace for the Irish Nationalist Volunteers'; once they had taken the initiative there was 'nothing to prevent the other twenty-eight counties from calling into existence citizen forces which like the Volunteers of 1782' could become the instrument of establising Irish self-government. MacNeill's well-remembered sentence, spoken at the Rotunda meeting on 25 November 1913 over which he presided, and repeated in the manifesto of the Irish Volunteers whose coming into existence was the consequence of that meeting – 'They have rights who dare maintain them' – showed once again

---

[2] A. S. Cohan, *The Irish Political Elite* (Dublin, 1972), pp. 59–60.

the force of Ulster Unionist example. With MacNeill, who somewhat paradoxically discounted the Orangemen, their actions provoked emulation rather than rivalry. 'We have nothing to fear from the Volunteers in Ulster', he declared, 'nor they from us.' Not all shared this *simpliste* view.

On other points Professor Martin's conclusions, broadly stated, are that MacNeill's article calling for the formation of the Volunteers 'happened to be the right message, at the right moment, by the right man', that MacNeill was again the right, indeed the inevitable, choice to preside at the Rotunda meeting and, for much the same reason, the obvious President of the Volunteers, hoping to guide a movement which he himself did not expect to control. If there was an acknowledged element of misjudgement on this last point – and not only on the side of MacNeill – Professor Martin makes clear that MacNeill was not prepared to be, and did not become, a figurehead or still less a 'front' behind which the radical separatist elements manoeuvred to further their plans and secure their control. But the large question remains, to what extent was MacNeill himself the man who sparked, if not the revolution, at any rate the creation of the force that was a condition of revolution? Professor Martin in effect would seem to advance two propositions – first that the originators and true founders by force of example were the Ulster Volunteers and second that it was in fact MacNeill who, 'apparently by accident, initiated the movement'. In so far as the two propositions are in conflict, and admittedly this is largely a question of emphasis, MacNeill himself would seem to have opted for the first. 'We of the Irish Volunteers', he declared at the Rotunda on 25 November 1913, 'must admit candidly that it is the Ulster Volunteers who have opened the way for the Irish Volunteers.' If this were even broadly speaking the case, then MacNeill must be thought of more by way of one who responded to a revolutionary situation brought into being by others than one who played a decisive part in its creation. Or to put it in other words, the more Professor Martin stresses his first proposition, the less significant does his second appear. And that would apply to others as well as MacNeill.

Professor Martin dwells little on Professor MacNeill's qualities of leadership – and indeed has little reason to do so for his detailed consideration of MacNeill's rôle as founder-President of the Volunteers ends in 1914. On the wrapper – if I may return to it again – MacNeill's countermanding order of Easter Day 1916 is reprinted in part with seemingly fitting appreciation of its key importance in MacNeill's public life and his place in history. But in the book there is here an astonishing lacuna – no consideration being given to this most decisive of moments in his life. It is as though a commemorative volume were produced on Mahatma Gandhi omitting his role in the 'Quit India' movement, 1942 – only more so! On one count, not least because it arose later in respect of the Boundary Commission, the omission is to be regretted. Such a reassessment, apart from reviewing a dramatic decision of which the surrounding circumstances are well known in more than outline, might have thrown more light on a question beneath the surface in a number of contributions in this book – how good an administrator was MacNeill? Criticism on this score is often discounted as retrospective but there is a letter from Alice Stopford Green, not quoted here, written before 1916 saying that MacNeill was not well fitted for any position requiring administrative gifts. The record suggests that there was something, perhaps a good deal, in this but it would have been interesting had occasion been taken to examine it more closely.

In the politico-historical conceptual field there could be no doubt of MacNeill's consistency or of his clarity of thought. He was, almost inevitably, given the source and inspiration of his pioneering historical work and his linguistic preoccupations, a believer in an Irish-Ireland. That belief – intense conviction might be a more appropriate description – was closely allied to, indeed inseparable from his concepts of nationality and nation, as Dr McCartney has shown in illuminating analysis. These concepts were of great importance. The former, i.e. nationality, he wrote of as the type of civilization which a people has developed, which has become that people's tradition and is distinctive of that people. It was will and spirit that made a nation and MacNeill conceived that by reason of their existence historically an Irish nation had existed from antiquity based on 'a positive conscious nationality', 'more real and concrete than was ever the conception of nationality in ancient Hellas'. There was no need to recreate the nation: it existed and Thomas Davis, singing of 'a nation once again', was accordingly to be rebuked for confusion in terminology. What had existed down the ages, the nation, did not need to be recalled into being; for 'nation' Davis should therefore have substituted 'state', and his poem would have gained in exactitude what it lost in euphony.

MacNeill, over and above his concern with definition of terms – and Dr McCartney has shown how deep that preoccupation was – had categoric opinions on the frontiers and true manifestation of the spirit of Irish nationhood. Every inch of the island was to be claimed as part of the Irish nation, and the Gaelic language was a principal distinguishing bond of the nationality comprising it, or, as MacNeill himself phrased it, the language was 'the chief thread', the most indisputable sign of an Irishman's nationality, with the Irish speaker as 'the truest and most invincible soldier of his nation'. Allied to this concept of an Irish-Ireland was the notion that each nation, Ireland not least among them, had a particular vocation, a special destiny which it was specially endowed by God to fulfil. This is precisely what Mazzini – though his name is mentioned by neither MacNeill nor Dr McCartney – had been unable to discern in the case of Ireland and by reason of which he had concluded that Irish claims to a separate nationality were not well founded. If it may now be thought that Mazzini's search to identify particular national vocations, or destinies, was misconceived that was clearly not MacNeill's view. Without apparent overt reference to Mazzini, he essayed a positive answer to a possibly misguided and certainly unhistorical question. Believing, as he did, the early Christian period, when 'the Irish were the schoolmasters of Europe', to have been the greatest in her history, MacNeill boldly concluded that Ireland's destiny was to be a teaching nation, setting an example to the rest of the world with 'our ancient ideals, faith, learning, generous enthusiasm, self-sacrifice – the things best calculated to purge out the meanness of the modern world'. It was a missionary concept to which many in theory subscribed – but MacNeill, though an academic, was little of a theorist. The world he thought of may be a world that is lost – but it was as a world that might be gained that he saw it. Here indeed both in his linguistic exclusivism – and his views on language were uncompromisingly exclusivist in tenor – and in his idealistic comprehensiveness he was in intent the scholar-revolutionary, drawing on the past for his inspiration for the future.

But it was not on a high visionary plain but amid the intractable thickets of partitionist politics that MacNeill for the last time appeared on the stage of history. There he lost his way. It may be there was no way out: if there was he did not find it nor was he the man to find it. It came about because the Cosgrave administration deemed it essential that their representative on the Boundary Commission should be a Catholic, a Northerner and a Minister. MacNeill alone fulfilled these essentials. That was his tragedy.

The Treaty could not have been signed but for Article 12. It contained, as was known at the time, political dynamite. Its purpose was to allow the Treaty to be signed, by postponing unresolved the explosive boundary issue with the remote possibility that with time its explosive content might even be defused. In fact, it achieved the first and, by a narrow margin and on a short term, the second also. But even so there were casualties, in reputation if not in life. Chief among them was MacNeill. The chairman, Mr Justice Feetham, emerged by no means unscathed. It was long supposed that Feetham had deliberately weighted the scales against the Irish Free State and its representative on the Commission. Professor Hand in his Introduction to the *Report of the Irish Boundary Commission 1925*, published in 1970, and again in his substantial, more personally angled, commentary in this volume, on the basis of a careful scrutiny of British records, supplemented by the use of Irish collections of private papers and personal interviews with survivors, has disabused us once for all, it would seem, of this notion and in so doing has placed modern historians, not for the first time, in very considerable debt to a medievalist.

What Professor Hand has written underlines once again, however regrettable the fact may be, the price that may be exacted in politics by high integrity when allied, as indeed it often is, to inflexibility. Feetham and MacNeill were alike in possessing both of these virtues coupled with devotion to right principles as they conceived them – and in paying the price. Feetham, apparently far from being susceptible to behind-the-scenes British pressures, was concerned above all to insist upon the application in practice of his own only too well-weighted restrictive interpretation of the Commission's terms of reference, whilst MacNeill was so impressed with what he deemed to be the 'judicial' aspect of the Commission's work that he declined absolutely to discuss its progress with his colleagues on the Executive Council. The consequence for MacNeill was rumour, resignation, reproaches – mercifully restrained – and retirement from politics. No doubt his own administrative deficiencies – it seems clearly established in Professor Hand's account that MacNeill was not only irregular but worse, unpredictable, in his attendance at meetings – added an element of unnecessary haste and confusion at the last. A more agile, if need be less principled Irish member would at least have ensured that this was avoided and that the break came earlier, when he had perceived the inevitable consequences for the Irish Free State of the chairman's reading of the terms of reference, and he would have made it at a moment favourable to the government whose representative he was. But in a sense all this is secondary for, given the chairman's legal interpretation of the terms of reference, break there was bound to be. That being so, the degree of foresight shown by the Cosgrave administration comes sharply into question. But it cannot be properly considered until the Irish official records for the period are opened. When is that going to be?

The public life of the 'scholar-revolutionary' is, however, to be thought of in larger contours than this. Essentially, in my judgement, MacNeill is not to be seen as the maker of revolutions: for in such a rôle he seems miscast. But certainly he was a man to be viewed in the context of the succession of revolutions at, or near, the centre of which he found himself and in which he sought to play out his part. Men who make revolutions are rarely in a predicament: men who find themselves in revolutionary situations very often are. This means that their contributions are to be studied in the context of those situations where the interrelation between the man and the situation gives to them their lasting and often very human interest for historians. MacNeill was one such and I suspect he would have asked no more.

16

EAMON DE VALERA:
Life and Irish Times

Many years ago I remember hearing Philip Guedalla telling of how he had asked George Moore for advice about the biography of the Duke of Wellington, on which he was at the time engaged, and of how, with an expressive movement of his hands, Moore had replied 'Mould it like a vase'. The implication of the advice was apparently that the biography should be securely but narrowly based on parentage, youth and early manhood; that it should expand to a well-rounded fulness in recording the achievements of maturity and then should taper away elegantly in the retrospects of age. To Guedalla the advice, conveyed with an air of remote but utter finality, seemed on inspection as impracticable as it was impressive. The Duke, alas, from the point of view of literary form, did not fade away after Waterloo; he moved on to become an unpopular Prime Minister and then a popular national symbol.

The same problem as that which confronted Philip Guedalla, in equal or accentuated form, has faced Lord Longford and T. P. O'Neill, the biographers of Eamon de Valera.[1] The subject of their study was thirty-four years old when first he became a national figure in the Easter Rising 1916 and fifty years later he was re-elected, at the age of eighty-four, to be President of Ireland for a further seven years. 'The century', say the authors, 'offers no parallel to such sustained pre-eminence.' Much depends

---

[1] The Earl of Longford and T. P. O'Neill *Eamon de Valera* (Dublin, 1970).

on the criteria used in such reckoning but in so far as this is just – and Smuts (State Attorney in Kruger's Transvaal government in 1899 which is apt to be overlooked outside South Africa) and Churchill alone may claim to have nearly approached it – it imposes the more exacting a test upon the judgement of the authors in respect of the design and presentation of their study. They have passed this test admirably. It is true there is no great centrepiece – as might aesthetically be most satisfying – but instead, as is a historical imperative, a series of high points: the Easter Rising, the negotiations with Lloyd George, the Treaty and the Civil War, the Fianna Fáil administration of the early thirties, the Constitution of 1937 and the Anglo-Irish settlement of 1938, neutrality sustained, the post-coalition government – in a lower key – and the symbolic climax of the Presidency. If there is a special emphasis it is upon pre-war relations with Britain and the vindication of de Valera's policy of independence for Ireland, unequivocally expressed in neutrality in a war in which Britain was fighting for survival.

The mere recital of the high points of President de Valera's career suffices in itself to indicate another of the problems facing his biographers – how to treat adequately of them all, while keeping the biography within reasonable compass. The book is, in fact, just five hundred pages, but on reading it the overall reflection for once must be that it is too short. There are topics of critical importance, notably the Civil War period, as well as matters of more general interest, such as the content of de Valera's concept of republican nationalism, which could with advantage have been more searchingly probed or more fully analysed. Then, too, while the book has some delightful pages on de Valera's youth and boyhood, it is later on, perhaps inevitably, thin on the personal side. What sort of letters did he write to his friends? We do not know, the veil comes down and no amount of assertions by the authors of his humanity quite compensate for the loss of the immediate flavour to be detected perhaps most of all in casual correspondence. Possibly he was not a writer of letters, even to colleagues on political issues, but, if so, it would have been of interest to know this.

Official Biography?

That brings one to a larger question. Is, or is not, the book to be regarded as an official biography? The authors say that the President consistently refused to write an autobiography but that, once he had agreed to the writing of an authoritative biography, he could not have been more helpful. His 'huge library' of private papers was made freely available to his biographers and they were always able to draw upon his personal recollections of the events in which he had played so momentous a part. In short, and in their own words, the biography 'could not have been written without the co-operation of President de Valera himself'. If there is a distinction between an 'authoritative' and an 'official' biography it is a fine one and presumably in this case it exists because the work, while based on authoritative sources is not, we are told in effect, to be taken as necessarily reflecting the President's own interpretation of particular events. This is perhaps a point for historians to note. A near-parallel, instructive where it departs from the line, is provided by *India Wins Freedom* which placed on record the views of Maulana A. K. Azad, the distinguished Muslim President of the Indian National Congress in the critical wartime years. Like de Valera, Azad declined to write an autobiography but in place of it described his experiences to Humayun Kabir who submitted to him his record chapter by chapter for amendment and final approval. The book was described as *An Autobiographical Narrative* and, though written by another hand, it carried the imprimatur of its subject. In this case, that is lacking. For while President de Valera gave every assistance, there is no indication that he questioned what he felt unable to accept.

In other respects the book carries not merely great but, for the time being and presumably for some time to come, unique authority. This is because the authors have had access not merely to the President's personal papers but also, for the long periods he was in office, to Irish state papers, copies of which no doubt are on his files. Such access enormously enhances the importance of the account given of events in the thirties and in the war years, since these papers are not available to other scholars. One's impression is that the authors in their privileged position have been at pains to give a fair and balanced account of events. Certainly the chapters dealing with these years, while clearly by no means exhaustive in their treatment of particular topics, are of absorbing interest. They have also a wide perspective since many of the American and the captured German official records, with their interesting if comparatively slight references to Irish affairs, have been published and the British official records, including the Cabinet papers with fuller references, are also available and, where relevant, extensively used by the authors. All of this broadens the range and deepens the interest of a biography of one who is on any reckoning to be numbered with the great men of our time, the more remarkable in one sense in that he became a world figure, not by playing any significant part in world affairs but by becoming by force of character and long survival symbolically representative of a twentieth-century nationalism that had at once discarded the liberal, internationalist trappings of much of nineteenth-century nationalism and sharply repudiated the ideological, left-wing, self-styled internationalism of the twentieth century.

De Valera's life has been so interwoven with the pattern of Irish history for half a century that many of the chapter titles of the book may well reappear in the appropriate volume of the forthcoming Oxford *History of Ireland*. In such circumstances a recital of the sequence of events is otiose. But it may be worth asking oneself the question – what aspects of de Valera's character, rôle or contribution are here placed in a new perspective or freshly illumined?

Force and Partition

Churchill once described the twentieth century as a century of war and, because this was so, he believed that familiarity with war was almost a necessary condition of political success at any rate in the Western world. De Valera possessed this qualification, not merely in the sense that he was a commandant in 1916 but, as is brought out clearly in the biography, in his resolve beforehand to train and equip himself for fighting. Indeed, like Smuts the philosopher, de Valera the mathematician might well have written the 'military life agrees wonderfully with me'. De Valera believed that certain ends could be achieved only by force and, belonging in essence to the physical-force tradition, Gandhian notions of non-violent resistance, in the abstract as well as in the particular, had no natural appeal for him. Since the illusion dies hard (except in universities) that men of an academic cast of mind are by nature pacific, when not pacifist, the point is worth establishing. Indeed in my judgement, as Smuts's early experiences in the South African war were far more important than his philosophy in shaping his outlook, so also I believe that de Valera's experiences in the Volunteers were more relevant than his mathematics to an understanding of his subsequent career.

The Ulster question affords the second point of interest. The book, which is in most other respects an impressive record of hard-won achievement, here indicates failure – and this is what merits special attention – where it was not anticipated. 'Let the Orangemen', wrote de Valera in the context of the South Armagh and East Tyrone by-election of the spring of 1918, 'fall back on their fortress of the two races, their fortress of partition – that has no terrors for us. Let them fall back on it, they will find it a Metz. It is after all only an old fortress of crumbled masonry – held together with a plaster of fiction.' An oratorical flourish, of course, but his biographers comment, and there is other evidence to support their conclusion, that from the first de Valera was sure that the struggle for Irish freedom would leave no insoluble problem in the north-east. Possibly, it now appears, by reason of that conviction, unity was subordinated to status in the negotiations that led to the Treaty, and it was only when, from President de Valera's point of view, status was satisfactorily disposed of with the passage of the External Relations Act in 1936 and the adoption of the new Constitution the following year that unity once more assumed priority. This is made very clear in the account of protracted discussions leading up to the 1938 Agreement with Britain, which are skilfully analysed with detailed reference to British official records of them, in Chapters 25 and 26. Unity was subordinated once again to neutrality, though in effect it was restored to a primary position after 1945 and Mr de Valera on a Commonwealth tour sought to enlist overseas Commonwealth opinion against partition. (In a curious oversight the authors (p. 435) write of de Valera's being in India 'on the last night of British rule' on his homeward journey in 1948. But India had kept her 'tryst with destiny' at the midnight hour of 14–15 August 1947.) But in office he had never sought to deploy the Commonwealth at the governmental level, as, for example, African governments have done in respect of Rhodesia, against the border presumably because *inter alia* it would have seemed inconsistent with repudiation of Commonwealth membership in any traditional form which then, consistently with his order of priorities, engaged his first attention. The wartime proposals for ending partition by a neutrality–border deal were a facile essay in the new style 'hustling' transatlantic diplomacy and, as presented, merited the unqualified rejection de Valera as Taoiseach meted out to them. But in respect of fundamentals, the fact remains that his earlier assessment of the dimensions of the Northern Ireland problem derived from a mistaken premise, and even though it is far from clear that had it been otherwise his order of priorities would, or could, have been different, there would have been differences, presumably, in emphasis and psychological predisposition.

The Treaty

The preliminaries to the Treaty had demonstrated once for all President de Valera's political sensitivity and ingenuity in matters of status and constitutional form. Here he was genuinely creative. In external association he formulated a new concept of interstate relations which attracted subsequent attention in many parts of the world, and most of all in renascent post-war Asia. It is historically important and revealing to have, in consecutive form, an account of de Valera's reaction to the Treaty negotiations. It would be in accord with normal political or diplomatic practice for a principal not to engage in direct negotiation unless there were reasonable assurance, as there was far from being in this case, of attainment of fundamental aims. On the other hand, with the publication of the biography, two new and more detailed questions open up. The discussions between overtired, overtaxed men on the evening of 2 December (1921) were followed by the Cabinet meeting of the following day, heavy with potential misunderstanding. Here two points seem important. Firstly, were Ó Murchadha's recorded six points of agreement approved by all members of the Cabinet before it broke up? And secondly, was the President's itinerary for the succeeding days known to the delegates in London and would he in fact have been available on the telephone in Galway, Ennis, and Limerick had the delegates desired to consult with him? The answers to both questions may well be in the affirmative but, if so, this would seem to merit explicit statement.

Neutrality

The sense of tragedy, in the Grecian sense of predestined doom, overhanging honourable men in the desperate climacteric of the struggle for freedom so present in 1921 was absent in the crises of the Second World War. That is partly because the ground for neutrality had been carefully prepared beforehand. The Treaty ports, which de Valera early and correctly judged to be a condition of detachment, had been restored by one of the rare exercises in skilled and constructive Anglo-Irish diplomacy, though whether the rôle of Malcolm MacDonald, however significant in an intermediary sense, was quite so important in that of principal, as is suggested here, may be open to doubt. It was diplomacy that again was required for the war years. De Valera not only represented the will of the people on the issue of neutrality, but he was furthermore the unflinching and ever-watchful repository of it. The authors in their account of the events of 1940–1, in a chapter entitled 'On Razor's Edge', seemingly subscribe to the view that there was a possibility, even a strong one, both of a German landing and, independently of it, of a British invasion to seize the ports, a view which may appear to receive some further support from more recently available British archives with their accounts of speculative Churchillian designs. Not everyone may concur in that judgement on the evidence available, including in it, as one must, a reasoned assessment of the balance of opinion in Britain, German strategic thinking and known Irish resolve to resist. For my part, I incline, *per contra*, to the conclusion that invasion by the one was as improbable as by the other, though for different reasons, and that in consequence there is some element of overdramatization by the authors here.

On this second view, though not on the first, de Valera's concern was to ensure that he was not moved by sentiment or stratagem from the stand he had taken. Provided, always provided, that this did not occur, the paradoxical result was that Ireland, in a position of superficial weakness, came to occupy, in effect, one of considerable diplomatic strength. This the Americans and the American Ambassador in particular were slow to grasp, and Churchill to recognize with good (as he did with ill) grace. Throughout de Valera was engaged in an exercise arising from, but also remote from the cataclysm that engulfed Europe, which required for its successful performance many of the arts of the so-called old diplomacy. Here the biography amply confirms that neither de Valera's concentration on an overriding aim, neutrality, nor his skill, nor his courage, failed throughout a demanding six years, which in most respects represented the apogee of both his power and his prestige. One consequence is that Ireland shares with Switzerland and Sweden, alone of all the countries of Europe, the advantage of not having been engaged in war, including in that term civil and colonial wars, for virtually half a century.

International Affairs

The authors regret that President de Valera had not the opportunity, as political leader of a small power, to demonstrate his political stature on a world stage. This, however, while substantially, is not wholly true. He attained, despite that handicap, the status of an international statesman, but the observation points to a curious lacuna in the biography. De Valera, as is recorded, was twice President of the Council of the League of Nations in the decade that preceded the catastrophe of war that was, in the strict sense, worldwide for the first time. He appears in one of many well-chosen illustrations in his presidential chair at Geneva in 1932 looking incredibly youthful and flanked by European leaders, von Neurath, Paul Boncour and John Simon, whose reputations were among the least of the casualties of that deluge. Yet, despite the position he occupied with general acclaim, little or nothing is said, except what has already appeared in speeches that reflected 'Third World' attitudes two decades before a 'Third World' assumed identifiable form, of his impressions at that time of men or politics in that early phase of the decline of the first system of international organization. He was President again in 1938 and at Geneva during the Munich crisis and, while it is true that Geneva was impotent, still recollections of men's fears and hopes would have added a further dimension to the book. As it is, the reader is left in some doubt about the depth of de Valera's interest in what was happening in Europe. It is clear that he felt keenly and spoke courageously when national rights were flouted, as in the Nazi invasion of Holland and Belgium, but there are no such comments recorded on Fascism or Nazism as systems of government or of crimes committed under the latter and there was one incident which might be taken to indicate either a certain unawareness of them, or a certain insensitivity to them born perhaps of a high degree of absorption in diplomatic manoeuvres.

The apotheosis of Eamon de Valera as statesman-President of a nation whose destinies he touched, or guided, over a period of half a century is apt to obscure, at least for a younger generation, the foundation of his achievement. One has already been mentioned. He was inured to and experienced in warfare. The second is that as a politician he had a mastery of strategy and usually of tactics – there were some lapses here, e.g. exposition of status in terms of a dictionary republic – which none of his rivals could match. The third was his long-term perspicacity. In 1921 he envisaged realistically the problems of the relationship between a republican state and a monarchical Commonwealth and India, if not Ireland, was to be a beneficiary of his first formulation of possible answers to them, just as in 1936–7 his sense of timing in respect of the External Relations Act and the new Constitution was very sure. The same appreciation of timing in respect of the 1938 Agreement has already been noted. Almost certainly 1938 was the only year in which British agreement to the return of the Treaty ports might have been obtained, the case for the appeasement of Ireland not being strong enough, given the Eurasian context (it seems not unlikely that the threat of war in the Far East, stretching British naval resources to breaking point, was an unstated but nevertheless decisive factor in British strategic thinking about the ports) for the Baldwin or Chamberlain administration to have been influenced by it earlier, and the likelihood of war too great for such a step to be taken later. The sense of timing was also evident in the war years, though a tendency here on the part of the authors to insist upon an almost exclusive degree of reliance upon principle has the effect of discounting what might otherwise be attributed to realistic assessment of the probable course of events.

Principles

Throughout the work, indeed, President de Valera's biographers underline his devotion to principle and in the concluding chapter they have some interesting reflections on the nature of his political thought from which these principles derived. They bring out the supreme importance to him of his religious faith – 'no famous statesman of our time can have centred his life more completely, or perhaps so completely, on religion'; his attachment to democracy, of the highest significance to his country in the early thirties; his rôle as a constitutionalist, manifested in the drafting of a new Constitution, and subsequent exposition of its provisions at meetings up and down the country during the referendum campaign,[2] both testifying

---

[2] On 24 June 1937 I heard him speak, so a diary entry reminds me, chiefly on the Constitution, at a public meeting by Kickham's monument in Tipperary from 11 p.m. till past midnight. He spoke, I noted, 'with warmth but without rancour' for about one and a quarter hours, giving 'a severe, unadorned, well-reasoned' exposé of the provisions of

to his sense of the great importance attaching to the form of a constitution – something which is unfashionable today, but not for that reason necessarily misplaced; and his republicanism, which in effect summed up for him his political beliefs, above all his sense of nationality.

On most, if not all of these questions, and especially on the nature of his republican views, one would have welcomed more searching analysis from his biographers. De Valera's cast of mind, it seems, was too practical for him to have adopted the 'utopian' eighteenth-century concepts of republicanism, too conservative for him to be carried along with the contemporary European social-democratic ideals associated with it, even when impeccably constitutional in their formulation – he had many discussions before 1916 with James Connolly, but if they touched on ideological questions their substance is not recorded – and perhaps essentially, making due allowance for the very different social patterns of their respective countries, he was here by contrast at heart something of a Gandhian looking back in his case to the hard, independent country life of his childhood at Bruree, freed from foreign influences, its indigenous character reinforced by the use of the indigenous tongue, as the source of national virtue and the ideal of national regeneration.

De Valera was not, it would seem, deeply interested in the socio-economic issues which have so greatly preoccupied the mid-twentieth century world, and, we are told, for example, that in the thirties he gave a virtually free hand to Seán Lemass at Industry and Commerce on industrial policy. Whether this indicated a certain detachment from such questions, or a political awareness that 'romantic' national issues – national independence, the language, the republic – had on the one hand a natural priority and on the other a unifying influence, whereas social issues are apt to be divisive, is not made clear. In any event the man who has played so great a part in national history will have many biographers and some questions must remain for later ones. However they treat of them, this biography will retain its unique status, if not as *the* authorized version, then at least as being as near as one will ever get to *an* authorized version.

---

2 (cont.)
the Constitution, especially those relating to the office of President, which was listened to with a respect that was the greater for his firm refusal, on a matter of the highest importance for the future of the country, to score debating points.

17

SOME REFLECTIONS UPON THE LOCAL DIMENSION IN HISTORY

Tipperary: History and Society is being launched upon a flowing tide. In the last twenty or thirty years there has been something of a revolution in attitudes to local studies, that is to say to studies relating to the origins, physical environment, development and distinguishing characteristics of a local, regional or otherwise identifiable social or administrative entity: in this case a county, the largest inland county in Ireland and the only one divided for administrative purposes into two ridings. That revolution is in part the consequence and in part the continuing cause of a greater awareness of the local community from which we spring and correspondingly a greater interest in its past. It has raised local history – and history is the lynchpin of local studies – from a little regarded position, altogether subordinate to national or international history, to one more nearly of parity and often commanding more sustained and authentic interest than either. After all, it is usually possible, and almost always rewarding, to see for oneself the sites or remaining evidence of events that took place within one's own county, but only infrequently, and with special intent, those elsewhere in the country, let alone across the seas. Enhanced status in its turn has brought more demanding standards which, in the words of one authority, have transformed local history 'from an amateurish *pot-pourri* into a recognised academic discipline'.[1]

---

[1] C. W. Chalkin and M. A. Havinder (eds.), *Rural Change and Urban Growth: Essays in Honour of W. G. Hoskins* (London, 1974), p. xix.

It has also introduced wider perspectives. To history in its traditional narrative form are now to be added archaeology, physical and human geography, and social sciences, in whose wide embrace demography, politics and economic factors may be enfolded. At first sight this may seem a hint forbidding, fragmenting older and simpler unities of experience and common memories by the casting of a cold analytical eye on the aspects into which they have been divided. Fifty years ago indeed any such breakdown would have seemed inconceivable. Local history, while it had passed from 'the drum and trumpet' stage, remained the preoccupation of devoted individuals working in isolation, carried along by their own conviction that what they were doing was worthwhile, but not necessarily endowed with all the qualifications or having at their disposal the equipment deemed desirable by the more rigorous demands of today for balanced reconstruction of the local past. But this has happened in most fields and in local studies, where so much remains to be done, the contributions of 'amateurs' are always likely to be welcome. For this reason, in hailing new departures I pause to salute the pioneers of other days and, more particularly, Paul Flynn who first introduced me to difficult questions, such as the original location of the settlement that became Tipperary town, and whose *Book of the Galtees and the Golden Vein* (Dublin, 1926) now enjoys a scarcity value. But they would, I am sure, have been among the first to welcome more recent specialisation and the greater depth and range of knowledge it has made possible.

However it is well also to continue to entertain a realistic sense of limitation. Historians are the victims of their own sources. We shall never recapture the past, only those parts of it which written records or collective folk memories have preserved. Both are apt to be highly selective. Local records were kept in medieval times, for strictly functional purposes – collection of taxes, discharge of obligations, determination of entitlement to privileges or land – with vital statistics in parish registers. In modern times such records have multiplied a thousandfold to serve as, so to speak, a collective official memory for the administration of local government, but their functional purposes and consequently their limitations remain. Social scientists of the future should be able, for example, on the basis of local authority records, to extract statistics on car ownership and compare the figures for town and country, but they would have to look elsewhere for enlightenment on the uses to which owners put their cars or to formulate answers to such questions as, in what ways did ownership alter the pattern of social life? There will, I assume, be no details in such records on preceding forms of transport – traps, donkey carts or for that matter bicycles. To catch glimpses of how our ancestors lived in medieval times, one would turn to chronicles as later to ballad mongers and for the last two centuries or so, to local newspapers notably the *Nationalist*. But, important as their contribution has been, if that were all, the more intimate and human sides of life would perforce pass undescribed. Happily, however, this is not altogether so. Such sources may be and often are richly supplemented by private letters, notes of shop or farm accounts, the occasional autobiography and above all oral evidence, which is at the heart of local history.

Such evidence generally falls into one of two categories, on the one hand stories of people and events handed down from mouth to mouth through the generations and, on the other, direct relation by a living person of events that took place and in which he participated or witnessed when he was young. In whichever category they fall, the important thing is that somehow or other, if they are of interest, they should be transferred from the oral to the written category and so preserved. In this respect, as was recognized in a paper read at the Fifteenth Congress of the Historical Sciences held in Bucharest in August 1980, the Irish Folklore Institute, formed in 1930, played a pioneering rôle in these islands, sending out interviewers into the country, so Congress delegates were told, armed at the outset with nothing more than an Ediphone recording machine and wax cylinders.[2] By the fifties and sixties interviews of individuals on topics ranging from high politics, to who cut the hay and with what machinery was it saved, were taking place and the records being placed in a depository. In turn this is being supplemented by film, with the result that future generations of historians should have evidence before them of a variety hitherto unknown. Fundamental questions of how to use it, however, remain much the same.

First one might pose that of nature. Has local history characteristics that place it somewhat apart from national or world history? I think one part of the answer might be that because of its more limited scope, it can afford to give more, sometimes overmuch, attention to detailed narrative or exact description. Some thirty years ago I remember hearing historians in general being dismissed by one among their number, trained in the methodological continental tradition, as mere antiquarians and anecdotalists. It is a charge that has been levelled with some force against local historians devoting time and energy to some disputed but unimportant site, while neglecting altogether what had been a major enterprise and was now reduced to an abandoned warehouse or factory. There is here a question of balance, one purpose at the outset being the identification and preservation of relics of the past that are likely to have enduring interest. They may range from horse-drawn turning machines (of which I was pleased to supply one to the agricultural machinery museum at Bunratty) to castles. Has not the restoration and the opening to the public of Cahir Castle, that

---

[2] *XV Congrès International des Sciences Historiques* (Bucharest, 1980), *Rapports I: Grands Thèmes et Méthodologie*, pp. 555–6; see generally pp. 558–69.

stronghold of the Butlers, done much to quicken our sense of the late medieval struggle for power in the area and does not the story of the cannon ball still to be seen lodged in the outer wall add a piquant flavour – it was fired by order of the Earl of Essex, Queen Elizabeth's favourite, in 1599 when Essex decided to march south though under royal command to go north, with the result that he captured Cahir Castle, only shortly thereafter to lose his head? Though they may find no place on a wide national canvas, such reminders of older farming methods or sieges some centuries ago are grist to the mill of local history, their importance being as much, or more, in the ambience they create as in the facts they represent or relate. But also in Cahir overlooking the river on the other side of the road are the old flourmills. They offer little by way of anecdote but how much do they tell of the amount of tillage in the area a hundred years ago and of its subsequent decline.

Secondly, there is the question of reliability where so much depends on imperfect records and the fallibility of human memories. History in all its manifestations is basically an exact study and readers very reasonably expect historians, local or otherwise, to have examined the evidence before them critically and to tell their tale on the basis of fact, being careful to indicate where lack of knowledge requires surmise or some degree of speculation and where reliance is based upon oral evidence. When old we remember selectively rather than forget. With such factors in mind historians then exercise their imaginative insights in interpreting the past. But it is not for them to invent; they are not, or should not be, composing a historical novel or writing a historical drama. Thucydides, reflecting on this at the dawn of history, tells us that even while recognizing that his history of the Peloponnesian War (431–404 BC) might be less attractive as a result, he had avoided 'all story-telling'. As a historian he required better evidence than that of poets 'who exaggerate their themes' or prose chroniclers 'who are less interested in telling the truth than in catching the attention of their public'.[3] By such constraints, local historians are bound equally with their colleagues in other fields, though because of the patchiness of the evidence before them, they have at least as great, if not greater demands imposed upon their judgement. For that reason, they may be accorded rather more latitude in interpretation. We would not wish them to be so preoccupied with facts as to be inhibited from painting in wider contours. And here one may remark that the local historian working intensively in a small area is not over-likely to be misled. He may have reason

---

[3] *The Peloponnesian War*, translated by Rex Warner (London, 1954). An earlier and more colourful translation by the political philosopher Thomas Hobbes was reprinted in 1975, editor R. Schlatter, by Rutgers University Press, New Jersey, and from which some of the quotations are taken.

to know that not all first-hand evidence is reliable. Thucydides made it a principle not to write down the first story that came his way, knowing well that different eye witnesses, from either partiality or imperfect memories, would give different accounts of the same events. A Hungarian delegate to the Bucharest Historical Congress (already mentioned) provided a gloss to this in telling of a policeman in Budapest who had listened attentively to the evidence of five witnesses to an accident he had not seen and then wrote down his own – the sixth – account which bore little or no resemblance to the others, but was the one that survived as the official report (I expect the story had political overtones partly lost on me, but not, I suspect, on the other East European delegates).[4]

Thirdly there is the question of range. It seems right to me that this volume should refer to disciplines other than history. Archaeology, which requires expertise and employs techniques unfamiliar to historians, is included as befitting a county so rich in archaeological remains. But this would not always have been so. In the Age of Reason there was contempt for what happened in the centuries following the fall of Rome and for the monuments they left behind them. 'I know nothing', wrote Horace Walpole in 1773, 'of barrows, of Danish entrenchments, and Saxon barbarisms . . . in short I know nothing of those ages that knew nothing.'[5] Nowadays, however, interest in excavations of such remains is worldwide; wherever found they are or will be seen as a rich part of the Irish heritage. The enlightened are not always as enlightened as they think! For our part, we may look forward to a time when further insight into the past comes from excavations of some of the sites of the many mounds and forts to be found in various parts of the county.

Fourthly there is the large question of overlapping frontiers of local with national history. One could perhaps break this down into the local aspects of national history, which is one thing, and local history in its own right having no such national significance, which is another. Dr David Fitzpatrick has written a study of *Provincial Experience of War and Revolution* (to quote the subtitle of his work)[6] on regional events 1913–21 in County Clare, which systematically analyses the interplay (or lack of it) between centre and region in troubled times and provides a very good example of a study of the former, i.e. the national aspect of local history in a period of momentous change. Even a particular local link with a matter of national significance is apt to be invested with special interest. My great-grandfather, Richard Martin Mansergh, was a lifelong friend of William Smith O'Brien. When O'Brien was arrested on 5 August 1848 and (with

---

[4] *Rapports I*, G. Ferenc, p. 570.

[5] Horace Walpole, *Letters*, Selected by W. S. Lewis (London, 1951).

[6] The title is *Politics and Irish Life 1913–1921* (Dublin, 1977).

T. F. Meagher and Patrick O'Donoghue) brought before the Grand Jury at Clonmel, it fell to his lot, as foreman, to announce the verdict. The sentence was death. That was commuted to transportation for life, partly or largely because of many representations, Richard Martin's among them, made to that effect. Smith O'Brien was later pardoned and released, but the anxieties connected with the trial and the fate of his friend are said to have undermined Richard Martin's health. An account of his part was written out by my mother some fifty years ago (an example in itself of family tradition being placed on record, before it had faded into the mists of time); otherwise I would have known nothing of it. But thus reminded, my wife and I went over to see what remains of the widow MacCormack's house, which stands well back from the road on the top of a hill at Boulagh Common, some four miles north of Ballingarry.[7] It is a two storey building with an enclosed yard behind it, better equipped to withstand a siege than I had supposed. The 'cabbage patch' is to the east of the house. All that needs to be said is written in fading letters but with a nice economy of phrase on a plaque over the door 'Remember '48'. Not unfittingly it was there that the Tricolour was first raised in County Tipperary, for the timing at least of the affray at Ballingarry was a by-product of the turmoil in Paris, which on 24 February 1848 had overthrown the Orleans Monarchy, led to the proclamation of the Second Republic and sparked off the Year of Revolution in Europe. What could be, and was, dismissed at the time as 'ludicrous' in the *Annual Register*, as an affray in a cabbage patch elsewhere, came later, as Professor Oliver MacDonagh in his *States of Mind* has noted, to take its place in a sequence 1798, 1803, 1848, 1867, 1916. 'After all', he remarks, 'the February Revolution of 1848 in Paris itself was a theatrical and a theoretician's affair rather than a professional conflict.'[8]

Almost every family will have its store of memories, especially of hard or troubled times spanning generations, maybe centuries, which collectively provide the basis for local history in its own right, i.e. my second category. They are part of a family's heritage. Sometimes they will be supplemented or underpinned by papers or letters, say to and from those who emigrated to North America or Australia or more recently worked in England. Almost

---

[7] At the time also I read an article by Michael Fitzgerald entitled 'A Shrine Neglected' in *The Sunday Press*, 14 August 1983, which further prompted me to visit it.

[8] O. MacDonagh, *States of Mind: 'A Study of Anglo-Irish Conflict 1780–1980* (London, 1983), pp. 66, 79. See also *The Annual Register* 1848, p. 95. The sentence read: 'The ignominious defeat of Mr O'Brien's ludicrous attack upon the civil power and the unresisted capture of his person annihilated at once the dignity and danger of the conspiracy'. However the *Annual Register* recognized the intellectual calibre of many of the conspirators including Smith O'Brien. It also reproduced the proceedings of the trial (pp. 364–445), itself an indication of the extent of contemporary interest.

always they will include some recollections of school as well as occupation and later experiences. The Abbey School in Tipperary, of which John O'Leary was the most distinguished product of what educationally is said to have been its best period and at which I like to think he acquired the independence of mind and Roman fortitude by which W. B. Yeats was so greatly influenced and inspired, has, as one of the Erasmus Smith schools, a place in past educational controversies. As the youngest boy at that school in the last days of its existence in that character, I feel tempted, however, to contribute an account in lighter vein of what might be classified as a local incident arising from its closure and one throwing light on railway transport in times of emergency. The school, which was dwindling away as the prospect of civil war approached – I remember spent bullets coming through the north window of the big schoolroom – closed abruptly. My brother and I had been taken home, but others from a distance learned one morning of a parting instruction from the headmaster, who had left for Dublin the night before, to do so as best they might. Among them were the four sons of Canon Pike from Thurles. They got as far as the Junction only to find that no trains were running because a bridge had been blown up at Knocklong. While the solitary porter obligingly looked the other way they unhitched an open railway truck, hoisted their luggage on board and, with the four of them pushing for a start and then by turn one by one with three on board, off they went past Dundrum, past Goooldscross – and then, faint at first but soon unmistakable came the sound of a train coming at speed behind them. They stood up on the truck waving and shouting. The driver of the Dublin express (for such it was) slowed down. They explained: he told them to get back on their truck and he pushed them ahead of the engine into Thurles station.

At the last you may ask what is the purpose of it all? Are local studies something to be undertaken by a select few for others likewise occupied? This is certainly one feature – local studies do have that comparative professional interest. But they have other aspects also and how you regard them depends very much on your view of history itself: it has been described 'as the most humane of the humaner studies, its subject being the story of man on earth itself'.[9] Unlike the natural sciences, its study requires not only detachment, but detachment with sympathetic insight into man's way of life, his preoccupations and concerns at points in time, stretching back to the prehistoric. In that sense, history is all-embracing, hence the vogue on the other side of the Atlantic for courses in world civilization, categorized by Professor Kenyon as 'Romulus to Reagan' surveys and thus concluding at the time of writing with one of Tipperary descent. But just

---

[9] A. F. Pollard on *Why we Study History*. Historical Association Publication, No. 131 (London, 1944), p. 14. See also *ibid*: essays by R. C. K. Ensor, D. C. Somervell and others.

because of the range of history, local history has its attraction for schools, not, I think, as a 'way in' to the subject – it is necessary first to have some broader framework of historical knowledge – but as a way of linking it to boys' and girls' own environment and experience. Young people in acquiring a sense of the past are the more likely to feel something of its reality by being told of what happened in places they have seen and with which they are tolerably familiar. At what times and by what stages was the town laid out as it is today? Where did the materials for building come from? Why on earth was the Limerick Junction station sited where it is? Is there any concrete evidence that the British army barracks in Tipperary were built in error to a design intended to help keep the troops cool in the near-tropical climate of Hong Kong? Did marauders, not only by land but also by water, come up the Suir as far as Athassel Abbey and did the Augustinian monks repel them from walls that have the strength of parapets? Once interested in what has happened locally in the past, one is apt to look with a fresh and more concerned eye on what is in prospect for the future and be the better qualified to express an opinion on transport, town planning and development in this age of extensive building on the perimeters of towns and to acquire informed judgement on what is of sufficient historical interest to preserve or even to restore (of which Holycross Abbey affords so striking an example) in times of straitened resources.

In a sense this longer perspective on change and how and why it has taken the form it has in one's own region may be thought of as one of the practical uses of local studies. Whether there are more intangible ones is a matter which has preoccupied historians from the time of Thucydides, who believed that those who read his narrative in after days would find it useful, because he was persuaded that human experience repeated itself and that therefore by precise knowledge of the past men would be the better equipped to solve the problems of the future. It is, as he wrote in a well-known paragraph (22) in his history of the Peloponnesian War, for those who 'desire to look into the truth of things done and which may be done again'. Nearer our own time, Samuel Taylor Coleridge, with qualified scepticism, thought of history as being like a lantern on the stern of a ship casting its light only on the waves behind. As one to be numbered with the more sceptical, I would none the less contend that knowledge of history should at the least help one to avoid courses that had proved unsatisfactory, or still more, disastrous in the past. But whatever shade of opinion one takes, local studies must add a dimension to one's life in the locality to which one belongs, not least where it is a county like Tipperary in which there are so many reminders that history often turbulent – Macaulay I suspect spoke for more than himself or his time when in 1833 he told the House of Commons that he would far rather have been in the Young Pretender's line of advance on Derby in 1745 'than in Tipperary now'[10] – passed this way. Finally – and it is no mean thing – such studies should bring many incidental and unexpected pleasures to readers.

---

[10] Hansard, third series, xi. 262.

Epilogue

18

'LETTERS THAT WE OUGHT TO BURN'

The lives of great men all remind us,
As we o'er their pages turn,
That we, too, may leave behind us,
Letters that we ought to burn.

The lives of many, if not all, great men do give us cause, as we read their papers, their biographies or even their autobiographies, to reflect with Father Ronald Knox, the author I believe of this parody, how much wiser they would have been, how much higher their reputations might stand, had they burnt this letter or that paper. It would have been good for them; but disappointing, very disappointing in many cases, for us. Historians, we feel, want to know, are indeed entitled to know, what were the inmost thoughts and motives of the great. And these, we are apt to assume, are revealed in all their nakedness and reality in personal, and preferably indiscreet, letters. I find it difficult to persuade a research student nowadays that the purposes and motives behind, let us say, a Prime Minister's policy on some particular and complex issue are more faithfully and carefully expounded in a paper circulated to the Cabinet or a speech given to Parliament than in a hurried note written to his wife late that night. I find it almost impossible if the note is written, not to his wife, but to a lady-friend. When, to speak of a period and a personality in whom I am interested, the latest biographer of Asquith, Roy Jenkins, in a book published a few months ago,[1] reveals, and reproduces extensively, the notes the Prime Minister sent to Miss Venetia Stanley, recording, shrewdly enough but with the evident purpose of entertainment rather than instruction, talks with colleagues or discussions in Cabinet, I find myself half wishing the letters had been burned. They will, I say to myself, distract attention from authoritative sources; they will distort historical perspective. But, of course, I am delighted they have survived; I shall hope to look and see if there are more to be traced; I shall, in brief, succumb to that most insidious of historical temptations; what Gibbon called, in warning us to be on guard against it, 'the pursuit of the curious'.

The injunction about letter-burning does not, I think, apply to men whose achievements and personalities are part of the history of a nation. 'Publish and be damned', said the Duke of Wellington to the lady who threatened to make known some letters of his earlier days. Clearly, and in more senses than one, he was right. Nor does it apply, or can it usually be applied, to the notoriously imprudent or indiscreet. If it did, almost all the letters of the Kaiser Wilhelm II among others would have to be destroyed. No, the letters which great men ought to burn are the letters which in one way or another expose unsuspected deviousness in action, deficiency in character or in other ways diminish their stature. That is why in such instances lesser men – and historians – treasure them. Yet, there is, inevitably, a large element of chance in what survives and what does not; in what is burned and what is not. That is something, I think, historians ought to remember but often overlook. I recall a sophisticated Foreign Office official saying, after a Greek Prime Minister had fallen from power because of the publication of an ill-advised letter, that stability seemed now to be reasonably assured because, according to Foreign Office sources, the new Prime Minister, a general, was not capable of writing a letter. On the whole, English prime ministers have tended to be, possibly rather dangerously, literate. Of none was this more true than of Gladstone, whose papers must be the most voluminous among English private collections and whose diary is now being edited for publication. He was by no means always well advised in what he wrote, though the ambiguity of ambiguity, as Lytton Strachey described it, through which his sentences uncoiled their slow length along, was in itself a certain safeguard. In the early forties, Peel complained that Gladstone's letters were hard to understand; in the critical autumn of 1885 Hartington said he found it impossible to comprehend what Gladstone was saying to him. What prompted Peel's observation was a letter Gladstone sent him, resigning from the Cabinet on the ground that while personally he approved of, and would vote for, an increased grant to the Roman Catholic seminary at Maynooth, none

---

[1] Roy Jenkins, *Asquith* (London, 1964).

the less because the principle of the grant conflicted with principles he had adumbrated in his work, *State and Church*, published many years before, he could not give it support as a minister. More than one hundred years later his resignation in such circumstances was held up by *The Economist* as a model of honourable political behaviour which ministers in this age of declining political morality should seek to emulate. I mentioned this one evening to the late Professor Sir Charles Webster. He told me that the episode reflected no credit on Gladstone and provided nothing worthy of emulation. In his work on Palmerston, he had come across a letter of Gladstone's, written many months earlier, saying that he was looking for an opportunity to resign from the Cabinet as soon as might be! If that letter had been burned!

Then take a better known and most dramatic case. In the summer of 1885 Lord Randolph Churchill came forward as the exciting protagonist of Tory–Parnellite understanding. He wooed the Irish, he spoke to the heart of the peasant masses. He, also, was of the land, he was their natural ally and champion against the superiority, indifference and incomprehension 'of the lords of suburban villas, of the owners of vineries and pineries'. Gladstone then came out for Home Rule. Lord Randolph became the champion almost overnight it seemed of minority interests in Ulster. He journeyed thither. He uttered stirring and memorable phrases. On landing at Larne, he declared 'Ulster will fight; Ulster will be right'. He concluded a speech at Belfast with words 'which are best expressed by one of our great English poets':

> The combat deepens; on ye brave
> Who rush to glory or the grave.
> Wave, Ulster – all thy banners wave
> And charge with all thy chivalry

Even the ranks of Tuscany, in this case the Irish Nationalists, if not prepared to cheer, at least were willing to concede that behind such eloquence must rest *deep* conviction. Unfortunately Lord Randolph had written two letters. Both survive. One, dated November 1885, complained to Lord Salisbury of the 'monstrous alliance' with 'these foul Ulster Tories' which 'has always ruined our party'. The second, written on 16 February 1886, to Fitzgibbon, stated, 'I decided some time ago that if the G.O.M. went for Home Rule the Orange card would be the one to play. Please God, it may turn out the ace of trumps and not the two . . .' Certainly a couple of letters that ought to have been burned.[2]

The element of chance in the destruction, even of letters of set purpose

---

[2] For texts of letters, see R. R. James, *Lord Randolph Churchill* (London, 1959), p. 223; and W. S. Churchill, *Lord Randolph Churchill*, 2 Vols. (London, 1906), Vol. II, p. 59.

preserved, is clearly high. When Lionel Curtis, the 'prophet' in Milner's 'kindergarten', joined his staff in South Africa, Milner said he felt like a country rector who had been sent the Prophet Isaiah as his curate – and later he became a member of Lloyd George's 'garden suburb' at No. 10 Downing Street in controversial Coalition days. When his Oxford home was burned down before the last war with all his papers, it was said that the sigh of relief in London could be overheard along the High in Oxford.

But more important for the historian are papers destroyed not by chance but by design. Within this category would fall assuredly letters that ought *not* to be burned – letters that is to say, using the same criteria of judgement, as in the case of letters that ought to be burned, that would have enhanced the reputations of the writers of them. Historians have, or in the course of time will presumably have, sufficient evidence to judge the parliamentary careers, to confine myself within my own field of study, of men like Botha and Smuts, de Valera and Jawaharlal Nehru. But the reputations of none of them were made in parliamentary assemblies. On the contrary, they were in each case first founded in the organization or direction of national, revolutionary movements or warfare. Yet the evidence here is thin – and of necessity so. Men engaged in hazardous enterprises are ill-advised to keep papers. De Valera, like Michael Collins, destroyed all incriminating documents of the years of the Irish revolution – and in old age, I have reason to suppose, senses with regret gaps in historical knowledge that can never be conclusively filled. Smuts was in some respects more fortunate. His wife rolled up and stuffed the secret telegrams that came to him as a member of President Kruger's government down the inside of the hollow brass Victorian curtain rods in their house, *one* day before the British soldiers came; and in 1951 she pulled them out to show them to his biographer, Professor Sir Keith Hancock. Smuts's wartime records concealed in the leather of his saddle-bags survived to our great profit, but his letters to his wife which she cut up and put inside a cushion were never found – she had mislaid the cushion![3] Of course, there are always other records, written or personal. But the first are rarely a complete substitute and the second often to be treated with some reserve. Unlike de Valera, Michael Collins did not survive the Irish Civil War, but like him he kept no important papers. Historically his reputation, I am sure, has been thereby somewhat diminished. Historical figures rarely remember the rôle of others as fully as their own. Nor indeed are their memories altogether reliable.

No man that I have met was, I think, more conscious, sensibly conscious

---

[3] *Selections from the Smuts Papers*, edited by W. K. Hancock and Jean van der Poel, 7 Vols. (Cambridge, 1966-1973) and W. K. Hancock, *Smuts: The Sanguine Years 1870–1919* (Cambridge, 1962), pp. 116–17 and 136–7.

may I add, than Pandit Nehru of walking upon the stage of history. In Delhi in 1951 and again in 1958 I asked him, quite by chance in the course of conversation, the same question. It was an important one. 'When', I said to him, 'did you first come to realise that the response to Muslim demands would have to be the partition and the concession of Pakistan?' On each occasion, he reflected carefully and answered with deliberation and much circumstantial and convincing evidence. But the dates he gave differed widely. On each occasion I went out into the sunshine and wrote my notes. As a result of two conversations, instead of one, I am a good deal less positive in my conclusions; but also, I suspect, that much nearer to the truth. One statement, once made, quoted and requoted by a succession of historians, is apt to assume the authority but rarely to possess the reality of truth. There is, and how I regret it, a conflict between the logic and lucidity that go so well with direct and easy narration, and the complexity of life as it is and it was in other days.

There is, also, evidence of set purpose destruction, but not for ends now thought to be so creditable as nationalist revolution. Here indeed Commonwealth history provides its classic example in the form of eight telegrams missing from the files of the Colonial Office. It will be remembered that Dr Jameson's Raid, launched in the early morning of 31 December from Pitsani across the high veldt of the Transvaal towards Johannesburg, the city of gold – and of other things besides – was intended to coincide with a rising organised by the wealthy, mining financiers within the city. We know now, in the words of a caustic contemporary commentator, that it is as sensible to rely upon millionaires to stage a successful revolt as it is to enter a carthorse to win the Derby. But it was apparently not appreciated then. The question that even now remains unresolved and undiminished in its historical interest is whether the Colonial Secretary, Joseph Chamberlain, who, on his own admission, knew all about the intended rising, as was right and proper, also had foreknowledge of Dr Jameson's filibustering incursion into the Republic from a base in British territories. The debate is by no means concluded. It was thought that the text of the missing telegrams would resolve it. Some, but not all, were reprinted in facsimile in a Dutch newspaper and they inspired a contemporary volume called *The History of the Mystery*. Some are only partly decipherable or in shorthand, and the interpretation of telescoped or missing words provides fascinating ground for speculation and for special pleading. All of them were said to be in the waistcoat pocket of a Liberal Member of Parliament (Mr Thomas) while Chamberlain was speaking to the report on the raid and, it was rumoured, it was arranged that Mr Hawksley, standing by the clock in the gallery was to give a sign, if Chamberlain did not exonerate Rhodes, to Mr Thomas who would then read them out. Chamberlain, in fact, spoke with surprising warmth of

Rhodes, but almost certainly not for that reason. Even if the wilder rumours be discounted, the missing telegrams and the overhanging questions remained. In recent years they have been interpreted in a sense adverse to Chamberlain by Dr Jean van der Poel of the University of Cape Town and favourable to him by Elizabeth Pakenham, now Lady Longford, and best known for her recent biography of Queen Victoria. It seems in a way a little inappropriate that Jameson's Raid, which, whatever you may think of it, was a *manly* affair, should now be the subject of learned and long-distance exchanges between two distinguished women. For my part I incline to the view that too much evidence was quite literally burned by too many people for the whole truth ever to be established now. When I had a look recently at the files of the Prime Minister's Office at Cape Town, for the years in which Rhodes occupied it, I was struck not so much by what was, but all that was not on them!

There remains in a rather similar category the official letters or documents destroyed many years after the events to which they relate, because of the embarrassment it is thought they might cause. I have been told of a number of such letters and papers deliberately removed from an archive and presumably destroyed. It would be wrong of me to be specific, yet it is right to reflect that the purposes of such abstraction will no doubt be successfully achieved. Clues which might guide historians through some labyrinthine maze are no longer there. Will they find their way? Frankly I doubt it. They will find a way certainly, but hardly the way. How could it be otherwise? The risk, indeed, is best diminished by the realisation of it.

Sometimes, of course, it is not destruction but chance oversight that may affect the writing of history and indeed history itself. Let me, in returning to where I began, give one strange illustration. In 1916, in the great English political crisis of the First World War, the Liberal Asquith was supplanted by the Liberal Lloyd George as Prime Minister of the wartime Coalition. The manner as well as this fact of the change left personal animosities between the two men and within the party. Asquith, moreover, was ousted but not altogether discredited. He remained the focus of discontent in the country, in the army, in the Liberal party itself. By early 1918, with victory seemingly no nearer and the dreadful slaughter on the Western Front continuing, the moment of challenge had come. General Sir Frederick Maurice, the son of a distinguished Victorian theologian and the father of a distinguished Cambridge economist, Mrs Joan Robinson, with his inside knowledge as a recently transferred Director of Military Operations at the War Office, felt it his duty to challenge a number of statements made by the government and particularly one by the Prime Minister. On 9 April 1918, Lloyd George, in reply to criticism, told the House of Commons that the army in France was stronger in January 1918 than it had been in January 1917. General Sir Frederick Maurice, still on the active list and in possession of knowledge officially acquired, knew that this was not true; and after much searching of conscience he decided that it was his duty to write to *The Times* and say so. This he did, after telling Asquith of his intentions but neither expecting nor receiving encouragement from him.[4] It was, of course, a grave step for a serving soldier to take – especially in view of Lloyd George's not ill-founded suspicion of military intrigue and his conviction of military incompetence in high places. The Prime Minister, in fact, did not credit General Maurice's patriotic intentions. He felt, too, that his honour was impugned. The government offered to set up a Court of Enquiry. Asquith, unwisely as both his biographer Roy Jenkins and that formidable critic Lord Beaverbrook allow,[5] refused. He demanded a debate and a Select Committee. The first was granted for a debate on the second. The great political crisis of the war had come. If it could be shown that Lloyd George had deceived the House, then the Coalition would fall. And could it be doubted that he had whether deliberately or by oversight misled it on a critical issue? After all, the man who was Director of Military Operations at the War Office at the time could hardly be mistaken on a matter of figures and facts. The debate took place in a highly charged atmosphere on 7 May 1918. Asquith, an honourable man concerned not to appear party, as he was not, to military intrigue, did not press home the indictment. Lloyd George enjoyed perhaps the greatest, certainly the most conclusive of his parliamentary triumphs. And what was his line of defence? It was that if the figures he gave the House were wrong, the fault lay with General Maurice. He had asked for them before he made them; the War Office had supplied them, General Maurice being still Director of Military Operations. When the House divided on Asquith's motion for a Select Committee, 293 members voted for the government, 106 for the opposition. Asquith and those who voted with him were not forgiven. In the so-called 'coupon' election of November 1918, they were refused the Coalition ticket and were everywhere denounced with an asperity rare in English public life. Asquith himself, Prime Minister for a longer consecutive period than any man since Lord Liverpool, with the greater part of his followers, lost his seat. Nor was the division in the ranks of the Liberal party ever healed or the followers of Lloyd George and Asquith, 'Squiffites' as they were called, ever reunited. Asquith himself was pursued to the end of his days by the bitterness aroused by the Maurice debate, and when, on Lord Curzon's death in 1925, he stood for election to the thus vacant Chancellorship of the University of Oxford, he was still shadowed by it. He, who had been foremost among the classical scholars of Balliol in its greatest age, was opposed by Lord Cave, the Lord Chancellor, a man

---

[4] See Jenkins, *op. cit.* p. 469 et seq.

[5] Lord Beaverbrook, *Men and Power 1917-1918* (London, 1966), p. 254.

of no distinction with a pass degree alone to his academic credit. Yet from town and country, and above all from country rectories, the 'Cavemen' as they were termed, emerged to deny to Asquith the last well-merited and much coveted honour that might have come his way.

But what, you may ask, has all this to do with destroyed or missing papers? In 1922, Sir Frederick claimed in a letter to the Prime Minister that his House of Commons statement on army strength relied upon an accidentally mistaken return which had however been corrected before 9 April. Had the Prime Minister seen it? What had happened to it? We know now. Lord Beaverbrook has printed an extract from the diary of the Countess Lloyd George, formerly Miss Stevenson, his private secretary. The diary date is 5 October 1934. The extract reads:

> Have been reading up the events connected with the Maurice Debate in order to help LL.G. with this Chapter in Vol V [of his War Memoirs] and am uneasy in my mind about an incident that occurred at the time and which is known only to J.T. Davies and myself. LL.G. obtained from the W.O. the figures which he used in his statement on April 9th in the House of Commons on the subject of man-power. These figures were afterwards stated by General Maurice to be inaccurate.
>
> I was in J.T. Davies' room a few days after the statement, and J.T. was sorting out red dispatch boxes to be returned to the Departments. As was his wont, he looked in them before locking them up and sending them out to the Messengers. Pulling out a W.O. box, he found in it, to his great astonishment, a paper from the D.M.O. containing modifications and corrections of the first figures they had sent, and by some mischance this box had remained unopened. J.T. and I examined it in dismay, and then J.T. put it in the fire remarking 'Only you and I, Frances, know of the existence of this paper.'

In the Senate at Cambridge not long ago it was alleged that historians were 'mere chroniclers and anecdotalists'. If after a paper such as this I cannot dispute, perhaps at least in conclusion I may temper the charge by offering a few final reflections. My theme is, I suppose, really not the familiar one of the unreliability of much of what passes for solid historical evidence, but the combined effect of chance and deliberate intent on the nature and substance of all the evidence that survives. What is there can at least be subject to critical scrutiny; what is not is discounted or altogether neglected. Yet clearly there are times when what is not is more important than what is. Yet the temptation must always be to rely upon the latter. That is likely to be more so in the future than in the past. Government departments and other organizations nowadays consciously build up their records. There are accessible and voluminous individuals on the other hand who no longer do so. Some years ago I spoke to a Cabinet minister of reasonably long experience about the richness of private collections of papers, I seem to remember alluding particularly to the Campbell-Bannerman and Asquith papers, and I asked him how often he wrote to colleagues on political matters. He was surprised by the question but emphatic in his reply. He could not remember, he said, in six or seven years of service in the Cabinet ever having written such a letter to a colleague. He discussed; he had not the leisure to write. If, as I suspect, this is generally true, there is some risk of undue dependence by historians, indeed I think there is already some evidence of it, on official files, upon what 'one damned clerk wrote to another'. So, all in all, if I have any conclusion to offer, which I rather doubt, it is that historians should not now, and still less in the future, overlook the unwritten, the mislaid, or the destroyed.

BIOGRAPHICAL NOTE
Nicholas Mansergh the Historian[*]

Nicholas Mansergh is one of Ireland's most distinguished historians with a worldwide reputation as a Commonwealth scholar. Since his first book, on the Irish Free State, was published at the age of twenty-four in 1934, Dr Mansergh has written or edited nearly thirty volumes. Since the announcement of his appointment by Harold Wilson in 1967, he has been editor-in-chief of the massive tomes of documents from the India Office Records on the transfer of power to India in the 1940s. From 1969 to 1979, he was Master of St John's College, Cambridge.

Born in Tipperary in 1910, troop trains leaving the town for the war in 1914–15 are among his earliest memories. After a brief period at school in the north, he went to the Erasmus Smith Abbey School in Tipperary. He was the youngest boy there when, in troubled times, the school abruptly closed. After the Civil War, he went with his elder brother to St Columba's College from 1923 to 1928. There Dr S. J. Willis, the mathematics master, was an outstanding influence.

Going up to Oxford to read modern history, he remembers that his interests were initially rather more literary than historical and that he became strongly interested in political science. At Oxford he came under the influence of R. B. McCallum (who coined the word, psephology, to describe the study of elections) and was supervised in research by W. G. S. Adams who had worked in Plunkett's IAOS and who had also been a member

---

*'The Saturday Interview' by Tom McGrath, *The Irish Times*, Saturday 11th June 1983.

of Lloyd George's garden suburb. Mansergh was also influenced by the works of James Bryce on modern democracies. All three were Scottish liberals.

Looking back now, fifty years later, Dr Mansergh comments: 'It seems to me unmistakable that my two earliest books were written by someone who was a political scientist rather than a historian. My interest moved rather sharply from modern history to political science in a way that I think would not be possible now, because the techniques of the historian and the political scientist have so much diverged'.

His first book on Ireland gave Dr Mansergh his earliest interest in the Commonwealth theme which he has pursued all his life. 'The Commonwealth for my generation', he notes, 'had something in common with the Common Market nowadays. I was interested in the Commonwealth to see if it would provide a way forward in Ireland itself. An inherent weakness in the Anglo-Irish Treaty was that the Dominion settlement was not consistent with Partition. I felt that Dominion status wouldn't work, which was obvious enough by 1934, but I wasn't sure whether any alternative to Dominion status would work in the Irish case.'

In 1940, Dr Mansergh published a seminal work on *Ireland in the Age of Reform and Revolution* (now available as *The Irish Question*), which was notable for bringing a European perspective to the study of modern Irish history. In this book, Mansergh analysed the Marxist-Leninist dialectic in respect of Ireland. He remarks wryly: 'I do note from time to time that because I wrote on Marx, Lenin and Engels that people have cursorily commented that I am a Marxist historian in bibliographies, which is nonsense'. Dr Mansergh was in Oxford until the war as a tutor in the school of Modern Greats and as secretary to the Oxford University Politics Research Committee.

During the war years in the Ministry of Information where fellow Tipperary man Brendan Bracken was Minister, Mansergh had for a time special responsibility for Anglo-Irish information services and cultural relations and in 1944 he was appointed head of the Empire division.

In 1947, Dr Mansergh was elected to the chair of British Commonwealth relations at Chatham House, Headquarters of the Royal Institute of International Affairs undertaking teaching responsibilities in the University of London. In the same year he went on the first of many visits to India as an observer at the Asian Relations Conference. Dr Mansergh explained that India before independence was a tremendously exhilarating place. 'It was the ending of imperialism in Asia and was compared in importance with the French and Russian revolutions.' That, no doubt, was exaggerated, but as Pandit Nehru put it, there was some magic in the air as India moved on to keep her 'tryst with destiny' at midnight on 14–15 August 1947.

In December 1946 Nehru, in moving the Objectives Resolution in the Constituent Assembly, had declared: 'India is bound to be sovereign; it is bound to be independent and it is bound to be a Republic', but he had also taken the occasion to remind the Assembly that 'even in the British Commonwealth of Nations today, Eire is a Republic and yet in many ways, it is a member . . . So it is a conceivable thing'. Mansergh himself was convinced that a relationship on an external but otherwise equal basis would be of advantage to India and might be the solution to this problem.

He recalls: 'When I came back from India I delivered a lecture entitled "The Implications of Eire's Relations with the British Commonwealth of Nations". Since the Cabinet papers for this period have become available, I have discovered that at the suggestion of Stafford Cripps this paper was sent to Attlee, who referred it to a committee who were examining Commonwealth relations. The Canadians became interested and something of this kind did emerge. India became as a republic a full member state, with an acknowledgement of the King as the symbol of the free association and as such Head of the Commonwealth – a further acknowledgement to Mr de Valera for his pioneering of the way would not have been unfitting. My lecture was referred to in the *Sunday Independent* and prompted questions to John A. Costello when he went to Ottawa – or so the Canadians tell me – on the question of whether the External Relations Act should be repealed or not. The repeal took effect in April, 1949, at which date the Indian republican membership which exists to this day was established.

In 1953 Dr Mansergh moved from Chatham House to Cambridge, where he was appointed Smuts professor of the History of the British Commonwealth. There he moved in the environment of scientists. One of his colleagues persuaded him to read the lives of mathematicians. 'It had an influence', he asserts, 'on my outlook. Among other things, I felt it enabled me to understand Mr de Valera better! Some people have detected a shift in my historical writing from that time. Possibly I do now pay greater attention to exact analysis as against literary form.'

In Cambridge, Professor Mansergh ran a special subject on the Anglo-Irish settlement which was taken by a large number of students reading for Part II of the Historical Tripos, and he supervised a number of research students of Irish history, including three from Australia. For some years he was an external examiner for the NUI. In 1969, he published his famous work *The Commonwealth Experience*, the title of which was suggested by his wife, Diana.

Sir Keith Hancock described this book in Mansergh's Festschrift as 'a magisterial work, the scholarly distillation of four decades of intellectual endeavour in Oxford, London and Cambridge'. In 1969, his colleagues elected him Master of St John's, the second largest college in the Oxbridge group, and he resigned from his chair so as to have a sufficient balance of time for his Indian editorial work. He served as Master for ten years.

Professor Mansergh divides his time between his home in Tipperary, Cambridge, where he is a fellow of St John's, and the occasional trip to India where he has been three times Visiting Professor at the Indian School of International Studies in New Delhi. Modest, humane and liberal in outlook, he described himself as someone who is a rare bird, interested in the Commonwealth and an anti-imperialist. 'I don't put it much stronger than that because I wish to remain a historian. In the latter part of my life what we have seen emerge is a Commonwealth which is an essentially anti-imperialist one', he suggests. He is contemplating another book on Ireland. Finally, he comments philosophically: 'As I get older, I tend on the one hand to move backwards in time and on the other hand, time is moving away from me'.

INDEX